Virginia at War, 1861

VIRGINIA
AT WAR
1861

Edited by William C. Davis
and James I. Robertson Jr.
for the Virginia Center for Civil War Studies

THE UNIVERSITY PRESS OF KENTUCKY

Publication of this volume was made possible in part by a grant
from the National Endowment for the Humanities.

Contents

Preface

Virginia's was a troubled course to disunion. As the mother state of independence, home of Washington and Jefferson and Madison, hers was an attachment to the nation unique among the states. As the sectional crisis grew in intensity after 1820, Virginia and its leaders increasingly sought ways to mediate between the antagonistic sections, perhaps knowing instinctively that if ever it came to blows, the Old Dominion could be caught in between, doomed to lose no matter who won. Once the secession juggernaut launched itself on its mad course, Virginians tried mightily to stay out of the coming storm. No other future Confederate state stepped back from the brink repeatedly as did Virginia, before events inevitably propelled her to secession.

Geography and events guaranteed that the state's history after leaving the Union would be just as difficult. No other state would be the scene of so much fighting. No other state would see so much destruction. By the end of the four-year conflict, Virginia was exhausted. Yet in the process she had done other things to give her a place apart. Here was the fabled Army of Northern Virginia. She gave to Confederate posterity names like Lee, Jackson, Stuart, and more. It was in her own capital city Richmond that the Confederate government lived its brief life and began to die its death. Behind all that lay the story of a common people at war, and that is the story that will be explored in Virginia at War, of which the present volume is the first of a projected five, each to deal with a discrete year of the Old Dominion's life as a Confederate state.

While each volume will present enough of the story unfolding on the battlefield to provide a backdrop, *Virginia at War, 1861* will look at other roads less traveled. It will present the stories of a civilian population struggling to continue life as normal, of industry pressed to the limit to cope with war's demands, of society strained beyond its usual bounds, of women taking on new roles while continuing the old, and of blacks, free and slave, defining new roles for themselves in a cultural unknown. Here, too, we will look at the changing role of the press in an embattled democracy, at the challenges to education, to communications, even to everyday family life for adults and children alike. The outcome of the war may or may not have been inevitable, but for Virginia, as for the other seceded states, there was never a doubt from the first that the war experience would change almost everything in the life it had known before 1861. Those challenges, the changes they wrought, and the ways in which Virginians coped with them then and into posterity, form the concept and the substance of Virginia at War.

Certainly that is evident in this first volume covering the year 1861. James I. Robertson Jr., Alumni Distinguished Professor of History at Virginia Tech and director of the Virginia Center for Civil War Studies, is well known to scholars and students alike for more than four decades of contributions to the field. Former executive director of the United States Civil War Centennial Commission, he is the author of a host of distinguished works, including the award-winning *Stonewall Jackson: The Man, the Soldier, the Legend.* Here he addresses the troubled course of the Virginia State Convention as it wrestled with the problem of secession in debates that mirrored the conflicted values of Virginians themselves in the most critical hour of their history.

Craig L. Symonds, for many years professor of history at the United States Naval Academy at Annapolis, is the author of several notable works including *Joseph E. Johnston, A Civil War Biography,* the finest work to date on the Virginian who sometimes commanded the second of the Confederacy's major armies. In an essay discussing the land operations in the state in 1861, Symonds provides the military background and context against which other events in the state unfolded in that first year of the war.

Currently professor of history at the University of North Carolina, Joseph T. Glatthaar has achieved signal distinction for his works *Forged in Battle: The Civil War Alliance of Black Soldiers and White Officers,* and *Partners in Command: The Relationships between Leaders in the Civil War.* He is among the most distinguished of American military historians today, and in his essay on the mobilization of Virginian volunteers in 1861 he looks at the motivations and experiences of the men who would be the backbone of the future Army of Northern Virginia.

Arguably the finest American museum devoted to the Civil War era is the Museum of the Confederacy in Richmond. John M. Coski, director of the library and research at the museum, is the author of *Capital Navy: The Men, Ships, and Operations of the James River Squadron,* and coauthor of *Four Days in 1865: The Fall of Richmond.* His essay in this volume on the short-lived Virginia State Navy is the only substantial work ever done on the subject, and an able example of the expedients necessary in Virginia and other seceded states during their brief careers as independent entities before being amalgamated into the new Confederate nation.

Ervin L. Jordan Jr. gives a voice to hundreds of thousands of other Virginians in his essay on black Virginians' attitudes toward secession and the war in 1861. He is the author of the pathbreaking *Black Confederates and Afro-Yankees in Civil War Virginia,* the most comprehensive look to date at the attitudes and roles of free and enslaved African Americans in the Old Dominion during the war era. He is Special Collections Librarian at the Alderman Library of the University of Virginia at Charlottesville.

William C. Davis, professor of history and director of programs at Virginia Tech's Virginia Center for Civil War Studies, has for some years made a special study of the Confederate government, including authoring "A Government of Our Own": The Making of the Confederacy; Look Away, A History of the Confederate States of America; and An Honorable Defeat: The Last Days of the Confederate Government.* In this volume he outlines the controversial and hardly inevitable course of Richmond from capital city of a state in the Union, to capital of the Confederacy itself.

Virginia was and is a state of distinct regions. In 1861 it included the Tidewater, the Piedmont, the western counties that became West Virginia, and in between, the Shenandoah Valley. Michael Mahon, author of *The Shenandoah Valley, 1861–1865: The Destruction of the Granary of the Confederacy,* provides an essay that assesses the distinctive features of Virginians caught between the unionist western counties and the more committed Southern rights counties to the east. Even within itself the Valley was divided, and would remain so throughout the contest.

As for those western counties, theirs was perhaps the strangest odyssey of all, from leaving the Union as a part of seceding Virginia, to readmission to that same Union as a new and independent state in opposition to the Old Dominion and the Confederacy. C. Stuart McGehee is Dean of the School of Social Sciences at West Virginia State College and author of *Bluefield, West Virginia, 1889–1999: A Centennial History.* His provocative work on the story of how those western counties came to become separated from the rest of Virginia and achieve statehood in their own right provides an important dimension to a portrait of *all* of Virginia in 1861.

One Virginian gets to speak for herself in these pages, and she represents the women of the Old Dominion as well. Judith Brockenbrough McGuire kept an extensive diary throughout the Civil War, which she published two years after the return of peace. It instantly became one of the standard sources for a look inside wartime Richmond and inside the war's impact on ordinary middle-class families. However, it has never been properly edited and annotated until now. James I. Robertson Jr. has undertaken the annotation of the 1861 portion of the diary that appears at the close of this volume, and hereafter in each of the succeeding volumes her annotated diary will also speak for the civilian role of Virginians in the trial of the war.

The editors and the Virginia Center for Civil War Studies wish to thank all of the contributors to this inaugural volume in the Virginia at War series. Thanks, too, go to the University Press of Kentucky and especially to director Stephen M. Wrinn and editor Joyce Harrison. To some it may seem peculiar that a book series on Virginia be published by a Kentucky press, but after all, there was a time when Virginia extended all the way to the Mississippi, and Kentucky's "dark and bloody ground" was simply an extension of the Old Dominion.

Finally and most profoundly our gratitude is extended to the William E. Jamerson family of Appomattox, for their generous financial support in underwriting the editorial expense necessary to produce these volumes. Their commitment to preserving the history of their state is emblematic of the ardent interest that all Virginians share in their common past.

Virginia at War, 1861

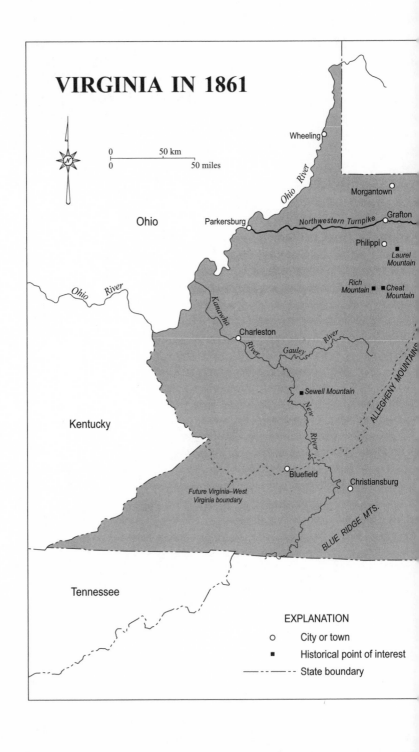

VIRGINIA IN 1861

0   50 km
0   50 miles

Wheeling

Morgantown

Ohio River

Ohio

Parkersburg

Northwestern Turnpike

Grafton

Philippi

Laurel Mountain

Rich Mountain

Cheat Mountain

Ohio River

Kanawha River

Charleston

Gauley River

ALLEGHENY MOUNTAINS

Sewell Mountain

New River

Kentucky

Bluefield

Christiansburg

Future Virginia–West Virginia boundary

BLUE RIDGE MTS.

Tennessee

EXPLANATION

○   City or town

■   Historical point of interest

– – – – –   State boundary

The Virginia State Convention of 1861

James I. Robertson Jr.

On Wednesday, April 17, 1861, an air of tension engulfed Richmond, Virginia. All eyes focused on the Capitol Building. There two months of seemingly endless debate by the Virginia State Convention was about to climax. A few days earlier, the artillery batteries of seven Confederate states had bombarded Fort Sumter, South Carolina, into surrender. The Union's new president, Abraham Lincoln, had responded with a call on all states for seventy-five thousand militia to put down an insurrection "too powerful to be suppressed by the ordinary course of judicial proceedings."[1]

Virginia—the "Mother State"—now was caught literally in the middle of disunion. She faced two choices, neither of which was pleasant. On the one hand, the overwhelming majority of Old Dominion citizens had shown a distaste for secession. On the other hand, Lincoln's proclamation clearly meant that Federal soldiers would cross Virginia's soil to wage war against Southern states. This was a program of coercion for which there seemed to be little constitutional warrant and no moral justification.

Early that Wednesday afternoon, the state convention took a second vote on union or disunion. A huge crowd surrounded the capitol in anticipation. Suddenly a man dashed outside with the news. Virginia had seceded! The Old Dominion had accepted war!

Cheers from the mob echoed down the capitol hillside. Thereafter, one Richmond newspaper stated, "the largest, longest and most demonstrative" procession ever witnessed in Richmond filled the streets. The great majority of paraders bore flags, banners, and torches. "The cheering was one continued vociferation along the whole route of the procession. One of the largest banners bore the inscription: 'Resistance to Tyranny Is Obedience to God.'"[2]

Another Richmond editor wrote soberly: "The great event of all our lives has at last come to pass. A civil war of gigantic proportions, infinite consequences, and indefinite duration, is on us, and will affect the interests and happiness of every man, woman and child, lofty or humble, in the country called Virginia. We cannot shun it, we cannot alleviate it, we cannot stop it. We have nothing left now but to fight our way though these troubles."[3]

John Janney, the venerable Loudoun County delegate who had presided over the Virginia State Convention, closed his next letter to his wife with the observation: "Perhaps some good may come out of this evil and bring the country to its senses. May God in his mercy grant it for the dry storm is raging and madness rules the hour."[4]

The implosion of Virginia had its beginnings with the 1860 presidential election. Nearly 90 percent of Virginia voters cast ballots against Lincoln's Republican policy of excluding slavery from the territories and Stephen A. Douglas's Democratic platform of allowing settlers themselves to exclude it. Third-party moderate candidate John Bell carried the state by a slim margin. South Carolina had been asking other slave states if they would secede should Abraham Lincoln win. No other states were ready to make the jump, so on December 20, South Carolina did it on her own. Many Virginia leaders condemned the action. Statesman John Minor Botts dismissed South Carolina as "a nuisance" that had been "disturbing the peace for thirty years."[5]

Some truth lay in that statement. Emotionalism was a primary factor in the coming of the Civil War. Too many people by 1860 were thinking with their mouths instead of their minds. What happened in Virginia during the first four months of 1861 is a classic illustration of feelings displacing logic.

Within a month of South Carolina's departure from the Union, secession swept through the Deep South. Its tentacles began stretching toward the Old Dominion. On January 7, the General Assembly went into session. One legislator told a friend: "Times are wild and revolutionary here beyond description."[6]

The first item on the legislative agenda was a proposal to summon a secession convention. Governor John Letcher saw no need for such a body.

At Virginia's initiative, a peace conference of all states had been summoned to Washington on February 4; and while this was a desperate, eleventh-hour effort to prevent what many considered unpreventable, Letcher urged a wait-and-see attitude.

Virginia unionists also opposed a convention. As one speaker put it, a special convention of "demagogues and extremists" might seize upon "popular excitement" to send Virginia down the road to secession.[7] Yet some 140 public meetings across the state had expressed a desire for a convention. One state legislator warned the "foot-draggers" that further hesitation by the General Assembly made the "Black Republicans jubilant."[8]

A compromise of sorts came forth. The General Assembly approved an act calling for the February 4 election of delegates to a secession convention that would meet ten days later. A total of 152 delegates (corresponding in number to the membership of the House of Delegates) would be chosen. Virginia voters would also be asked on the ballot to state whether the convention's recommendations should be submitted to a popular referendum by Virginia citizenry.[9]

Three weeks of local but intense campaigning followed. Candidates ran as secessionists, unionists, or moderates. Local newspapers took sides. For example, the usually calm *Richmond Daily Whig* editorialized: "Rain or shine, let the conservative voters of Richmond rally to the polls and visit upon the Disunion Precipitators in Virginia an overwhelming defeat!" The great Democratic standard-bearer, Stephen A. Douglas, then released a public letter to the nation. "There is hope of preserving peace and the Union," Douglas wrote. "All depends on the action of Virginia and the Border States. . . . Save Virginia, and we will save the Union."[10]

February 4 was a cold, overcast Monday. Snow was falling over most of the state. Some 145,700 voters trudged to the polls. How they voted made it clear that party organizations and political platforms meant nothing. Voters gave more attention to individuals and personalities—in part because many people were themselves undecided on the issues and preferred entrusting settlement to their representatives. Further, Virginia citizens felt all along that the final say would be theirs to make in a popular referendum.

The election of delegates showed no mandate for secession. Less than 20 percent of those elected were avowed secessionists. Unionists were delighted and momentarily optimistic. However, the term "unionist" had an altogether different meaning in Virginia at the time. Richmond delegates

Marmaduke Johnson and William McFarland were both outspoken conservatives. Yet in their respective campaigns, each declared that he was in favor of separation from the Union if the federal government did not guarantee protection of slavery everywhere. Moreover, the threat of the federal government's using coercion became an overriding factor in the debates that followed. One author summed up the situation succinctly: "The thought of leaving a Union in which Virginia had played such a conspicuous and glorious part was almost unbearable, but the idea of turning their arms against their sister states of the South was altogether unthinkable."[11]

The makeup of the convention included ex-President John Tyler, ex-Governor Henry Wise, two former cabinet members, two former lieutenant governors, plus retired judges, legislators, and members of previous constitutional conventions. Delegate Robert H. Turner (Warren County) considered his elected colleagues "of the highest and most honorable type of men . . . able statesmen of large and long experience, chosen as such by an anxious people."[12] One Richmond editor, however, dismissed the delegates as "old fogies who had not represented Virginia in the past thirty years."[13] The thirty secessionist delegates were principally from the Tidewater and Piedmont. Their floor leader was Lewis E. Harvie of Amelia County; their principal spokesman was Henry Wise of Princess Anne, whose thin frame, wrinkled face, and long white hair made him appear much older than his mid-fifties. Constituting only a fifth of the membership, the secessionists planned a strategy of agitation. As long as they made motions and noise in the convention, secession sentiment could not be ignored.

Unionist delegates, also thirty in number, came from the northwest and the Shenandoah Valley. Their floor leader was George W. Summers (Kanawha); their chief spokesmen, John S. Carlile (Harrison) and A.H.H. Stuart (Augusta). In the unionist view, secession was blatantly unconstitutional. Disunion meant revolution. In the middle of convention thinking were 92 moderates. Their number seemed overwhelming, and as the middle ground they kept the other two factions contained. Yet they were never a united faction. They agreed on certain basic principles, and they acknowledged cause for alarm. However, they wished to employ every means for peace short of secession. Robert Y. Conrad (Frederick), James Barbour (Culpeper), and William Ballard Preston (Montgomery) were their chief spokesmen. The moderates would gradually lose members and strength as emotions grew hotter in the weeks ahead.

At noon on Wednesday, February 13, the convention began in the chamber of the House of Delegates. Daily sessions were to run from 10 A.M. to 2 P.M. and from 4 P.M. to 6 or 7 P.M.[14] The first surprise for outsiders was the election of Loudoun County's John Janney as president of the body. Janney was then sixty-one and a quiet but longtime veteran of Virginia politics. His career included a dozen years in the House of Delegates, Whig candidature for the 1840 vice-presidential nomination, sitting in the 1850–1851 Virginia Constitutional Convention, and acting as a Whig elector in four presidential elections, in addition to which he was a much sought-after attorney and orator. Known as a "white-haired old Virginia gentleman," Janney was a "tall, spare figure" with "high, courtly old-time manners."[15] Far from an exciting or dominating figure, Janney owed his election to his conservative views and tactful demeanor. His colorless inaugural address to the convention appealed to calmness and love of state. The speech lasted only five minutes and brought mixed reactions.[16]

Janney's first major action as president was the appointment of a twenty-one-member Federal Relations Committee. All resolutions and petitions bearing on relations with authorities in Washington would be referred without debate to the committee. It in turn would report on a regular basis to the convention as a whole. Four secessionists, ten moderates, and seven unionists comprised the committee. It immediately decided to play a holding game for a month while awaiting the results of the Peace Conference in Washington and Lincoln's inaugural address.[17]

Indeed, all factions in the convention initially favored delay. Unionists wanted more time to search for support; moderates were hopeful that the Peace Conference and/or Lincoln would bring a solution to the crisis; secessionists saw in delay a means to heighten impatience for their cause.[18] Such nonproductivity created instant agitation across the state. Firebrand Edmund Ruffin snorted that the convention had spent "as much time to elect door-keepers . . . as the Convention of S.C. used to dissolve the Union." Inside the convention, the equally forceful Henry Wise wondered aloud if discussing minutiae was not "fiddling while Rome is burning."[19]

The activities of the Virginia State Convention ultimately fell into three distinct periods. The opening stage extended from the February 13 convening of the assembly to March 9, when the Federal Relations Committee made its first official report. In this period, conservatives changed from a position of inactivity to a definite plan of compromise. Delay and deliberation became one and the same. The usual order of business was for delegates to introduce resolutions and then follow them with long speeches. Most early recommendations dealt with the attachment of Virginia to the South, the right of secession, and possible federal intervention by force.

"Coercion" is a word that appears in convention proceedings almost as much as the word "secession." Virginians adhered strongly to a tradition of state sovereignty. They adamantly refused to accept the idea that federal authorities could employ force to override the liberties of a state. At any point in the convention, one observer wrote, "the advent of a Union army upon the soil of Virginia would have set the state ablaze and thrown it into the arms of the Southern Confederacy within twenty-four hours."[20]

Speech-making was constant and interminable. Visitors who daily packed the galleries often added their voices to the verbiage below. Three days into the convention, President Janney informed his wife: "Mr. Wise took his seat yesterday morning & has been talking almost all the time. Of course he raised a row in the galleries and this morning I announced if it was repeated today I should order them to be cleared. They have since behaved very well."[21] Such good conduct was sporadic.

February 16 produced the first fireworks by word and action. Moderate John Quincy Marr (Fauquier) began the day by urging the convention to declare itself in favor of the Union. A few minutes later, George Richardson (Hanover) offered a resolution calling for secession. Samuel Moore (Rockbridge) expressed his intent to oppose any move to take Virginia out of the Union. This provoked an angry outburst by Henry Wise, a man who seemed always to crave attention. The convention at that point adjourned for the day. That night an angry secessionist mob stormed the American Hotel where Moore was staying. Fortunately, the crowd confined its actions "to groans and hisses."[22]

It was near the end of the first week's proceedings that representatives of three seceded states arrived in Richmond to present their credentials. Over the objections of unionist delegates, the three commissioners were invited to address the convention. Fulton Anderson of Mississippi spoke first. He attacked Republicans for being hostile to the South and slavery. An "infidel fanaticism" in the North held all Southern states in contempt. Anderson urged Virginia to join the South by secession, thereby "placing our institutions beyond the reach of further hostility." Henry L. Benning of Georgia made a more substantive address. Secession, he stated, had removed slavery from Northern threats. The stronger the South, the less interest the North would have in Southern affairs. Virginia could become the leader of a new nation. "In such a cause," Benning exclaimed, "cowards will become men, men heroes, and heroes gods." John S. Preston of South Carolina, a transplanted Virginian and the best orator in the trio, spoke last. Preston fired the convention with a long speech mixing history, political science, Southern nationalism, and self-pride. To a rousing ovation, Preston repeated Patrick Henry's impassioned plea for liberty or death. He closed by asking convention delegates whether they would "skulk for protection beneath the crumbling fragments of an ancient greatness . . . or whether you will step forth . . . and keep the ancient glory of your name."[23]

The three presentations provoked strongly contrasting reactions. Some thought the speeches "of surpassing eloquence and power . . . rhetorical and convincing."[24] Unionist Robert Conrad called the oratory "the harangues of the ambassadors from the cotton states." President Janney informed his wife that after the addresses, "there is no body on our side either killed, wounded or frightened."[25]

With that, the convention returned to what it did best: talk and talk. Virginia fire-eater Edmund Ruffin snarled in his diary: "The Va. Convention continues to do nothing, & the worthless legislature of Va., which now has nothing to do, continues in session, so as to be spectator of the Convention." Even a weary John Janney conceded: "We have done nothing today but receive and refer resolutions and listen to a few gentlemen who are always ready to talk about nothing."[26] On February 23, the presiding officer had to take forceful action. Janney described the incident to his wife: "To-day we have a spicy dispute between Mr. Moore of Rockbridge and Mr. Goode of Bedford. While the 1st was speaking there was a [round] of applause in the men's gallery and in execution of a threat which I made last week I finally ordered the sergeant at arms to clear the galleries. Some of the members appealed to me to withdraw the order but I positively refused to. . . . The galleries were cleared and the doors closed for the balance of the [day's] session. I expect to be abused in round style . . . but I don't care for that."[27]

Soon came news that the Peace Conference in Washington, after three weeks of meaningless debate, had adjourned in failure. Aged John Tyler had pioneered the meeting. He returned to Richmond and told an audience that "our mission" was "a poor, rickety, and disconnected affair." One of the local newspapers lamented: "Virginia called the Peace Conference, and Virginia laid it away in the winding-sheet to-day."[28] Secessionists felt strengthened by the collapse of the Washington meeting. They argued that Virginia had made a supreme effort to restore the Union but Northern abolitionists had wrecked the conference. Hence, Virginians could and should move forward with a clear conscience of having done their best for the nation. A small stream of resolutions calling for secession became part of the convention's daily agenda thereafter.

It was the failure of the Peace Conference that caused moderates in the convention to begin wavering. To Robert E. Scott (Fauquier), the conference's failure and Northern indifference "extinguished all hope of a settlement by the direct agency of those States, and I at once accepted the dissolution of the existing Union . . . as a necessity."[29] A sense of urgency gripped Virginia unionists and moderates as March 4 and President Lincoln's first address to the nation approached. If the new leader made any conciliatory gestures, the further disintegration of the Union might be avoided. Yet what many Virginians wanted to hear was never spoken. Most Southerners found Lincoln's speech argumentative, if not defiant. An observer at the inaugural ceremony noted: "Mr. Lincoln raised his voice and distinctly emphasized the declaration that he must take, hold, possess, and occupy the property and places [in the South] belonging to the United States. This was unmistakable, and he paused for a moment after closing the sentence as if to allow it to be fully taken in and comprehended by his audience."[30]

In Richmond, Lincoln's determination to hold onto the Union at all costs created an explosive reaction. Secessionists asserted that Lincoln had declared war. Richmond newspapers leaped forward with criticism. The *Enquirer* let loose the first blast. It had biblical overtones and was aimed at the Peace Conference, Republicans, and state unionists. "We have asked for bread and they have given us a stone; for fish and they have given us a serpent; and yet there are men in Virginia, and unfortunately in the Convention, who will gladly accept the stone and serpent and return thanks to Black Republican bounty for providing so dainty a repast."[31]

The consistently inflammable *Examiner* aimed its sharpest arrows at "a Virginia convention which imprudently pretends to represent her people. The 'scarlet letter' of submission to Lincoln has been burnt into [Virginia's] brow, and whatever her future career may be, she has lost that which seven of her sisters gained by prompt and decided action." A day later, the *Exam-*

iner dismissed the convention as "the Rump Parliament at the Mechanics' Hall."[32]

Secessionist delegates were adding their fuel to the fire. Amelia's Lewis Harvie said of Lincoln's remarks: "We have just heard the trumpet sound of war thundering in to our midst, by our servant not our master, at Washington. . . . When the Federal Government has exceeded the limits of propriety and its limit of power . . . Virginia will clothe herself in the panoply of her arms to maintain her rights." To loud applause, Harvie called for the immediate raising of a Virginia army.[33]

With the Peace Conference's failure and Lincoln's hostility to Southern rights, moderates in the convention quickly sought an alternative action short of secession. The day after Lincoln's address, delegates James Cox (Chesterfield) and William Goggin (Bedford) introduced resolutions calling for a conference of the eight border states such as Virginia, Maryland, and Kentucky. The dual purpose of the gathering would be to check any coercive move by Lincoln and to unite the border states for secession, if necessary.[34]

Although some leaders such as Governor Letcher still believed that "patience and prudence" would "work out the results," a growing, uncontrollable attitude for war was sweeping through the state. Militia units were organizing from the mountains to the Tidewater. Newspapers in Richmond and elsewhere maintained a steady heat, noisy partisans filled the convention galleries, and at night large crowds surged through the capital streets "with bands of music and called out their favorite orators at the different hotels."[35]

Emotionalism, personal pride, a volatile atmosphere—all seemed to have merged into a highly inflammable situation. In the convention on March 6, secessionist John Goode (Bedford) challenged the truthfulness of a statement by unionist Jubal Early (Franklin). Tempers flared. Friends interceded to avert what might have become a duel. The two men made mutual apologies. That night President Janney told his wife: "We had some tolerably respectable 4th of July orations today intended for the galleries," yet the speeches made "very little effort" on the convention.[36]

The same cannot be said of the next day's proceedings, when John S. Carlile took the floor. A forty-three-year-old politician from Clarksburg (the same town where future general "Stonewall" Jackson was born), Carlile had many of the attributes of a hypocrite. He owned slaves and opposed coercion, but he was an outspoken unionist who seemed to delight in making people angry.[37] His March 7 address was one of the longest ever made in the convention. Carlile began by accusing the *Richmond Enquirer* of scheming to force Virginia from the Union. What do secessionists want? Carlile asked rhetorically as he looked at Henry Wise and his bloc. "To make war against the Constitution of our own country; to destroy . . . the work of our own revolutionary fathers?" Carlile asserted that the federal government "has never brought us anything but good. . . . [Now] we are called upon in hot haste, to destroy the Government that shielded us from the injurious consequences of our own mistaken conduct." Secession would bring an end to slavery. Further, Carlile insinuated, leaving the Union was treason. "And I denounce all attempts to involve Virginia to commit her to self murder as an insult to all reasonable living humanity, and a crime against God."[38] After Carlile had taken his seat, Janney noted: "Mr. Carlile made us a very good speech today and as I would not let [those in the galleries] express their disapproval, the mob hissed him as he came out on the pavement though he had two ladies with him."[39]

To this point, convention delegates had taken turns giving speeches that voiced personal and constituents' opinions. Subject matter varied, but progress toward anything was absent. This first stage of the convention ended March 9 with the preliminary report of the Federal Relations Committee. (The full report was submitted ten days later.) For almost a month, every idea and proposal of importance had been referred to this committee. Now it came forward with a series of resolutions that kept the convention fully occupied for a second month. The twenty-one committee members were far from unanimous with their report. Twelve endorsed the document, two opposed it, and seven abstained from committing one way or the other to it. The committee's report was neither a statement nor a compact; rather, it was a series of fourteen recommendations, each of which could be voted up or down by the convention as a whole. The key proposals affirmed the institution of slavery and upheld the sovereignty of states' rights. If secession of a state occurred, a resolution stated, all federal forts and arsenals reverted back to the state because it had ceded the properties to the government in trust, not as gifts. One recommendation urged Congress to pass a new and more effective fugitive slave law; another proposed a meeting in May of eight border states to discuss common feelings and common actions. Meanwhile, the report concluded, "the people of Virginia" would regard any coercion against the Southern states by the federal government "as aggressive and injurious to the interests and offensive to the honor of the Commonwealth."[40]

This report of the Federal Relations Committee contained two distinct categories: an explanation of the nature of the Union, and a list of Southern grievances. It was also apparent that the fourteen proposals were intended to be a middle path between diehard unionists and firebrand secessionists. The report waffled on the propriety of secession, but was clear that any federal coercion was unacceptable. In short, the conservative majority switched its position from delay to action. Now those delegates advocated quick adoption of the resolutions. That would keep the moderate majority occupied and less swayed by the always-active secessionist delegates.[41] Richmond's pro-secession newspapers, waiting impatiently for the committee report, resented its compromising tones. The *Enquirer* dismissed the proposals as "indefinite, incomplete, and imperfect." The committee's work, said the *Examiner*, showed only that the convention "determines to do nothing" and called on other border states "to help it in that profitable occupation."[42]

The second stage of the convention's work began on March 15 with the full report of the Federal Relations Committee, and it would last until April 4. Unionists and moderates pushed hard for acceptance of each of the fourteen resolutions. The hopes of these conservatives lay in compromise and the presumed cooperation of the other border states. Secessionist delegates, on the other hand, championed delay on the resolutions and agitation for leaving a shattered union. They began an almost daily habit of presenting petitions from mass meetings throughout the state. At least thirty-seven counties instructed—and in some cases demanded—that their convention representatives "dissolve the odious connection of Virginia and the Federal Government." The time for adjustment had passed, local petitions argued. Honor should be paid to South Carolina and other Confederate states "for their wisdom, their decisive boldness, and their human forbearance." Eleven such resolutions came to the convention in one six-day period.[43]

Meanwhile, all attention had turned to the fourteen recommendations. A gloomy John Janney told his wife: "From all indications now, there must be at least fifty speeches to be made."[44] Among the first to take the floor was unionist leader George W. Summers. The Charleston jurist had an aristocratic bearing that gave him a Tidewater appearance. He was confident that peace would prevail if the federal government would quietly evacuate Fort Sumter, now the focus of national concentration. In a four-hour speech spread over two days, Summers rambled from history to politics to philosophy to patriotism. "The duty of Virginia," he said toward the end, is "to be faithful when all others have been faithless." The state's chief responsibility is "not to fly from, but to stand by, these monuments of her glory—the Constitution and the Union—constructed by herself more than by all others."[45]

Such high-toned sentiments were commendable, but they illustrate the fatal weakness in the thinking of Virginia unionists. Summers and his bloc considered peacekeeping and reunion a long process involving careful deliberation. They would pursue such a course. That a sense of urgency, fed by growing emotions, was storming across the fractured nation, that secessionist warnings and warlike alarms went far deeper than mere hearsay, were realities far beyond the dreamworld in which unionists seemed to dwell.[46] Lincoln's new administration aided that scenario appreciably. Throughout the first three weeks of March, Secretary of State William H. Seward repeatedly assured Virginia conservatives that no Southern forts, especially Sumter, would be reinforced. Only five days after his inauguration, Lincoln told Senator Stephen A. Douglas that "the fort shall be evacuated as soon as possible." Unionists in the convention eagerly accepted such statements. On March 19, Summers wrote to a friend that reassurances from Washington "acted like a charm" and "gave us great strength." Virginia unionists, Summers added, "are masters of our position here, and can maintain it if left alone."[47]

For three weeks, the convention leisurely debated each of the fourteen resolutions. "Great heat and great ability on both sides" characterized the arguments, a pro-Union contemporary noted. "The vehemence and malignancy of the [secessionists] was met by the sturdy determination and eloquence of the Unionists."[48] One day when the Albemarle County delegate finished a speech on the advantages of slavery and the Southern Confederacy, "considerable applause" came from the galleries. President Janney ordered the area cleared of visitors. Squalls of protests followed, in which delegates pointed out that members on the floor were making far more noise than witnesses in the galleries. This time Janney recanted and allowed the balconies to remain filled.[49]

Richmond newspapers were goading the convention at every opportunity. On March 21, the *Examiner* sneered: "Five weeks of twaddle have dragged their weary length along, and the Convention [has] done nothing but impose upon an over-taxed State the heavy burden of paying for every dull . . . speech which has been delivered. . . . The conceited old ghosts who crawled from a hundred damp graves to manacle their State and deliver her up as a hand-maid to the hideous Chimpanzee from Illinois have determined that not one word of their rubbish and gabble will be lost to posterity."[50] This type of ridicule was precisely what the secessionists wanted. They knew back in February that taking Virginia out of the Union was well-nigh impossible. "We must train the popular mind and heart," fire-eater Henry Wise had stated. This meant external agitations and internal delays.

The secessionists were good agitators. In mid-March, delegate Marshall M. Dent (Morgantown) wrote his local newspaper: "Your readers cannot imagine the state of things here from the reports of the Convention in the newspapers. Every means is used to intimidate the [unionist] members of this Convention. Meetings are held nightly. Bands are hired who parade the streets followed by a motley crew of free negroes, boys and mad cops, who go around to the different hotels calling upon the well known Secessionists for speeches . . . and every Union man is denounced as an abolitionist! The members from the Northwest are compelled to daily hear citizens of Richmond . . . point them out with the remark that 'there is where the abolitionists sit.'"[51] Inside the convention, Wise and his followers performed their delay duties well. Endless resolutions were introduced. Delegates insisted on reading every bit of information, especially minutiae. Speeches became longer and more shallow. A day's session might be cut short because the scheduled speaker had suddenly fallen ill or else forgotten his notes. Questioning a quorum (which necessitated a rollcall), offering what Robert Conrad called "100s of meaningless propositions," challenging the ruling of the chair—these all became part of a policy of obstruction. Daily attendance began dropping as patience wore thin.[52]

The secessionists were achieving their objective of igniting public opinion for strong and immediate action. Not all of the pro-Confederate delegates were good history students, but their leaders were well versed in the antics and tactics of Samuel Adams, Patrick Henry, and the revolutionary Sons of Liberty. March 26 was a typical day. The session began with James C. Bruce (Halifax) giving a speech on the blessings of the Union. He was often interrupted with meaningless questions. Then delegates got into a sometimes sober, sometimes sarcastic, argument over points of order. Adjournment late that day was relatively painless, for only 91 of the 152 members were in attendance.[53] A few days later, Janney observed: "A more desperate faction never existed in any country than the occupants of the South, but they can't move old Virginia yet awhile."[54] The convention president was grossly mistaken—and had been for much of the past two months.

Professor William Freehling has provided a cogent analysis of the Virginia Convention. Looming over everything in that body was "an expectation that Virginia could once again master her destiny and dominate the nation. Most speakers assumed that all eyes were riveted on their Convention and that decisions reached in Richmond would control policy in Washington and Montgomery. . . . What mocked this tone and in the end reduced it to shrillness was the increasingly obvious fact that the Convention was itself at the mercy of decisions made elsewhere."[55]

April 3 was a day of extremes. Delegate George Richardson (Hanover) assured his colleagues that no war would come from secession. "War is contrary to the spirit of the age. The people of the North are people of commerce and of peace. They will not support a large standing army."[56] The *Daily Examiner* stated that day: "Language cannot describe the disgusting peculiarities of the famished pack of wolves, jackals, foxes and hyenas, now howling and ravaging after the crumbs and scraps from the table of the Abolition Kangaroo of the White House." Also on April 8, the *Enquirer* repeated a rumor that Lincoln was preparing to reinforce Fort Sumter at Charleston. Verification was not immediately possible, but the issue was perilous enough for secessionist Lewis Harvie. The next day, he introduced a motion for the prompt secession of Virginia. Bedlam followed as several delegates sought compromise or delay. Finally the chair called for a vote. Harvie's motion—the first formal vote by the convention on secession—failed, 45–88.[57]

The third and final stage of the State Convention now began. It consisted of the breaking up of the conservative coalition and the state's last steps in the secession crisis. Rumors quickly spread of a Northern buildup of munitions of war. William Ballard Preston (Montgomery), a former secretary of the navy, now emerged as leader of the moderates. He proposed sending a three-member delegation to Washington. It would "respectfully ask" President Lincoln to "communicate to this Convention the policy which the authorities of the Federal Government intend to pursue in regard to the Confederate States." Preston hoped that Virginia might yet influence Lincoln to maintain the peace.[58]

Unionists bitterly opposed the idea. It was an impolite demand on Lincoln, who probably would not give a straightforward response. The result could be a secessionist stampede inside the state. At the height of the debate, John Carlile added fire to the heat by seeking unsuccessfully to have a similar delegation sent to the new Confederate capital at Montgomery, Alabama, to ascertain Confederate intentions. The motion to send three representatives to Washington passed on a 63–57 vote. Preston, Richmond secessionist George Wythe Randolph, and Staunton unionist A.H.H. Stuart would form the delegation.[59]

For several days thereafter, heavy rains followed by severe flooding isolated Richmond. The telegraph was the single communication with the outside. It only heightened the rumormill.[60] On April 12, after lengthy discussion, the convention approved the fourteenth and final resolution of the Federal Relations Committee. The timing was ironic, for in the predawn hours of that day, Confederate guns opened fire on Fort Sumter. Flooded conditions delayed the Preston emissaries from seeing Lincoln until April 13. By then, telegraph keys nationwide were clicking details of the gunfire in Charleston harbor. Lincoln received the three Virginians, then read from a prepared text to avoid any misunderstanding. He had made it plain in his inaugural address, he said, that forts and arsenals in the South were the property of the federal government. Now, Lincoln continued, "if . . . an unprovoked assault has been made upon Fort Sumter, I shall hold myself at liberty to re-possess, if I can, like places which have been seized before the Government was devolved upon me."[61]

By the time Preston, Randolph, and Stuart returned to Richmond, the capital was in a frenzy of excitement. Secessionist mobs filled the downtown streets. Earlier, on April 13, the convention had received official bulletins about Fort Sumter. The first reaction, as expected, came from Henry Wise. The convention's leading secessionist asserted sarcastically: "I should think now, that war is flagrant, it should have some impression, and make a little change in our action." Wise then thundered to the chamber: "I hope now that the fire is applied to the terrapin, he will crawl, at last, and that you will heat the poker till you fry the very fat off his vitals." John Carlile urged continued respect for the Union. His pleas fell on deaf ears, even when he resorted to poetry by exclaiming: "You may break, you may ruin the vase if you will, But the scent of the roses will hang 'round it still."[62]

Highlighting the weekend of April 13–14 were reports that the Fort Sumter garrison had surrendered. The news, exclaimed a Richmond newspaper, "was greeted with unbounded enthusiasm in this city. Everybody we met seemed to be perfectly happy. Indeed, until this occasion we did not know how happy men could be."[63] Monday morning, April 15, came, and so did Lincoln's call on all loyal states for soldiers to quell the Southern uprising. In Richmond, this pronouncement "threw the whole city into a flame." People everywhere made spontaneous "declarations of independence." Everyone who had ever been known to make a speech was exhorted to make one now. Confederate flags appeared in windows and doorways. A wild excitement swept over the city—"a hysteria in the mass release from indecision." The now-disillusioned unionist John Janney asserted that he would have considered the federal call for troops "a forgery but Abe Lincoln is fool or knave enough to commit any absurdity or folly."[64]

In that atmosphere, the convention went into session at 10 A.M. Observers expected an ordinance of secession that day because so many moderates had swung into the ranks of the secessionists.[65] The pro-Confederates were now ready to take a calmer course for the sake of the strongest backing when a secession motion did come forth again. Doubts about the authenticity of Lincoln's call for soldiers, plus a motion that any movement toward secession be delayed until the cooperation of the border states could be obtained, led to adjournment after a mere three hours of discussion. The *Examiner* asked impatiently if these were not times "when the outburst of revolution becomes the path of duty? . . . Shall tens of thousands of honest and valuable citizens be driven into exile, or shall the Convention be given notice to quit?"[66]

On April 16, a rainy Tuesday, a feeling of inevitability seemed to settle over the convention. George Randolph, of the three-man commission just returned from Washington, urged immediate secession. His commission colleague A.H.H. Stuart advocated restraint until the border states could confer. Other unionists submitted motions aimed at compromise. All were soundly rejected. At that point, William Ballard Preston obtained the floor. In careful tones void of emotion, the Montgomery County delegate introduced a formal ordinance of secession. The heart of Preston's motion lay in these statements:

The people of Virginia, in their ratification of the constitution . . . having declared that the powers granted under the said constitution were derived from the people of the United States, and might be resumed whensoever the same should be perverted to their injury and oppression; and the Federal Government having perverted said powers . . . Now, therefore, we the people of Virginia do declare that the ordinance . . . whereby the constitution of the United States of America was ratified and all acts of the general assembly . . . adopting amendments to said constitution, are hereby repealed and abrogated; that the union between Virginia and the other states . . . is hereby dissolved, and that the state of Virginia is in full possession and exercise of all the rights of sovereignty which belong and appertain to a free and independent state.[67]

At that point, President Janney received the official request from the federal War Department for Virginia to supply 2,340 men to the Union army. This new element sent desperation into the ranks of the unionists. Western Virginia delegates, opposed to Preston's motion for secession, spoke with a deeper earnestness. Waitman T. Willey (Monongalia) pled for caution. "In all sincerity, from the depths of the belief of my heart," Willey declared prophetically, "I say that if this ordinance of secession goes out naked and alone, it will either be voted down by the people, or it will dissolve this State. . . . It will destroy the loyalty of the best friends that ever your slaveholders had; it will destroy the sons of sires who shed their blood in your defence, and whose bones now lie along your sea-shore."[68]

The convention adjourned early to allow members to think individually on the issue of secession. That was a good move on Janney's part, for the Wednesday, April 17, session lasted ten and a half hours. It opened with the reading of Governor Letcher's response to the federal War Department for soldiers. The governor not only refused to send Virginia soldiers to Washington; the once-moderate Letcher also told the Lincoln government: "You have chosen to inaugurate civil war, and, having done so, we will meet it in a spirit as determined as the administration has exhibited towards the South."[69] Events began in earnest, a unionist wrote, when "Henry A. Wise came into the hall, carrying a large horse-pistol, which, with a flourish, he placed before him on his desk, and proceeded to harangue the Convention in the most vehement and denunciatory manner, and, looking at his watch, he declared that at that very hour events were occurring 'which caused a hush to come over his soul.'"[70]

Such antics did nothing to stop the debate that followed. Delegates who had previously not spoken in convention sessions obtained the floor to voice opinions. Even Janney left the president's chair to urge consideration over emotion. "The Confederate army never will and never can march to our assistance," he declared, because "they will use all their means and power to protect themselves at home." How then can Virginia "defend our people who live upon the [Northern] frontier, who are exposed to the assaults of the enemy, and upon whom they will come thick and heavy?"[71] Call for the question on Preston's ordinance of secession came in early afternoon. The vote was eighty-eight for leaving the Union, fifty-five against. (However, changes in votes plus absentee ballots made the final vote 103–46 in favor of disunion.) As a Richmond newspaper concluded, "Lincoln gives us no alternative but to fight or run."[72]

How the original 88–55 vote broke down regionally provides interesting numbers for thought. Of the eighty-eight affirmative votes, fifty-five were from east of the Blue Ridge Mountains, ten were from the Shenandoah Valley, eighteen came from the southwest, with only five from the northwest. The fifty-five delegates who voted against secession included twelve from east of the Blue Ridge, seventeen from the Valley, three from the southwest, and twenty-five from the northwest. More intriguing was the delegate-vote from forty counties that later became West Virginia. Twenty-one of those counties voted for secession, while nineteen counties were unionist. There was an even more ironic statistic. The Shenandoah Valley voted almost two to one to remain in the Union; while across the mountains, the majority of counties that would leave the "Mother State" saw their representatives at the convention vote to go with the Southern Confederacy.[73]

The convention spent the remainder of Wednesday appropriating $100,000 for defense of the state, suspending all federal authority in Virginia until ratification by the people of the secession ordinance, and authorizing Governor Letcher to inform Confederate President Jefferson Davis of Virginia's desire to become part of the Confederate States of America. By nightfall, Virginia militia units were moving speedily to seize the federal arsenal at Harpers Ferry and the Gosport Navy Yard at Norfolk. Overnight Richmond became "a city of soldiers." One newspaper chortled: "If the northern madmen, who have so promptly responded to the summons of the modern Nero, desire the honor of a grave in the soil of Virginia, let them come on in any number."[74]

Western Virginia delegates had departed for home by April 23, when former U.S. Army Colonel Robert E. Lee came before the convention to accept command of all Virginia military forces. The distinguished Virginian received a warm welcome. The convention adjourned a week later, its work basically completed. The May 23 statewide referendum on secession created enthusiasm rather than excitement. Just before the voting, a Petersburg matron asked Virginia statesman Robert M.T. Hunter if the citizenry might reject secession. "My dear lady," Hunter chuckled, "you may place your little hand against Niagara [Falls] with more certainty of staying the torrent than you can oppose this movement. It was written long ago in the everlasting stars that the South would be driven out of the Union by the North."[75]

Hunter's optimism was well grounded. Virginians approved secession by a vote of 125,950 to 20,373. However, this six-to-one margin was not spread evenly across the state. Eastern Virginians overwhelmingly endorsed secession, while the four counties of the northwestern panhandle voted against ratification by a twenty-to-one ratio.[76] In the first months of 1861, Virginians felt an obligation to remain loyal to a longstanding state rather than to a young, still somewhat untested country. The past was visible; the future was not. John Janney touched on this fact in his farewell speech to the convention. "Gentlemen, the clouds are lowering . . . and the muttering thunder is heard in the distance. By the blessing of Providence upon the arms of our brave defenders, the storm may yet be averted; but, if not, and it shall burst with fury upon us, don't turn your backs to it—turn your faces."[77]

With those remarks, the speeches of the politicians were done. The sacrifices of the soldiers now began.

Notes

1. Roy P. Basler, ed., *The Collected Works of Abraham Lincoln* (New Brunswick, N.J.: Rutgers University Press, 1953–1955), IV, 332.

2. *Richmond Daily Whig,* April 20, 1861.

3. *Richmond Daily Examiner,* April 17, 1861.

4. John Janney to Alcinda Janney, April 19, 1861, John Janney Papers, Special Collections, Newman Library, Virginia Polytechnic Institute and State University, Blacksburg, Va.

5. Henry T. Shanks, *The Secession Movement in Virginia, 1847–1861* (Richmond: Garrett and Massie, 1934), 134.

6. James E. Walmsley, ed., "The Change of Secession Sentiment in Virginia in 1861," *American Historical Review* 31 (1925): 83.

7. Daniel W. Crofts, *Reluctant Confederates: Upper South Confederates in the Secession Crisis* (Chapel Hill: University of North Carolina Press, 1989), 137.

8. *Richmond Enquirer,* January 10, 1861; *Richmond Daily Dispatch,* January 14, 1861. Prince George County representative Timothy Rives was typical of the activists in the General Assembly. The people, he shouted, are for "secession, disunion, war, anything you might call it, to assert and defend their rights. I have heard too much talk. I and my people are for action now! Now!! . . . I will die before I submit to the Lincoln administration." *Richmond Enquirer,* January 14, 1861.

9. Virginia State Library, comp., *Proceedings of the Virginia State Convention of 1861* (Richmond: Virginia State Library, 1965), I, iii. Cited hereafter as *Convention Proceedings.* The work of the General Assembly practically ended with that bill. All attention thereafter until secession focused on the special convention.

10. *Richmond Daily Whig,* February 3, 4, 1861.

11. *Richmond Daily Dispatch,* January 26, 1861; James C. McGregor, *The Disruption of Virginia* (New York: Macmillan Company, 1922), 121–22.

12. Robert H. Turner, "Recollections," typescript (Richmond, Va.: Virginia Historical Society), 1. See also statement of Governor Letcher's secretary in S. Bassett French, *Centennial Tales* (New York: Carlton Press, 1962), 5.

13. *Richmond Daily Examiner,* February 28, 1861.

14. The opening session of the convention was in the House of Delegates chamber. Yet with the General Assembly in special session, the convention moved the next day to the nearby Mechanics' Hall. That was the regular meeting site until early April, when the convention returned to the House chamber.

15. *New York Times,* November 6, 1862.

16. *Convention Proceedings,* I, 7–9; *Richmond Daily Whig,* February 14, 1861; McGregor, *Disruption of Virginia,* 127–28. Janney and his wife had been married for thirty-five years. They had no children but were devoted to one another—as is evident in the letters Janney wrote her almost daily from Richmond.

17. *Convention Proceedings,* I, 24–29.

18. For example, see David Conrad to Robert Y. Conrad, February 16, 1861, Holmes Conrad Papers, Virginia Historical Society, Richmond, Va.

19. Edmund Ruffin, *The Diary of Edmund Ruffin,* William Kauffman Scarborough, ed. (Baton Rouge: Louisiana State University Press, 1972–1989), I, 550; *Convention Proceedings,* I, 22.

20. McGregor, *Disruption of Virginia*, 129.

21. John Janney to Alcinda Janney, February 16, 1861, Janney Papers, Virginia Tech.

22. *Convention Proceedings*, I, 15–29, 40–48; *Richmond Daily Dispatch*, February 20, 1861.

23. The three addresses are in *Convention Proceedings*, I, 50–93. For an excellent analysis of the visit of the three commissioners, see Charles W. Dew, *Apostles of Disunion: Southern Secession Commissioners and the Cause of the Civil War* (Charlottesville, Va.: University Press of Virginia, 2001), 59–73.

24. John Goode, *Recollections of a Lifetime* (New York: Neale Publishing Company, 1906), 48–49; Turner, "Recollections," 37. See also *Richmond Daily Dispatch*, February 18, 1861.

25. Robert Y. Conrad to Elizabeth Conrad, February 18, 1861, Robert Young Conrad Papers, Virginia Historical Society, Richmond, Va.; John Janney to Alcinda Janney, February 18, 1861, Janney Papers, Virginia Tech.

26. Ruffin, *Diary*, I, 555; John Janney to Alcinda Janney, February 20, 1861, Janney Papers, Virginia Tech. Two days later, a still-bored Janney wrote home: "I get almost every mail a half peck of pamphlets & essays from all sorts of people in all parts of the country, all suggesting their crude remedies for the times. They don't want their wisdom to die with them and knowing nobody here they address them to me. . . . I am obliged to open them to see what they are. Then 4/5s of them go into the fire." Ibid., February 22, 1861.

27. John Janney to Alcinda Janney, February 25, 1861, Janney Papers, Virginia Tech.

28. *Richmond Daily Examiner*, March 1, 1861; *Richmond Daily Whig*, March 4, 1861.

29. *Convention Proceedings*, I, 340, 347–50; Shanks, *Secession Movement*, 174.

30. *Diary of a Public Man and a Page of Political Correspondence, Stanton to Buchanan* (New Brunswick, N.J.: Rutgers University Press, 1946), 86.

31. *Richmond Enquirer*, March 5, 1861.

32. *Richmond Daily Examiner*, March 5 and 6, 1861. The *Daily Dispatch* regarded Lincoln's address as a virtual war measure, while the *Enquirer* reported the president's statements in a black-bordered edition. *Richmond Daily Dispatch*, March 5, 1861; *Richmond Enquirer*, March 7, 1861.

33. *Convention Proceedings*, I, 387–88. For similar sentiments, see Joseph A. Waddell, *Annals of Augusta County, Virginia, from 1726 to 1871* (Richmond: W.E. Jones, 1886), 455–56.

34. *Convention Proceedings*, I, 379–80, 385–86.

35. F.N. Boney, *John Letcher of Virginia* (University, Ala.: University of Alabama Press, 1966), 110; Goode, *Recollections of a Lifetime*, 51–52.

36. *Convention Proceedings,* I, 437–38, 486–88; *Richmond Daily Dispatch,* March 9, 1861; John Janney to Alcinda Janney, March 6, 1861, Janney Papers, Virginia Tech. By the end of March, Early was termed "the strongest Union man in the Convention" with the exception of George W. Summers (Kanawha). *Convention Proceedings,* III, 40.

37. Carlile increasingly became a source of derision in the convention, a target for laughter and insults outside the hall. He later claimed that a mob on one occasion surrounded his Richmond boarding house with the intent of hanging him. McGregor, *Disruption of Virginia,* 161n.

38. *Convention Proceedings,* I, 449–82; *Richmond Daily Dispatch,* March 9, 1861. The day following Carlile's drum-thumping address, delegates from Pulaski and Washington counties submitted motions for secession. *Convention Proceedings,* I, 489, 492–93.

39. John Janney to Alcinda Janney, March 7, 1861, Janney Papers, Virginia Tech.

40. *Convention Proceedings,* I, 523–28, 70, 1–16; Granville Davisson Hall, *The Rending of Virginia: A History* (Chicago: Mayer and Miller, 1902), 520; Henry A. Wise, *Seven Decades of the Union* (Philadelphia: J.B. Lippincott & Company, 1881), 277.

41. James M. Brown lived in a house adjacent to Mechanics' Hall, the convention's meeting site. Each morning Brown placed a Confederate flag in his front yard as a reminder to the delegates. *Richmond Daily Whig,* March 14, 1861.

42. *Richmond Enquirer,* March 18, 1861; *Richmond Daily Examiner,* March 19, 1861.

43. Hall, *Rending of Virginia,* 521; *Convention Proceedings,* I, 585–88, 630–36, 655–60, 590–92, 695–700. "If a general election for delegates to the convention had been held" in mid-March, one author asserted, "Secessionists would have swept the state east of the Allegheny Mountains." McGregor, *Disruption of Virginia,* 152–53.

44. John Janney to Alcinda Janney, March 11, 1861, Janney Papers, Virginia Tech.

45. *Diary of a Public Man,* 108; *Convention Proceedings,* I, 549–78, 590–629. The night after Summers finished talking, Janney wrote home of the address: "It was one of great prowess and consummate ability and cannot fail to have a good effect. . . . Poor old Mr. Tyler got the floor and will attempt a reply tomorrow. He is very feeble and I believe every body pities his condition." John Janney to Alcinda Janney, March 12, 1861, Janney Papers, Virginia Tech.

46. See Crofts, *Reluctant Confederates,* 308–9. One moderate Richmond newspaper continued to stand firm in the face of mounting secessionist feel-

ing. The *Richmond Daily Whig* observed on March 16: "To break up a government is an easy task—a child may apply the torch to a castle, but when thus consumed, it requires men of skill and ability to reconstruct it," 33.

47. *Diary of a Public Man,* 101, 106; Shanks, *Secession Movement,* 182–83, 264.

48. Hall, *Rending of Virginia,* 521.

49. *Convention Proceedings,* II, 136–38.

50. *Richmond Daily Examiner,* March 21, 1861. On the following day the same paper editorialized: "Nothing since the fiddling of Nero, while Rome was blazing, furnishes a parallel to the Dead Sea of pointless, vapid, dull, tiresome, dreary rigamarole with which the Convention is delaying the country."

51. Reprinted in *Richmond Enquirer,* March 26, 1861.

52. Shanks, *Secession Movement,* 186–88, 197, 265–66. Janney observed bitterly: "It is the general opinion that if Gov. Wise had not been in the Convention that we might all have been at home 4 weeks ago." John Janney to Alcinda Janney, April 11, 1861, Janney Papers, Virginia Tech.

53. *Convention Proceedings,* II, 249–337; Virginia State Library (comp.), *Journals and Papers of the Virginia State Convention of 1861* (Richmond: Virginia State Library, 1966), I, 118–19. Cited hereafter as *Convention Journals.*

54. John Janney to Alcinda Janney, March 31, 1861, Janney Papers, Virginia Tech.

55. William W. Freehling, "The Editorial Revolution, Virginia, and the Coming of the Civil War," *Civil War History* 16 (1970): 67.

56. *Convention Proceedings,* III, 106.

57. *Convention Proceedings,* III, 153–63. Three unionists and three secessionists paired their votes, while fifteen other delegates failed to vote for varying reasons. Janney voted against both formal motions for secession. The outspoken *Examiner* unloosed a broadside of criticism at the conservatives who voted in the negative. "The Federal majority . . . is responsible for civil war. . . . Their cowardice, their folly, their criminal delay and wicked, selfish, base calculations of what was or was not popular at the moment, makes the war! . . . Never was a greater trust committed to a nation's hand, never was it more despicably betrayed." *Richmond Daily Examiner,* April 8, 1861.

58. *Convention Proceedings,* III, 272–76.

59. *Convention Proceedings,* III, 271, 282–87, 290, 362–69.

60. Robert Y. Conrad (Frederick), chairman of the Federal Relations Committee, informed his wife that "telegrams are read in the house, and rumors are circulated—none of which I listen to but with a smile of incredulity." Four days later, Conrad reported: "The telegraph is beginning to tell some—though not the whole—truth." Robert Y. Conrad to wife, April 9 and 13, 1861, Robert Young Conrad Papers, Virginia Historical Society.

61. Shanks, *Secession Movement*, 196–97, 268; Basler, *Collected Works*, IV, 330.

62. *Convention Proceedings*, III, 678–79, 720.

63. *Richmond Daily Examiner*, April 15, 1861. Editor John M. Daniel then showed a sad ignorance of the situation by adding: "We are in the midst of war. War, so far, between seven rich and powerful Confederate States, on the one hand, and a handful of Federal mercenaries on the other. The Federal troops skulk and hide themselves in forts. In a fair and open field the troops of the Confederacy would in a single week surround and capture the whole army of the United States." In stark contrast was an April 14 letter from Alcinda Janney to her husband. "Virginia would not allow the seceded states to be coerced but is not the boot on the other foot when they begin hostilities? I only wish S. Carolina had to bear the whole weight on her own shoulders. I have no pity or sympathy with her in any way, I only feel contempt and am sorry she is in N. America." Janney Papers, Virginia Tech.

64. John Janney to Alcinda Janney, April 15 and 16, 1861, Janney Papers, Virginia Tech; Clifford Dowdey, *Experiment in Rebellion* (Garden City, N.Y.: Doubleday, 1946), 23. See also John B. Jones, *A Rebel War Clerk's Diary at the Confederate States Capital* (Philadelphia: Lippincott, 1866), I, 19–20.

65. Bedford delegate John Goode stated that Lincoln's call "destroyed all hope of a peaceful settlement" in Virginia. "The middle men, so called, who had held on to the Union as a shipwrecked mariner holds to the last plank when the midnight storm and tempest are gathering around him, were swept away by the overwhelming tide of popular excitement." Goode, *Recollections of a Lifetime*, 51.

66. *Richmond Daily Examiner*, April 12, 1861.

67. *Convention Proceedings*, IV, 4–17, 24–25.

68. Ibid., 26–27, 52. Willey's remarks, said one of his supporters, was "his last thrilling appeal to his colleagues to stand by the Constitution and the Union. During its delivery, there were all over the hall old men, with the frosts of winter on their heads, sobbing like children." Hall, *Rending of Virginia*, 526.

69. *Convention Proceedings*, IV, 75–76.

70. Hall, *Rending of Virginia*, 525. For a different version of Wise's intentions and actions, see McGregor, *Disruption of Virginia*, 173–76.

71. *Convention Proceedings*, IV, 138–39.

72. Ibid., 144; *Richmond Enquirer*, June 18, 1861; *Richmond Daily Whig*, April 18, 1861.

73. Shanks, *Secession Movement*, 204–5; McGregor, *Disruption of Virginia*, 176–77.

74. *Richmond Daily Whig*. April 23, 1861.

75. Roger A. Pryor, *Reminiscences of Peace and War* (New York: Macmillan Company, 1905), 124.

76. McGregor, *Disruption of Virginia,* 180–81.

77. *Convention Journals,* I, 456.

Land Operations in Virginia in 1861

Craig L. Symonds

On April 17, 1861, three days after Confederate forces fired on Fort Sumter in far away Charleston, South Carolina, the delegates to Virginia's state convention, who up to that moment had generally opposed disunion, passed an ordinance of secession by a vote of 88 to 55. Most Virginians had been willing to adopt a wait-and-see attitude toward the new Republican president, and believed that the precipitous secession by seven southern states that winter had been, at best, premature. But after Fort Sumter when Abraham Lincoln called for seventy-five thousand volunteers to "suppress" the seceded states and "to maintain the honor, the integrity, and the existence of our National Union," opinion in Virginia shifted decisively. The choice now seemed to be subjection or defiance, and the delegates voted accordingly. Virginia's decision provoked despair in the North and jubilation in the South. Many Southerners believed that with Virginia in their camp, independence was as good as won.[1]

From the very start, Virginia occupied center stage in the war that ensued. Aside from Texas, Virginia was the largest state in the Confederacy. It was also the most populous and the home of both its most valuable shipyard, Gosport near Norfolk, and its only cannon foundry, the Tredegar Iron Works. In recognition of Virginia's importance, the Confederacy moved its seat of government from Montgomery, Alabama, to Richmond, and that summer the first great battle of the war was fought along the banks of Bull Run near Manassas. Four years later, Lee's surrender at Appomattox Court House in Virginia marked a symbolic end to the war. Scholars of the Civil War point out quite rightly that the campaigns in the West were critical, even decisive, in determining the outcome of the war. But with the opposing capitals only about one hundred miles apart, the popular attention of both sides, as well as that of the international community, focused heavily on the campaigns in Virginia so that even small engagements there had a disproportionate impact on public opinion, and therefore on politics and policy.

Though the Civil War was a milestone event that transformed both the nation and indeed the nature of war itself, this fact did not become fully evident during the fighting in Virginia in 1861; the first eight months of the war witnessed more harbingers of change than change itself. The armies in Virginia, though large by prewar standards, were small in comparison with the hosts that fought in 1863 and 1864; and the number of casualties, though horrifying at the time, were relatively modest by the later standard of Fredericksburg or Chancellorsville. Moreover, the early months of war in Virginia betrayed the inexperience of the volunteer officers and the lack of clarity in command relationships on both sides. While these campaigns witnessed the emergence of several of the elements of "modern" war such as the telegraph, the railroad, and even semaphore signal flags, the full application of these revolutionary changes in warfare came later. Even the revolutionary impact of the rifled musket and the minié ball did not become fully evident during these early campaigns. What did become evident, however, even in these early battles, was the complex and often contentious relationship between strategy and politics, and the squabbling between generals, many of whom had agenda of their own.

From the very outset, the man who was charged with principal responsibility for orchestrating the defense of the state was Robert E. Lee. As a major general in command of the state's militia, Lee began planning the defense of his native state even before Virginia formally adhered to the Confederacy. His role changed in the second week of June when on the eighth of that month, the military forces of the state were formally transferred to the Confederacy. Lee was unsure what his new position would be within the Confederate military architecture, but in a few days he received an appointment as military adviser to Confederate President Jefferson Davis, and in that capacity Lee continued to oversee the defense of Virginia. As he saw it, danger threatened from four directions:

> The greatest menace was from the north. Union officials were gathering a large army at Washington just across the Potomac, and to

defend against this threat, Lee ordered a concentration of forces around Manassas Junction, forces that were eventually entrusted to the hero of Fort Sumter, Brig. Gen. Pierre G.T. Beauregard.

Another danger was that Federal forces would seize the arsenal at Harpers Ferry and drive south-eastward up the fertile Shenandoah Valley. To forestall this, Lee sent the former Virginia Military Institute mathematics professor Maj. Thomas J. Jackson to Harpers Ferry with orders to take command of the 2,500 or so men who had gathered there.

The third threat came from Federal forces in Ohio who could invade across the Ohio River into western Virginia. Invaders from that quadrant would have to deal with the inhospitable terrain of the Allegheny Mountains, but they could take encouragement from the fact that many of the inhabitants of western Virginia were strong unionists.

Finally, Lee had to worry about an invasion from the east. Union naval forces might test the defenses of Virginia's rivers, and Federal forces still held Fort Monroe at the tip of the peninsula formed by the James and York rivers, from which they were only a few days' march from Richmond.

During 1861, all four of these potential dangers were realized. One by one, and sometimes simultaneously, Federal forces moved toward the heart of the state from each of these four directions. Only to the south, along the boundary with North Carolina, was Virginia relatively secure.[2]

It did not take long for the Federals to test Lee's defensive arrangements. The first "invasion" of Virginia soil came on May 24, the day after Virginia voters ratified the convention's decision to secede. Lincoln had declined to send Federal forces into the Old Dominion while the vote was still pending, but once Virginia's departure from the Union was confirmed, he ordered the Forty-fourth New York Regiment (the so-called Fire Zouaves) across the Potomac into Alexandria. The commander of this unit was Col. Elmer Ellsworth, a handsome twenty-four-year-old who had studied law under Lincoln in Springfield and whom the president considered a personal friend. In Alexandria, Ellsworth noted a Confederate flag flying over the Marshall House Hotel, and he personally climbed to the roof to remove it. On his way back down he was shot and killed by the hotel manager. The news was a blow to Lincoln and brought home to him the reality of war in a very personal way. Ellsworth's death made headlines in the North (his body lay in state in the White House before being removed to New York for burial), but this initial Federal foray into Virginia did not lead immediately to a larger campaign. The first serious Union thrust into Virginia came from the east.

The Federal garrison at Fort Monroe was virtually unassailable. The gigantic masonry fort sat at the end of a spit of land cut off from the mainland by the marshes of Mill Creek and accessible only by a narrow causeway. It was a Union thorn stuck firmly in the side of Confederate Virginia, and since it was also easily accessible by sea, the Union Navy could keep it supplied and reinforced. It was, therefore, a natural staging base for a Federal assault against Richmond. In the second week of June, the commander of the Federal garrison at Fort Monroe was Maj. Gen. Benjamin F. Butler, one of the first of the so-called political generals: a Massachusetts Democrat who had subdued the hostile citizenry of Baltimore and declared runaway slaves to be "contraband." For all his lack of experience as a military commander, Butler was not the type to sit by and await orders. On his own initiative, he decided to send about 4,400 troops under Brig. Gen. Ebenezer Peirce to attack Confederate forces near Big Bethel on the northern branch of Back River a little less than halfway to Yorktown.

This initial Union offensive of the war demonstrated just how much field commanders had to learn about warfare. Because Peirce's forces were to advance at night along converging roads, he ordered his men to tie white strips of cloth around their arms so they could identify each other. As a failsafe, they were to yell out the password "Boston"—which he calculated no Rebel was likely to utter—to confirm their identity. Despite this, when the two Union columns came together, they immediately opened fire on one another. The white armbands were not visible in the predawn darkness, and any cries of "Boston" were drowned out by the sound of gunfire. Two men were killed and nineteen wounded before the mess could be sorted out, and of course the enemy was fully alerted, making surprise impossible.[3]

In spite of the confusion, Peirce decided to go ahead with the attack, and at daylight on June 10 he sent the Fifth New York Zouaves against the Confederate right and the Third New York Infantry against the left. During the advance, one company from the Fifth got separated in the thick trees, and when it reappeared on the regiment's flank, the regiment's commanding officer, Col. Frederick Townsend, mistook it for an enemy force and fell back. Confusion reigned on the left as well when the Zouaves assailed the Confederate line only to be thrown back by the North Carolina and Virginia troops under Col. John B. Magruder. Peirce decided to call off his offensive and ordered a retreat. The result was even more confusion as the troops straggled back to Fort Monroe in disorder. Butler put the best face he could on the fiasco by reporting that "we have gained more than we have lost" because "our troops have learned to have confidence in themselves under fire." Perhaps. But their confidence in their commanders could not have been enhanced.[4]

For their part, the defenders were jubilant. Magruder reported that the enemy had been "repulsed at all points and totally routed." Not only had the Yankees been thrown back, they had been defeated by a force barely a third their strength. One Reb really could whip three Yanks, it seemed. Magruder reported euphorically to Richmond that the battle at Big Bethel was as decisive as any in the Mexican War. The *Richmond Dispatch* called it "one of the most extraordinary victories in the annals of *war.*"[5]

In fact, however, the Battle of Big Bethel barely qualifies as a skirmish in the long history of the American Civil War; if it had taken place in 1864, it would not have attracted any attention at all. The attacking Union force lost eighteen killed, fifty-three wounded, and five missing; Confederate losses were one killed and seven wounded. But because the battle took place early in the war and relatively close to Richmond, it received big play in the Richmond papers, and indeed all across the South. The one Confederate fatality, Pvt. Henry L. Wyatt, became nearly as famous in the South as Colonel Ellsworth had in the North. His native North Carolina even erected a statue of him that still stands. Moreover, the skirmish had a disproportionate effect on morale, especially in the South, where it quieted latent unionism and energized Confederate recruiting. For the rest of the war, the Confederates who had fought at Bethel took pride in being the "first to fight."

Far more important strategically than the fight at Big Bethel was the campaign for western Virginia that got underway at about the same time. There in the hills and valleys of the Allegheny Mountains, the sparse population was both sympathetic to the Union cause and resentful of the Tidewater and Piedmont aristocrats who ruled the state from Richmond. The local citizenry was likely, therefore, to greet Union forces with enthusiasm; hundreds of them even volunteered for Union regiments. These troops fell under the overall command of Maj. Gen. George McClellan, who would make his name in this campaign and use it as a springboard to both fame and controversy. McClellan's Department of the Ohio encompassed not only Ohio, Illinois, and Indiana, but also western Virginia. When pro-Confederate forces burned several of the bridges on the Baltimore & Ohio Railroad just west of Grafton, Virginia, McClellan got orders to clear western Virginia of rebel troops and secure the railroad.[6]

McClellan had two options: He could invade Virginia along the Kanawha River Valley toward Charleston, or he could strike due east from Parkersburg along the line of the Baltimore & Ohio Railroad toward Grafton. He preferred the northern route to Grafton since from there he could command not only the B&O, but also the rail line that ran north from there to Wheeling in the thin finger of Virginia that jutted up between Ohio and Pennsylvania. Moreover, the area was strongly Union in sentiment. Only a dozen miles west of Grafton was the town of Clarksburg, whose 1,200 voters had voted unanimously against secession.[7]

McClellan opened the campaign by ordering a single regiment of pro-Union Virginia volunteers under Col. Benjamin Kelley southward from Wheeling to Grafton. There they were joined by an Indiana regiment and combined under the command of Brig. Gen. Thomas A. Morris. Falling back from this threat, the six hundred or so Confederates at Grafton under Col. George A. Porterfield retreated two dozen miles southward to Philippi, and Morris, who had upwards of three thousand men, prepared to assail him there. On June 2, Morris sent two columns toward Philippi on a night march. Mirroring Peirce's approach to Big Bethel, the Union advance on Philippi was marked by confusion and delay. In spite of that, Morris somehow managed to achieve surprise, though in the confusion of a night attack in rainy weather the much smaller Confederate force mostly escaped. Morris had hoped to block its escape and bag the whole force, but the blocking column did not get into place on time. The result was the "Philippi races" as the Confederates fled, with Union troops in close pursuit. There were no fatalities in this confused little skirmish, though one Union solider was killed when he accidentally shot himself during the march, and Morris himself was slightly wounded. This so-called Battle of Philippi initiated the campaign for western Virginia.[8]

That same week, Union Brig. Gen. Lew Wallace faced only nominal resistance while capturing the town of Romney more than halfway between Grafton and Harpers Ferry. Federal forces now controlled not only the Baltimore & Ohio Railroad, but also the entire length of the Northwestern Turnpike from Parkersburg to the Shenandoah Valley. These circumstances triggered two events: First, they convinced Maj. Gen. Joseph E. Johnston, who had succeeded Jackson in command at Harpers Ferry, to withdraw from that site and occupy Winchester, where the Northwestern Turnpike struck the Valley Pike. And second, they led Lee to dispatch reinforcements of several Virginia regiments (plus one from Georgia) along with a new commander for the Confederate forces in the Alleghenies. The man Lee chose was Robert S. Garnett, who had been the commandant of cadets during Lee's superintendency of West Point and who up to now had been acting as Lee's adjutant. Lee hoped that Garnett, promoted to brigadier general, would bring order and purpose to the defense of the western counties.

Garnett placed most of his forces, augmented to just over 5,000 men, in a blocking position athwart the turnpike a dozen miles north of the town of Beverly, where the road passed through a gap between Rich Mountain to the west, and Laurel Mountain to the east. Garnett arrayed nearly 4,000 men across the gap in a defensive position. But to guard against a flanking movement around his left, he put another 1,200 men under Lt. Col. John Pegram ten miles to the south to cover a gap through Rich Mountain.

Meanwhile McClellan arrived personally in the theater bringing the rest of his army with him: some twenty-seven regiments and a total of perhaps 20,000 men. In the first manifestation of what would become his most salient characteristic as a commander, he estimated Garnett's force at about twice its actual strength, and he therefore decided to feint against the Confederate main body with a single brigade while sending the bulk of his army to attack Pegram's 1,200 men at Rich Mountain. A sympathetic local farmer showed the Federals a path to Pegram's rear, and Brig. Gen. William S. Rosecrans led about 1,900 men on an early morning flanking movement on July 11 along a narrow mountain path in a driving rainstorm. Arriving near the summit around noon, Rosecrans found a much smaller Confederate force of about 350 men.

The original Federal plan was that McClellan was to join the fight with the Federal main body when he heard the sound of Rosecrans's assault. But the rainstorm and the trees muffled the sound and McClellan heard nothing. Rosecrans and Pegram were therefore left to fight it out atop Rich Mountain. When the outmanned Confederates finally broke, it split Pegram's command in two. One group fled southward down the turnpike; the rest, including Pegram himself, surrendered. With Rosecrans holding the pass through Rich Mountain, Garnett's flank was turned and he had to give up his position near Laurel Mountain. Fearing incorrectly that the route south had been blocked by McClellan's forces, he turned east and found his way into Cheat Valley. In this Battle of Rich Mountain McClellan took 555 prisoners at a cost of 12 dead and 62 wounded.[9]

McClellan pursued Garnett's retreating army, though both forces were slowed by continuing rain as well as difficult terrain. The Federals finally caught up with Garnett's rear guard on July 13 at Corrick's Ford on the Cheat River. There, the Twenty-third Virginia under the command of William B. Taliaferro held off the Yankees for several hours. Garnett came back from the main column to supervise the defense, and just as he was ordering the rear guard to fall back, a bullet struck and killed him. The Confederates got away again, but the death of Garnett was a psychological blow, similar in its impact on Robert E. Lee to the blow Lincoln had felt upon hearing the news about Elmer Ellsworth.

Just as Southern newspapers had trumpeted Big Bethel as a monumental victory, so did Northern newspapers elevate the modest Union success in western Virginia into an American Austerlitz. McClellan encouraged the comparison. Each of his reports was more triumphant than the one before. The day after the battle at Rich Mountain, he reported that his army had gained "a decisive victory." McClellan also made it evident where the credit for that victory belonged; in a report consisting of fourteen sentences, he used the word "I" eleven times. The next day in reporting the success at Corrick's Ford, he finally employed the plural pronoun in asserting that "we have driven out ten thousand of the enemy," and the day after that, he reported that "our success is complete." He claimed that the rebels had lost 150 killed and wounded, numbers that eventually proved to be overstated. Southern papers dismissed his claims and accused him of sending out his bulletins of victory before the battle had been decided. But exaggerated or not, McClellan's success in western Virginia was welcome news in beleaguered Washington, and it would resonate all the more when news arrived of the fiasco that took place the next week along the banks of Bull Run Creek.[10]

While McClellan was pursuing Garnett, events were moving to a climax in the central theater of Virginia. Beauregard's forces at Manassas Junction had been augmented to some twenty-two thousand, but in Alexandria, Maj. Gen. Irvin McDowell commanded a Union army of thirty-five thousand. Many of McDowell's soldiers were ninety-day volunteers, however, and those ninety days were swiftly running out. Lincoln urged McDowell to do something with his soldiers before their enlistments expired. McDowell was reluctant, reminding the president that his troops were untested in battle. In a famous riposte that he perhaps came to regret, Lincoln replied that "You are green, it is true; but they are green, also; you are all green alike."[11]

Thus prodded, McDowell consulted with commanding general Winfield Scott and developed a sound strategic plan. Recognizing that Union forces had to operate on exterior lines, he ignored the Rebel forces in western Virginia and on the Virginia peninsula as too small and too distant to matter, and focused instead on those in northern Virginia: Joseph E. Johnston's army of about twelve thousand men in the Shenandoah Valley and Beauregard's twenty-two thousand at Manassas Junction. As long as they could be kept apart, McDowell could count on having numerical superiority. His plan therefore called for the eighteen thousand Union soldiers under Robert Patterson in western Maryland to make a credible demonstration that would hold Joseph E. Johnston's army immobile in the Valley while McDowell's own force assailed Beauregard at Manassas.

McDowell's army reached Centreville, five miles north of Manassas, on July 18, five days after Garnett fell at Corrick's Ford. The Union army commander sent a column probing toward Blackburn's Ford over Bull Run where the Federals found the ford strongly held, and as a result McDowell determined to abandon a frontal assault in favor of a flank march to find the enemy rear. Ever since the invention of the minié ball in the 1850s, professional officers had known that frontal assaults were likely to be suicidal under all but the most favorable circumstances. Both sides, therefore, sought to maneuver to find the enemy flank or rear. In spirit and design, McDowell's move around Beauregard's flank in the First Battle of Bull Run was identical to Stonewall Jackson's flank march at Chancellorsville two years later. While McDowell sought a route to Beauregard's flank, Beauregard himself was sending frantic telegrams to Richmond asking for support. Davis, acting as literal as well as constitutional commander in chief, ordered Joseph E. Johnston to go to Beauregard's aid. Patterson's half-hearted maneuvers in the lower Valley that were supposed to keep Johnston in check were so unconvincing that even the cautious Johnston concluded that Patterson was not serious. When he got the telegram from Richmond, therefore, Johnston did not equivocate, wiring back at once: "We shall move toward General Beauregard tomorrow."[12]

In fact, he started that night. Johnston's four brigades marched eastward from Winchester, through the Blue Ridge at Ashby's Gap, and then south to Piedmont on the Manassas Gap Railroad. There they boarded trains to make the rest of the trip by rail, the first of them arriving on the afternoon of July 19. It was the first tactical use of the railroad in military history, and, arguably, it changed the outcome of the battle. That same night, McDowell spread a large map out on the floor of his command tent at Centreville and instructed his subordinates in the plan that they would execute the next day. Three brigades under Daniel Tyler would proceed directly along the Centreville turnpike and assault the Stone Bridge that spanned Bull Run Creek; another brigade would feint toward Blackburn's Ford. Both of these moves, however, were only diversions. The bulk of the army would undertake a lengthy roundabout night march to the north and west to cross the creek at Sudley Springs Ford two miles upstream, then swing southward to attack Beauregard in flank and rear. When the attack cleared the turnpike, Tyler's men would cross the bridge and join in the general assault. Beauregard's line would be rolled up north to south.

Ironically, Beauregard, too, was planning an offensive. With three of Johnston's four brigades at hand—Kirby Smith's was still en route—Beauregard wanted to cross Bull Run at Blackburn's Ford the next morning and assault the Federal left. Though Johnston was senior to Beauregard in rank, he had just arrived with his men and did not know the ground, and he therefore allowed the hero of Fort Sumter to write the orders for the next day. Those orders were all but incomprehensible and almost certainly would have led to confusion and perhaps disaster, but they were soon overtaken by events.[13]

McDowell's flanking movement began at 2:00 A.M. At first light, just past 6:00 A.M., Tyler's men fired the opening shot of the battle at the Stone Bridge. Three hours of desultory fighting ensued around the bridge before the Federal flanking column reached Sudley Springs Ford, crossed the stream, and started southward toward Beauregard's flank. If the Union attack was tardy, Beauregard's attack never got started at all. After some early morning confusion, and with the sound of battle rising to the north, he finally gave up on the whole idea and called it off. Meanwhile, Brig. Gen. Nathan Evans—known as "Shanks" for his long strides—commanded the lone Confederate brigade defending at the Stone Bridge. He was already facing long odds against Tyler's long-range bombardment when he was warned by the first known battlefield use of the signal flag that he was about to be flanked by the approaching Federal main body. Evans reoriented his brigade to face northward along the crest of what was known locally as Matthews' Hill to confront the new threat. Two of Johnston's brigades, those of Brig. Gen. Barnard E. Bee and Col. Francis P. Bartow, and the "Legion" of Col. Wade Hampton rushed northward to support him.

The soldiers in McDowell's flanking column still had numerical superiority, but they had been up since midnight and had been on the march and without food for more than eight hours. When they encountered the three Confederate brigades on Matthews' Hill, they stalled. They regained the momentum only after Tyler brought his three brigades across Bull Run to add their number to the battle. Gradually at first, then precipitately, the three Confederate brigades on Matthews' Hill began to fall back. Watching their flight, McDowell waved his hat and shouted, "Victory! Victory! The day is ours."[14]

Perhaps because he thought the battle was already won, or perhaps because he wanted to ensure that his army did not get out of control, McDowell hesitated before sending his forces up Henry House Hill in pursuit of the fleeing Confederates, and the delay was crucial. Johnston and Beauregard galloped up to the crest of that hill and took charge of the defense, assembling a more-or-less continuous defensive line across the crest. The Confederate survivors of the fighting on Matthews' Hill rallied on Henry House Hill where Johnston's other brigade, that of Thomas J. Jackson, had deployed. The retreat had severely disorganized the inexperienced Rebel troops, and Bee's South Carolinians in particular had been roughly handed. Seeking to rally and encourage them, Bee pointed to Jackson's Virginians, who, he said, were "standing like a stone wall," and ordered his men to "rally behind the Virginians." Thus was born the legend of "Stonewall" Jackson.[15]

By the time the Federals finally charged up Henry House Hill, at about 2:00 P.M., they discovered a new line of troops confronting them. For over an hour, the fighting surged back and forth across the undulating hilltop. Bee fell in the first fury of battle. Another victim was Judith Henry, whose house gave the hill its name; she became the first civilian battle casualty of the war. There was much confusion amid the thick white smoke and various uniform styles on both sides. At one point a blue-clad regiment appeared out of the woods near a Union battery. McDowell's chief of artillery, William Barry, assured the gunners that it was their own infantry coming up in support. It was, however, the Thirty-third Virginia, which delivered a volley followed by a bayonet charge.

Even then, however, the battle was still very much in doubt until late in the afternoon when, at about 4:00 P.M., Johnston's fourth brigade, that of Edmund Kirby Smith, arrived on the field. Kirby Smith fell wounded almost at once, but his senior colonel, Arnold Elzey, led the brigade into the fight, and it was enough to tip the balance. After marching and fighting for over fifteen hours, the Union forces could not hold up against a fresh attack on their flank. They gave way, and their retreat soon turned into a rout as they tried to crowd over the narrow stone bridge.

At the moment of victory, President Jefferson Davis arrived at Manassas by train from Richmond. He commandeered a horse and rode out to the battlefield to learn that the enemy was in full flight. That night he and his two generals shared mutual congratulations at Beauregard's headquarters. By the standards of 1861, the losses seemed high: 387 Confederates and 481 Federals were dead; nearly 2,000 had been wounded. Though the disparity in casualties was not great, the Rebels also captured thirty-eight cannon and nine battle flags—the greatly venerated tokens of victory in the nineteenth century. There was some talk at Confederate headquarters that night about a pursuit, but nothing came of it. Later there were recriminations on all sides about whose fault it was that no effective pursuit was undertaken. Most such discussions, however, were the product of hindsight, and it is unlikely that a pursuit could have been organized anyway, for the Confederates had been as disorganized by victory as the Federal army had been by defeat. Only later when the war dragged on into its second and third years did it seem that somehow an opportunity had been missed in the aftermath of the Confederate victory along the banks of Bull.[16] In the weeks after the battle, Johnston cautiously directed the combined forces of his army northward to Fairfax encountering no opposition. It remained there for only a month, however, because Johnston felt the position was too exposed, and on October 19, he moved the army back to Manassas.

If the news from Manassas electrified the South, the news from western Virginia was more sobering. After Garnett's death at Corrick's Ford, the Confederate defense of western Virginia became the scene of an absurd personal feud between two fractious and ambitious political generals. Jefferson Davis was under as much pressure as Abraham Lincoln to grant general's commissions to men of political influence but little military ability, and in consequence he had made brigadier generals out of former Virginia governor Henry A. Wise and former secretary of war John B. Floyd. At the same time, each of these men received permission to raise forces for a campaign in western Virginia.[17]

Wise got there first. In mid-July, as the opposing armies converged on Manassas, Wise led his small "legion" of perhaps 2,500 men westward along the Kanawha River Valley to Charleston. Though he occupied the city briefly, he could not hold it with such a small force amid a hostile population, and he fell back in late July. Then Floyd brought his little army into the region. At once the two political generals began to quarrel. Floyd, who had seniority, insisted that Wise's "legion" be made part of his command; Wise insisted that his was an independent command. Pleas from Richmond to cooperate for the sake of the cause went unheeded. Floyd won a small skirmish at Cross Lanes, on August 26, that encouraged him to think unrealistically about an advance to the Ohio, but instead he found himself attacked.[18]

By this time, Federal command in the Kanawha River Valley had passed from McClellan to Rosecrans who acted mostly on the defensive, guarding the railroads and establishing a chain of posts across the region. In early September, however, Rosecrans advanced against Floyd's position with three brigades. Floyd had foolishly entrenched his army with its back to the Gauley River, and but for a premature attack by one of Rosecrans's brigadiers the Confederates might have been overwhelmed. Instead, Floyd was alerted to his vulnerability and withdrew during the night of September 10. After this Battle of Carnifax Ferry, Floyd retreated out of the area, blaming all his problems on Wise's refusal to cooperate. The two men virtually stopped speaking to one another and made independent decisions despite the threat of a renewed Union offensive.[19]

This chaotic command situation was somewhat rectified by three events that took place in late September: First, Lee arrived in person to coordinate the two forces; second, Davis recalled Wise to Richmond; and third, William Loring arrived with nine thousand Confederate reinforcements. Before the Confederates could take advantage of their new circumstances to strike at Rosecrans, however, he fell back to his established defensive positions, having determined that the rainy weather and coming winter made a campaign unpromising. Soon afterward, Davis recalled Lee to Richmond, and the campaign in western Virginia ended for 1861.

There was one more act to be played out in Virginia before the end of the year. Like Big Bethel, the Battle of Ball's Bluff on October 21 was a small engagement measured either in terms of the number of troops involved or the number of casualties, but it was important, even decisive, for its long-term political consequences.[20] After the Union defeat at Bull Run, McClellan was recalled from western Virginia to take command of Union armies in the East. He set about reorganizing and drilling the Army of the Potomac. But while he did so, the fine late summer and early fall weather passed without any forward movement, and both the press and the administration became impatient. Pressed to take action, McClellan ordered a reconnaissance across the Potomac toward Dranesville on October 19, the same day that Johnston began his withdrawal from Centreville. At the same time he alerted Charles P. Stone of his plans, and on October 20 he suggested—but did not order—that Stone make a "slight demonstration" in the direction of Leesburg to see if McClellan's feint toward Dranesville had encouraged the enemy to evacuate it.[21] Stone's scouts got a late start and returned late that night to report that they had marched to within a mile of Leesburg and had encountered nothing more threatening than an abandoned enemy campsite. Armed with that information, Stone decided to send four companies, about three hundred men under Col. Charles Devens, on what amounted to a reconnaissance in force: a night march to destroy the camp at daybreak and return the next day.[22]

To cover this sortie, Stone sent two companies across the river at Edwards' Ferry and he ordered Col. Edward Baker to have the so-called California Regiment ready for service in case Devens found that the enemy had fled altogether.[23] The first report from Devens indicated that not only were there no enemy forces at the reported campsite, but the first scouting party had apparently mistaken trees for tents and there were no rebels there at all. Baker reported that his command was ready—not only the California Regiment, but his entire brigade—and he asked Stone for orders. It must have been an interesting conversation, for the command relationship between Stone and Baker was an awkward one. Baker was still a sitting Republican senator from Oregon. He had been offered a major general's commission, which would make him senior to Stone, but he had not yet accepted it because he could not hold any rank above colonel without giving up his Senate seat, which he did not want to do. Merely by saying so, however, Baker could resign and become a major general and Stone's superior. In addition, Baker was a close personal friend of the president who had named his second son after him. As a result of all this, Stone's "orders" to Baker may have been somewhat discretionary. Stone later claimed that all he told Baker was that he was to occupy Harrison's Island in the middle of the Potomac River, and that he was to make "no advance . . . unless the enemy were in inferior force, and under no circumstances to pass beyond Leesburg."[24]

Baker had an amateur warrior's enthusiasm but also an amateur's foolishness. He had only three small boats to ferry his four-regiment brigade of 1,640 men to Harrison's Island. But he did not stop on the island. Instead, he sent his entire command across to the southern side. Once across the river, he formed his brigade atop Ball's Bluff and assumed personal command. While he was forming up, Devens's scouting party finally found some enemy soldiers. They were Mississippians under the command of "Shanks" Evans, who had not only a full brigade of soldiers on hand and a better position from which to fight, but also the benefit of his experience at Bull Run. Unaware of this, Baker decided to move his command forward to support Devens; Evans brought his brigade forward as well, and all of a sudden the reconnaissance turned into a sharp little fight.

Instead of fulfilling the responsibilities of brigade commander and organizing lines of supply—and retreat, Baker went to the fighting front, sword in hand, to direct the action. Inevitably, perhaps, he became a casualty of the fighting, killed by a Confederate minié ball. Now his leaderless and disorganized command found itself in a very tight spot with its back to an unfordable river and assailed by what appeared to be a superior force. The two sides fought at relatively long range for about three hours before it became obvious to all that the Union position was untenable. In the ensuing retreat, some Union soldiers tried to scramble down the bluff behind them; some jumped, hoping to land in the river. Even those who made it safely to the boats overcrowded them in their panic, and the boats swamped or capsized.

By nightfall, it was over. Over half of Baker's command had been lost. Official Union casualties were 49 killed, 158 wounded, and 714 captured.

Confederate casualties were 33 killed and 115 wounded. The news of Baker's death was particularly shocking; it stunned Lincoln, who wept openly. Baker received a state funeral and became a martyr to the Union cause. Republicans could hardly pin the disaster on the martyred Baker; he was, after all, one of their own. Instead they directed their anger at the Democrat McClellan and at Stone. The investigation into the disaster at Ball's Bluff created the Joint Committee on the Conduct of the War, which played an important and not always positive role for the rest of the conflict. Stone was relieved of command and arrested by order of McClellan, who could see which way the wind blew. Indeed, McClellan was quick to recognize the danger of his position and immediately washed his hands of any responsibility. He denied that he had wanted Stone to send soldiers across the river. "My telegram [of October 20] did not contemplate the making [of] an attack upon the enemy or the crossing of the river in force," he insisted in post-battle testimony.[25]

Stone was left to be the scapegoat. He was arrested and imprisoned for 189 days without any charges ever being preferred against him. After his release, he returned to active duty and served as Nathaniel Banks's chief of staff for a few months in 1863, though soon afterward he was stripped of his volunteer's commission and reverted to his substantive rank. Eventually, the constant suspicion and distrust led him to resign. In an ironic twist, it was Stone who, in the 1880s, supervised the construction of the platform for the Statue of Liberty in New York Harbor.

The last action in Virginia during 1861 was the Battle of Dranesville on December 20, 1861, an accidental collision between scouting parties. Gen. James Ewell Brown "Jeb" Stuart, with 1,800 horsemen, was covering a foraging expedition northward on the same day that a Union infantry brigade under Edward Ord was embarked on the same mission southward. Ord's infantry got to Dranesville first and were able to withstand Stuart's attempt to drive them off. Finding it tough going, Stuart called off the attack and escorted his forage wagons back to Leesburg. Ord fell back toward Alexandria, and the two armies called it a season.

The year 1861 had served as an introduction to war for both sides. Despite Big Bethel, Confederates now knew that one Reb could not whip three Yanks, at least not every time. The Federals had learned that the rebellion would not be put down by ninety-day volunteers in a single summer. Officers on both sides had learned valuable lessons not only about the management of troops, but about the care and feeding of political superiors. Both sides looked to a longer struggle conducted by increasingly professional armies. Both sides now knew that the campaign would be renewed in the spring on all four of the battle fronts in Virginia: the Allegheny West, the Shenandoah Valley, the Manassas front, and the Virginia peninsula. The fighting in 1861 had merely set the stage for the more decisive—and far bloodier—campaigns of 1862.

Notes

1. Roy P. Basler, ed., *The Collected Works of Abraham Lincoln* (New Brunswick, N.J.: Rutgers University Press, 1953), IV, 332.

2. Jeffrey D. Wert, "Lee's First Year of the War," *Civil War Times Illustrated* 13 (December 1974): 7–8; Douglas Southall Freeman, *R.E. Lee: A Biography* (New York: Charles Scribner's Sons, 1934), I, 472–90, 530–31.

3. William J. Kimball, "The Little Battle of Big Bethel," *Civil War Times Illustrated* 6 (June 1967): 30–31.

4. Butler's report is in U.S. War Department, *War of the Rebellion: A Compilation of Official Records of The Union and Confederate Armies* (Washington, D.C.: Government Printing Office, 1880–1901), series I, vol. 1, 77–80. (Hereafter cited as *OR*.) The quotation is from p. 80.

5. Magruder's Report is in *OR*, series I, vol. 1, 91; *Richmond Dispatch*, June 12, 1861.

6. The most complete account of the western Virginia campaign is in Clayton P. Newell's book, misleadingly named *Lee vs. McClellan: The First Campaign* (Washington, D.C.: Regnery Publishers, 1996). See also Jacob D. Cox, "McClellan in West Virginia," in *Battles & Leaders of the Civil War* (New York: Century Company, 1894), I, 128–48.

7. Newell, *Lee vs. McClellan*, 64.

8. Ibid., 85–107.

9. Cox, "McClellan in West Virginia," 130–33.

10. McClellan's three reports are in *OR*, series I, vol. 2, 203–4. See also *Richmond Examiner*, July 16, 1861.

11. Quoted in T. Harry Williams, *Lincoln and His Generals* (New York: Knopf, 1952), 21.

12. Samuel Cooper to Joseph Johnston, July 17, 1861, and Joseph Johnston to Samuel Cooper, July 18, 1861, both in *OR*, series I, vol. 2, 478, 982.

13. Beauregard's orders are in *OR*, series I, vol. 2, 479–80.

14. The best summary of the First Bull Run (Manassas) campaign is still William C. Davis, *Battle at Bull Run: A History of the First Major Campaign of the Civil War* (Garden City, N.Y.: Doubleday, 1977).

15. P.G.T. Beauregard, "The First Battle of Bull Run," *Battles & Leaders,* I, 120.

16. Joseph E. Johnston, "Responsibilities of First Bull Run," *Battles & Leaders,* I, 252.

17. Freeman, *R.E. Lee,* I, 579–82; Newell, *Lee vs. McClellan,* 75.

18. Newell, *Lee vs. McClellan,* 197–202.

19. Cox, "McClellan in West Virginia," 144–46.

20. The only full-length work on the Battle of Ball's Bluff is Byron Farwell, *Ball's Bluff A Small Battle and Its Long Shadow* (McLean, Va.: EPM Publications, 1990).

21. A.V. Colburn to Charles Stone, October 20, 1861, *OR,* series I, vol. 5, 290.

22. Charles Stone to George McClellan, October 29, 1861, *OR,* series I, vol. 5, 294.

23. The so-called California Regiment, in fact, contained only a handful of volunteers from the Golden State; most of the soldiers in the ranks were Pennsylvanians.

24. Charles Stone to George McClellan, October 29, 1861, *OR,* series I, vol. 5, 295–96.

25. George McClellan to Simon Cameron, November 1, 1861, *OR,* series I, vol. 5, 290.

Confederate Soldiers in Virginia, 1861

Joseph T. Glatthaar

Most scholars and students of the Civil War simply assume that soldiers from rural areas were vastly superior to the urban enlistees. They believe that those from farms and the country had greater familiarity with weapons from hunting, and they unquestionably rode horses better. We presume that farmers were jacks-of-all-trades, people who could fix almost anything. While he might lack the sophistication and education of his urban counterparts, the rural soldier had developed his own horse sense, a kind of good-judgment compass that steered him through the morasses of military life. Surely those many days out hunting game taught them a familiarity with the woods, camping, and the outdoors—experiences that would dominate life as a soldier. So, too, would a sense of independence, a confidence in decision making and problem solving born of small-time success in their chosen occupation.

Perhaps we accept this superiority because the Army of Northern Virginia, predominantly rural in its composition, held a much larger and more urbanized Union army at bay for four long years. Or maybe we assume so because the Union western armies conquered the West and had marched all the way to central North Carolina by the end of the war. But are these assumptions justified? How knowledgeable and experienced were these rural men who fought for the Confederacy in Virginia, and did those prewar practices prepare them for the vicissitudes of military service? Whether from rural or urban areas, volunteers entered military service woefully unprepared physically, emotionally, and attitudinally. Yet that first year offered the officers and men who soldiered in Virginia some invaluable experiences. Most importantly, they taught themselves how to administer and care for themselves. Often that learning curve extracted a hefty price in lives lost and in human suffering. Those who emerged from the process, however, were far more ready emotionally and physically for the cataclysmic battles and hardships of the next three years.

While scholars have detected resistance toward secession from Southerners who possessed loose allegiances to the institution of slavery—effectively, those who lived in areas where few people owned slaves—the opposition was not a result of urban versus rural sensibilities. Slave ownership, as many scholars have indicated, had taken firm root in cities. In fact, the ratio of slaves to whites was the same in urban areas as it was in the countryside. Secessionists, whether urban or rural, saw themselves as defenders of principles. Both Northern and Southern states had endorsed a Constitution that yielded to states the power to permit the ownership of slaves. Residents of slave states had the legal right to own people of African ancestry as property, to take that property with them, and to use that property as they saw fit. Over the years (and with increasing ferocity), Northerners attacked those rights, thereby challenging the sanctity of that Constitution and endangering Southern whites by promoting servile disturbances.

Ironically, Southern whites believed that their freedom depended on the institution of slavery. Not only did slave labor prove economically viable, providing a high standard of living for those who owned slaves, but it also elevated all white men. Historical examples, they argued, demonstrated that some element of society had to function at a subservient level, so that others could reap the benefits of a privileged state. Menial labor debased workers. By having African slaves perform the lowliest tasks, all white men were lifted to a status that allowed them to enjoy and preserve their civil liberties. In white Southerners' eyes, because Africans were an inferior race, they were ideally suited to perform this function.

Under duress from the Northern onslaught, Southerners had two choices as they saw it. They could remain in the Union and permit Northerners to strip them of their constitutional rights, making them little more than slaves themselves. After all, a man without rights is nothing more than a slave, and a man who permits another to deprive him of those rights has no honor, no character worthy of a free man. Or, they could secede from the Union and found a Slave Confederacy, with their principles intact, as they did. Like their revolutionary ancestors, secessionists believed they were building a nation that others should emulate. Southerners had founded a "New Jerusalem" for people to enjoy the blessings of liberty under God's watchful eye, so asserted a soldier to his wife. It was "the last hope of free Government."[1]

When the administration of Abraham Lincoln announced that the U.S. government would block secession, with force of arms if necessary, Southerners determined they would fight in defense of hearth and home and also to preserve that freedom their ancestors had bequeathed to them. War fever was everywhere. "It seemed to me that the people were crazy and we were wild crazy," a Georgian wrote. From Alabama, a new soldier destined for the Virginia theater described the scene to his sister: "All is excitement hear—war—war—war—is the continued topic of evry days conversation."[2] Once Virginia seceded and the Confederacy moved its capital to Richmond, the state became a primary target for Union offensives. Virginians rallied to the banner in defense of their beloved homeland. Secessionists from other states, too, flocked to the Old Dominion. While it was not quite the same as defending one's own homeland, Virginia held a special place in the hearts of these soldiers. It was the land of revolutionary leaders; the cradle of the Old Republic; the birthplace of Thomas Jefferson, James Madison, Patrick Henry, and, most importantly, George Washington. Like these past leaders, secessionists sought independence and preservation of their liberties. Washington became their model—a citizen who picked up his sword and risked all for freedom. Henry's immortal words, "Give me Liberty or Give me Death," fired their hearts. In Richmond, they viewed St. John's Church, where Henry articulated those potent words, and around the city and in the army they occasionally caught a glimpse of Robert E. Lee, the son of the Revolutionary War hero, or John A. Washington, the first president's nephew. The sites and people reminded them of their obligation to preserve that legacy.[3]

Southerners brought with them into military service several advantages, not the least of which was motivation. "Our cause is a glorious & holy one," justified a Louisianan, "and I for one am willing that my bones shall bleach the sarced [sacred] soil of Virginia in driving [away] the envading host of tyrants." Another soldier, a Virginian, defended his decision to risk his life in military service, writing home, "Ma I intend to die *worthy* of the Mother who bore me and of the Father that taught me to be a *free man,* & to have honor." One South Carolinian informed his wife that he would fight till death, and when his son grew up, he expected that young man to take his place in the ranks "and fight until he dies, rather than be a slave worse than a slave to Yankee masters."[4]

In a war for independence and rights, the Confederacy must inevitably win, Southerners insisted. "Remember that the Straggle we are engaged in is a noble and a just one," a North Carolinian reminded his wife, "and that God is on our side and if he is for us who can be against us." Secessionists reasoned that surely a just God, surely the inevitable progress of mankind, would favor an attempt to preserve freedom. "*We are right!*" proclaimed a Mississippian, "and sooner or later right must triumph!"[5]

It was not just the notion of fighting for freedom that gave Confederates a sense of superiority. Those troops destined for Virginia battlefields believed that Southern society, with its emphasis on individualism and freedom, produced better men and women who would make superior warriors. "There is not a man in the Southern Army," boasted a Virginian to his mother, "who does not in his heart believe that he can whip three Yankees, he would consider it beneath his manhood to count upon whipping a less number in any sort of a fight." This Union attempt to conquer them boggled his mind. "How they can ever hope to subdue us is beyond my comprehension." So convinced was he of Southern superiority that he even doubted the entire world could defeat them in ten years.[6]

In addition to the emotional or psychological edge, these Rebels had other advantages that they hoped would offset Union manpower and materiel superiority. "We have the best portion of the old army, I mean not in numbers, but in talent," asserted future division commander Cadmus Wilcox to his sister. Many Confederates and Federals considered Lee, Joseph E. Johnston, P.G.T. Beauregard, and even Thomas J. Jackson among the very best the U.S. Military Academy produced.[7] Dozens of militia units throughout the South had formed in the wake of John Brown's 1859 raid on Harpers Ferry, and they continued to drill until they went on active service in 1861. The state of Virginia had allocated $320,000 to refurbish the Virginia Manufactory Armory in January 1860. On campus at the University of Virginia, two companies of eighty students each drilled every evening for ninety minutes. By early March 1861, a student-soldier noted, they were "getting to be pretty well drilled."[8] Other regiments and artillery batteries, especially those of Virginia and South Carolina, also benefited from former students of the Virginia Military Institute and the Citadel. During their school days, they had mastered drill and acquired a familiarity with tactics and military weapons. As the Confederacy raised units, these individuals could teach fresh enlistees close-order drill, military practices, and weapons use and care.[9]

Yet for all their motivation and prior training, Confederate officers and men who served in Virginia had no inkling of the scale and scope of the problems they would encounter. None of them had ever served in an army larger than ten thousand men—the one Winfield Scott commanded in his advance on Mexico City. By the end of July 1861, the Confederate command at Manassas Junction alone tripled that manpower strength. The flood of military personnel and civilians taxed the agricultural and industrial base beyond its capacity, and railroads and roads struggled to deliver the necessary food and supplies to the army. Commanding and controlling these men, especially with the sense of independence and individuality that they had absorbed from civil life, proved extremely burdensome, and in some cases almost impossible.

Nor had Confederates carefully thought through the problems of warfare on such a large scale. Misguided notions about war at virtually all levels inflicted painful, sometimes fatal, lessons. Even their peacetime life on Southern farms and in rural areas, which we often associate with inculcating soldierly qualities, prepared them inadequately—perhaps no better than the city soldiers—for the hardships and hazards of military life. That farming background provided few clues to anticipate these difficulties, and cultural attitudes resisted efforts to adapt the troops and cope with military realities.

In organizing an army in northern Virginia, Confederates were actually forming a city, with all the complexities and troubles of an urban environment. By the summer of 1861, the army around the Centreville-Manassas axis was larger than the population of 1860 Richmond. It would continue to increase in strength until by the summer of 1862 the Army of Northern Virginia as Lee styled it was twice the size of prewar Richmond. Unfortunately, Confederates had very little experience coping with urban life. Richmond was the twenty-fifth largest city in the United States in 1860, ranking immediately behind the hardly bustling metropolis of Troy, New York. New Orleans, ranking sixth, and Charleston, at twenty-second, were the only other cities in seceding states that outranked Richmond. Barely 4 percent of all Confederates lived in cities with ten thousand people or more, by any standards hardly a benchmark for a substantial urban environment.[10]

Nonetheless, military demands forced personnel to concentrate in densely packed areas. For days after the victorious Battle of First Manassas, Confederates lived on the field in numbers close to 10,000 per square mile. Keep in mind, too, that Civil War armies organized in a linear fashion, with less attention to depth. By comparison, 1860 Richmond had a density of about 6,000 per square mile. A little over a week later, the army dispersed along a fifteen-mile front, which reduced the density to 2,000 to 3,000 men per square mile, still a heavy concentration. By December, the command had 76,000 officers and men present, with the largest concentration crammed into a nine-square mile area around Centreville.[11] To make matters worse, nonmilitary personnel crowded into the area. Many of the troops brought slaves as servants, to take care of their personal needs during their days in the army. Visitors flocked to Manassas, to meet with loved ones and see for themselves this giant and triumphant army that their fledgling nation had created. Some even came to scavenge for mementoes. All of them taxed supplies, occupied valuable cargo space on trains and wagons, and spread illness to the city of Richmond and the army.

On better days, soldiers marveled over these massive "canvass" cities. From a hilltop, you could gaze across the landscape and literally see thousands and thousands of troops milling about camp, drilling, and performing sundry other chores. But these bivouacs, clumped together so tightly, acted as a biological time bomb. Medical studies have discovered a very high correlation between population density and the rate of illness. Thus, Union and Confederate camps would suffer from a high incidence of sickness. What made these Rebel camps particularly lethal was that the troops came almost exclusively from rural areas, where they had little prior exposure to these deadly agents.[12]

By the time they reached adulthood, most city dwellers had survived bouts with the usual assortment of childhood illnesses, and many had endured the likes of typhoid fever and other potentially lethal ailments. As a result, they developed resistance to these viruses and bacteria. Often, too, if their ancestors had come from urban areas, they had passed on some resistance to the illnesses to their descendants. Medical scholars call this seasoning. Those people who lived in farming communities frequently escaped the childhood illnesses and seldom developed resistance or seasoning to the kinds of harmful agents that spread through the water supply or that required intensive or lengthy exposure. In camp, living in tight proximity to thousands of others, with huge numbers of soldiers drawing from the same water supply, disease spread like wildfire.

The numbers were utterly astounding. In June, a Mississippian complained that his regiment had between 350 and 400 sick. In mid-August, the Fifth North Carolina reported 800 sick out of a total of 1,100 men. Eight men turned out for dress parade in one man's company; everyone else was sick. The Seventh Georgia could assemble 300 of the original regiment for dress parade, and of those 300, 100 were so sick they could not have performed active duty. "As summer diseases pass away," commented a young North Carolinian, "Winter ones takes its place." In December, the Fourteenth Alabama had 500 sick men. Nearly all the healthy ones had to devote their day to caring for the ill. That January, out of 700 on the rolls in the Eighth Virginia, only 264 could assemble for duty. At one point, army commander Joseph E. Johnston complained to President Jefferson Davis that of the 45,000 men he had with the army, almost 10,000 were sick, and that did not include 5,000 in hospitals away from camp.[13]

Measles, mumps, and typhoid fever were the greatest culprits. Pneumonia, dysentery, and diarrhea took their share as well. Funeral dirges became more familiar than "Dixie." The problem became so widespread that one soldier predicted, "those Yankees are going to try to whip [us] with *disease* instead of the Powder."[14] Medical authorities could do little to check the epidemics. Some regiments had no physicians; others lacked competent ones. But even the best doctors could not cope with the staggering number of cases. Good nurses would have helped to ease the burden by at least keeping the sick soldiers clean and fed, although they, too, were in short supply. As a captain in the Fourteenth Louisiana whose regiment suffered from a massive outbreak of typhoid fever explained, "the Regimental Surgeon seems unable to treat the disease successfully. The men have become very much alarmed and dispirited." Efforts to remove the sick and place them in hospitals merely shifted the site of agony. It took twenty-four to thirty-six hours to transport sick and injured soldiers by train from Manassas Junction to Charlottesville, where officials had temporarily converted dormitories and other facilities into hospital buildings. Seldom did they receive food or care on the trip, according to a physician. Others traveled to Richmond, a fourteen-hour journey on what one soldier called "filthy cattle cars." Overwhelmed as were the regimental facilities, off-site hospitals had an even more checkered record of success. Small wonder that soldiers deserted the hospital trains, despite their ailments.[15]

The best means of combating illness was to police camps. Unfortunately, rural living did little to develop concern over sanitation. In the early 1840s, a physician named John H. Griscom embarked on a pathbreaking study of sanitary conditions for the laboring class in New York City. Griscom blamed the high rate of disease on poor sanitary and living conditions. It took a few years to convince authorities, but Northern cities began to clean streets, build sewage lines, remove waste, and concern themselves with proper sanitation. The same month that the war broke out, a group of Northerners formed the U.S. Sanitary Commission, based on a model in the Crimean War. The Sanitary Commission was an advisory and watchdog group to ensure that the health and welfare of the Union army was preserved. Drawing on prewar experiences, Federals dealt with health problems early on. With its few urban areas, the South, however, lagged behind.[16] Farms on which most Southerners lived had few serious sanitary problems. To measure up to mid-nineteenth century standards of sanitation, they needed to know little more than not to build the outhouse next to the well and to keep the livestock out of the house. Since Joseph Lister did not develop his germ theory and antiseptics until after the war, they could do little else to maintain a healthy environment.

This lackadaisical attitude spilled over into military service. Unaccustomed to much discipline and unschooled in field hygiene, soldiers' sanitary practices lapsed as they responded anywhere to nature's call. "On rolling up my bed this morning," a soldier penned home, "I found I had been lying in—I wont say what—something that didn't smell like milk and peaches." Medical officers called for the digging and regular use of sinks, but enforcement was lax. Severe sanitation problems erupted in the aftermath of the Battle of First Manassas. In victory, the Confederates were unprepared to cope with the thousands of killed and wounded soldiers and animals. While Rebel soldiers received preferential treatment, quite a number obtained such scant attention that maggots infested their wounds. Meanwhile, human and animal bodies lay on the field decaying for days. The smell, recorded a Georgia captain, resembled a "butcher's pen." Millions of flies and thousands of scavenging birds picked at the decomposing flesh. In Bull Run, where most soldiers had drawn their water, deceased Yankees and horses rotted, breeding pestilence throughout the rivulet. Nine days after the battle, a Mississippian and his comrades had to wade across Bull Run. He complained that they "were much annoyed by the bad smell of the water, as we crossed below the battlefields, and the creek was perfectly impregnated with the smell of the bodies of dead men, & horses." "As soon as I could," he continued, "I went to a spring branch, and washed off the smell, & put on clean clothes." After some days, the army dispersed, but some remained encamped on the battlefield and continued to suffer the consequences.[17]

Sloppy, almost unconscionable sanitary conditions continued to plague the army. The department medical director complained in mid-November that offal from the slaughter pens and camp kitchens was not buried daily and that soldiers did not dig sinks "at such a distance from camp as to prevent the deleterious effects of miasma naturally arising from the deposits." Two months later, the Second Corps medical director grumbled that the troops failed to bury offal and deceased horses, and "the use of privies seems to have become a matter of Regimental history, and the claim of commanders to approval for observances of the Regulations in this respect appears to be entirely based upon the past." That month, the First Corps assigned a "Police Officer" with a party of men for daily duty to ensure proper practices in camp.[18]

Despite their days in the countryside, Confederate soldiers had little experience living outdoors. Often they positioned camps in unhealthy locations or in clumps of trees, proceeding to chop them down for convenient firewood. What they did not realize was that an adult tree drinks about thirty gallons of water a day. Without the timber for drainage, they converted their camps into mud baths. "I thought I had some very respectable mudy roads in Alabama," a soldier wrote, "but Virginia mud, is so decidedly mudy, of such unmitigated depth and stickiness as to render comparison impossible." Some complained that it was ankle deep—in their tents.[19] Creeks and streams always run along the lowest piece of ground; soldiers almost always fortify on the high ground. When they dug trenches, soldiers covered the grass and promoted runoff. Without well located and universally used sinks, soldiers relieved themselves just outside the defensive position. Rains then washed the waste down into the streams, contaminating the water supply.

Nor did soldiers demonstrate much interest in caring for themselves in camp. Removed as they were from traditional society, practicing personal cleanliness became a thing of the past. Soldiers seldom bathed and infrequently shaved. Dirt and mud—the Virginia form that had no parallel—dusted and caked onto uniforms, yet soldiers continued to wear them, undeterred by the filth. "You ought to see some of the soldiers in this regiment," one exclaimed to his parents. "Some of them I dont believe have had on a clean shirt in two months, one of them told me he had'nt washed himself *since he left home* (more than three months ago), he was decidedly one of the 'great unwashed.'" Part of the blame rested with the quartermaster department, which failed to issue soap for two months. But soldiers used soap sparingly even when readily available.[20]

With little experience living outdoors, regardless of their backgrounds, most soldiers struggled to perform the most elementary tasks, such as building proper campfires. Soldiers burned themselves by tossing on too many logs, roasting their feet, and singeing their hair. Some men in the Rockbridge Artillery positioned their fire too close to a wood. In the cold January air, they piled on too many logs, and the roaring flames spread to the trees. Frantic troops had to scurry about to remove the animals, guns, and ammunition—and nearly a ton of gunpowder—before the flames consumed them.[21]

At home, cooking had been women's work. Nearly all the troops were inexperienced when it came to food preparation. Some of course had the benefit of black servants, but they were usually selected on the basis of loyalty and heartiness, rather than culinary expertise. Once again, had the government provided them with satisfactory ingredients to prepare balanced meals, it would have helped somewhat. Still, their utter incompetence converted a reasonably healthy meal into unpalatable fare. One mess thought a container of tallow was lard, stole it, and baked biscuits with it. A Georgia private grumbled of eating biscuits so hard "i could nock a bull down with one." A soldier named Bacon had quite a time with bread making. "The first time I made up dough," he explained to a friend, "I had a mess of it; stuck to my hands and I hardly could get it off. Then I tried to bake it, but I could not get it done; some was burnt up and some was raw." He then concluded, "what a mess I had." Another soldier complained to his aunt that "the only thing that hurts me is the food I have to eat. It keeps my stomach out of order all the time. The bread is burned out side & raw in side, & the meat is so strong & salty that I dont pretend to eat it. The two comprise our bill of fare." The problem became so serious that Johnston

and Beauregard blamed the poor cooking for the massive diarrhea out-
breaks and had ovens built to furnish soldiers with decent bread a few times
per week.[22]

It is often assumed that men in the 1860s had extensive experience with
firearms. Although many Confederates in that day had hunted and knew
how to shoot well, like people of today few of them had any day-to-day
experience carrying weapons. All too often careless soldiers left their muskets loaded, with percussion caps on the firing nipple. A slight jarring of
the hammer sent a projectile roaring through camps, occasionally with fatal consequences. Others did not bother to remove the powder and ball
before cleaning the weapon, or were careless in the loading process. And
nothing was sadder than to lose a friend or comrade at the hand of someone on your own side through accident or negligence.[23] Quite a few Rebels,
regardless of rank, brought pistols with them. Unstable weapons when
loaded, these pistols went off far too frequently in camp, usually maiming
or killing the owner, but sometimes taking someone else's life. The problem became so serious that a Georgia officer wrote an Atlanta newspaper,
urging volunteers to leave those weapons at home.[24]

Early in the war, the urban soldiers were probably a bit better social-
ized than their rural counterparts. A small family farmer, a category that
encompassed a majority of Southerners, could and often did go days without seeing someone who did not live in his household. Urbanites inter-
acted with nonfamily members every day. They were more accustomed to
crowds and the hustle and bustle of city, or camp, life. They also had greater
exposure to the sorts of vices that tempted Civil War soldiers. For all Southerners, whether urban or rural, slavery was a steady reminder of their independent status. It elevated them in their own eyes and sensitized them to
the importance of treatment as free men, with dignity and respect. As
such, few of them were predisposed to endure army discipline. Discipline
in rural communities was largely self- or family-imposed. But urban living requires greater accommodation, a more structured way of life. Along
with the individual and his family, urban residents endured discipline
from external sources, like local law enforcement and social pressure from
neighbors.

That urban-rural distinction, however, did not last long. Military service acted as a great leveler, placing men from all sorts of backgrounds in
the same conditions. As soldiers encountered the discipline of army life, as

officers whom they deemed no better than themselves ordered them about and directed them to perform menial labor like digging trenches, or burdensome chores like guard duty in the pouring rain or freezing cold, they reacted as if someone had stripped them of their civil rights. "I am sure there is no field negro that has not more liberty than we have," grumbled a young Virginian. A Georgian complained to his sister that the army stripped him of his right to make decisions. "I don't like the idea of being ordered about like a slave, & being treated as a mere tool or machine," he groused. "I think I am a reasonable being, but some fools in authority think that a private soldier has no right to think at all." Excessively sensitive to slights, unaccustomed to being ordered about by fellow citizens, and wary of any violations of their rights as freemen, Confederates responded far too often with violence.[25]

Interestingly, of all the soldiers in Virginia during the first year, the most unruly were the Louisiana troops. Two-thirds of them came from New Orleans. Ethnically mixed, with large contingents of Irish and French, neither the urban nor the rural soldiers demonstrated much discipline or self-control. They embarked on a drunken riot en route to Virginia, and from late September to early October, portions of three different regiments launched armed mutinies. An officer was court-martialed because he refused to put down one of the riots, exclaiming he "was worn out" trying to control his men. On December 9, the Third Louisiana Battalion erupted in a major gunfight, leaving one enlisted man dead and three officers and a servant seriously wounded. Soldiers from Louisiana even tried to assassinate an officer who headed a general court-martial that ordered the execution of two Louisiana men.[26]

Clearly, these Louisianans were an extreme case, but tempers flared readily and misbehavior abounded throughout the army. Over the course of a week, a Virginia regiment had seven different brawls. An Alabamian informed his parents that the guardhouse covered about an acre and "sum times it is ful. Sum times there are nearly hole company put in at once princepaly for geting drunk and fiteing." Brig. Gen. James Longstreet himself had to disarm one mutinous Virginia company and threatened to disband an entire Virginia regiment. When a general court-martial convened on November 27, 1861, five of its ten cases dealt with assault with a deadly weapon or manslaughter.[27]

Removed from traditional social controls and with too much time on their hands, young men—rural or urban—responded with extreme behavior. "I have often heard it said that man when taken away from female society will soon become like a brute," a Virginian commented to a friend, "& I am forced by experience to acknowledge it to be true." Here they learned, a South Carolinian explained to his folks, "who are the friends and who are the rascals."[28] Wild drunkenness, gambling, and prostitution abounded around the army. "Constantly exposed to danger and disease," a Virginia officer explained, "the men and (I blush to say it) very many officers give way to excess and dissipation." Drunken frolickers in the Rockbridge Artillery kept everyone up one night. The next day, the drivers were so drunk they mired wagons and teams in mud. In Fredericksburg, some soldiers became "intoxicated and riotous." According to Brig. Gen. Theophilus Holmes, their behavior was "outrageous & shameful." A Virginian discouraged his wife from visiting him, fearing she would be identified as a prostitute. "I am fearful this country is filled up with Prostitutes who pass as soldiers wives," he lamented.[29]

Sacrificing time from loved ones, risking their lives to enemy bullets and disease, and enduring untold hardships, soldiers indulged in immediate gratification. In their shortsighted quest to ease their own burden, they cut across planted fields, rather than walk around them, damaging the future food supply. They raided vegetable gardens; stripped fruit trees bare; pilfered and consumed livestock and poultry; dismantled fences, barns, and "abandoned" homes for firewood; and stole bedding and garments for their own comfort. "The stories of out rage, theft & destruction by our men are truly horrible," an officer wrote disgustedly to his wife. "Women have escaped thus far, but property of every kind is taken without hesitation." Troops justified their conduct by believing that everyone in the Confederacy should be making sacrifices. As soldiers, they gave the most to the cause; others should contribute to their well-being, they felt. By the time the army abandoned the Centreville line in the spring of 1862, the area was one of wholesale devastation.[30]

Over time, military service and its various hardships blurred any distinctions between rural and urban soldiers. All of them lived in the open air, or under tents that a Texan claimed, "are no more protection than one of your fine cambric pocket hankerchief might be for an Elephant." They suffered from the same diseases, endured the same hunger and thirst, went shoeless, coatless, and hatless with the same frequency, marched the same number of miles, floundered in the same mud, shivered in the same freezing rain, and frolicked in the same snow.[31]

The rural soldiers had a decided edge, however, when it came to combat. Having used weapons for hunting and shooting much of their life, they tended to be better marksmen. But during that first year of war in Virginia, Confederates fought comparatively little. Only the Battle of First Manassas in July 1861 could be designated a major engagement, and even it paled in comparison to the magnitude of clashes in the later years. Barely thirty-two thousand Confederates saw action that day, and while the long list of casualties shocked the Southern public, in time they would come to endure lists that included ten times as many names. The scale and scope of the war eclipsed First Manassas the next year, and participants themselves would look back on that battle in late July 1861 as a strange episode of naïveté and confusion, almost to the point of a dark comedy. As a South Carolinian commented after the Seven Days' Battles in mid 1862, "we used to think that the battle of Manassas was a great affair, but it was mere child's play compared with those in which we have been lately engaged." Over time, city soldiers would hone their shooting skills, just as the rural men would harden to disease. The price for experience might be painfully high, but come it did nonetheless.[32]

The hardships of that first year and the military setbacks in early 1862 in Tennessee and North Carolina convinced avid Confederates they must redouble their efforts, and that everyone must contribute if the new nation were to survive. "The Great Washington went hungry and raged [ragged], lay on the coald, frozen ground without blankets," a Virginia private explained to his mother and sister, "then why not mee be lik Washington." None other than Robert E. Lee hoped that Southerners would learn a valuable lesson from the hardships and setbacks. "If it will have the effect of arousing them & imparting an earnestness & boldness to their work," the general intimated, then the struggle would have been worthwhile.

The men in what Lee later called the Army of Northern Virginia did just that. During the first year, they absorbed the painful lesson that much of war is not fighting battles. Soldiers learned to ease the burdens of military life by cooking properly, abiding by proper sanitary practices, preserving some semblance of military discipline, and performing the sundry duties that helped them in camp and on the field of battle. While they never quite mastered that alien concept of discipline, they did stop killing each other, recognizing that the true enemy were those fellows clad in blue. Plundering was one of those pastimes they never could break, but they did preserve enough military discipline to be excellent combat soldiers. They also taught these skills to newcomers, so that recruits did not have to learn the same harsh lessons for themselves.

Most importantly, those men of 1861 adjusted their attitudes. They steeled themselves for the incredible hardships and brutalities that they would face over the next three years. "All we can do," a Virginian advised his wife, "is to endure privation without murmur and with stout hearts and strong arms make ourselves worthy of victory and independence." It was just the sort of attitude and approach his future commander Lee recommended.[33]

Notes

1. John Winfield to Wife, September 2, 1861. John J. Winfield Papers, Southern Historical Collection, University of North Carolina, Chapel Hill (SHC, UNC).

2. H.W. Barclay Reminiscence, p. 5. H.M, H.W. Barclay Papers, Center for American History, University of Texas at Austin (CAH); Jesse to Sister, April 15, 1861, Jordan-Bell Papers, Virginia Historical Society, Richmond, Va. (VAHS).

3. John L. Hardaman to Uncle, August 22, 1861, in Atlanta, *Southern Confederacy*, August 1861, 28; Letter of August 13, 1861, in Atlanta, *Southern Confederacy*, August 16, 1861; George [Robertson] to George Lee Robertson, CAH; James W. Baldwin to Lee, August 15, 1861, Lee Headquarters Papers, Bound Series, Box 1, VAHS.

4. John Winfield to Wife, September 2, 1861, Winfield Papers, SHC, UNC; G.M. Lee to Jordan, August 26, 1861, Frank E. Vandiver, "A Collection of Louisiana Confederate Letters," *Louisiana Historical Quarterly* 26, no. 4 (1943): 941; Jimmie [Langhorne] to Mother, June 12, 1861, Langhorne Family Papers, VAHS; Husband [J. Griffin] to Leila, February 26, 1862, *Civil War Times Illustrated* Collection (CWTIC), U.S. Army Military History Institute, Carlisle Barracks, Pa. (USAMHI).

5. John Futch to Martha, March 9, 1862, Futch Brothers, North Carolina Department of Archives and History, Raleigh, N.C. (NCDAH); Will [Crutcher] to Darling, October 26, 1861. Crutcher-Shannon Papers, CAH.

6. James Langhorne to Mother, June 26, 1861. Langhorne Family Papers, VAHS. For more on superiority, see *Richmond Dispatch*, September 21, 1861.

7. Cadmus M. Wilcox to Sister Mary, November 18, 1861, Cadmus M. Wilcox Papers, Library of Congress, Washington, D.C. (LC).

8. John W. Davis to Brother, March 3, 1861, John W. Davis Papers, University of Virginia, Charlottesville, Va. (UVA). Also see J. Thompson Brown to Wife, November 27, 1859, J. Thompson Brown Papers, VAHS; A.B. Francis Reminiscences, in Kate Mason Rowland Papers, Museum of the Confederacy, Richmond, Va. (MC); B.F. Howard Record Book, MC; Edward Baker Loving Reminiscences, p. 2, Edward Baker Loving Papers, Virginia State Library, Richmond, Va. (VASL); Wilbur Davis Reminiscences, p. 35, Davis Family Papers, UVA; R.L. Dabney to Rev. Hodge, January 23, 1861, Box 2, F 4, Robert Lewis Dabney Papers, Union Theological Seminary, Richmond, Va.; Giles Cromwell, *Virginia Manufactory of Arms* (Charlottesville, Va.: University Press of Virginia, 1975), 61–62.

9. Richard M. McMurray, *Two Great Rebel Armies: An Essay in Confederate Military History* (Chapel Hill, N.C.: University of North Carolina Press, 1989), 99–104.

10. Emory M. Thomas, *The Confederate State of Richmond: A Biography of the Capital* (Austin: University of Texas Press, 1971), 128.

11. Richmond was 6.12 square miles. Conversation with John Hennessy, April 20, 1999. See also U.S. War Department, *War of the Rebellion: A Compilation of Official Records of the Union and Confederate Armies* (Washington, D.C.: Government Printing Office, 1880–1901), series IV, vol. 1, 822.

12. John Fort to Kate, July 15, 1861, Tomlinson Fort Papers, Emory University, Atlanta, Ga. Also see Wm. E. Bird to [Sallie], August 19, 1861, John Rozier, ed., *The Granite Farm Letters: The Civil War Correspondence of Edgeworth & Sallie Bird* (Athens, Ga.: University of Georgia Press, 1988), 15.

13. John Sewell Anglin to Parents, November 27, 1861, John S. Anglin Papers, LC. Also see A.L.P. Vairin diary, June 14, 1861, A.L.P. Vairin Papers, Mississippi Department of Archives and History, Jackson; R. Channing Price to Mother, August 18, 1861, R. Channing Price Papers, SHC, UNC; J.B.H. to the Editor, August 31, 1861, Atlanta, *Southern Confederacy,* September 6, 1861; R. Taylor Scott to Fan, January 13, 1862, Keith Family Papers, VAHS; D.W. Baine to Colonel, December 28, 1861, Pettigrew Family Papers, NCDAH; Johnston to Davis, August 23, 1861, C.C. Jones Jr. Papers, Duke University, Durham, N.C. (Duke).

14. Richard to little Brother, August 25, 1861, Richard Habersham Papers, LC. Also see John Sewell Anglin to Parents, November 27, 1861, John S. Anglin Papers, LC.

15. Thomas G. Rhett to General, September 5, 1861, Order Book, Thomas H. Williams Papers, Schenectady County Historical Society, Schenectady, N.Y.

See also Dr. J.L. Cabell to Surgeon Samuel Moore, September 30, 1861, Confederate States of America Archives, Hospital Records, Duke.

16. John H. Griscom, *The Sanitary Condition of the Laboring Class of New York, with Suggestions for Its Improvement* (New York: Arno, 1845, 1970).

17. W.H. Mitchell to Doctor, August 12, 1861, Atlanta, *Southern Confederacy,* September 12, 1861; J. Hays to Mother, August 4, 1861, James Hays Papers, VAHS. Also see James G. Hudson Journal, July 1861, in James G. Hudson, "A Story of Company D, 4th Alabama Infantry Regiment, C.S.A.," ed. Alma H. Pate, *Alabama Historical Quarterly* 23, no. 1 & 2 (1961): 174.

18. Thomas Williams to Sir, November 19, 1861, Report of the Medical Director of 2nd Corps, in Thomas H. Williams to Sir, January 22, 1862, Letters Sent, Medical Director's Office, Army of Northern Virginia, Record Group (RG) 109, National Archives, Washington, D.C. (NA); General Order No. 2. Head Quarters, 1st Corps, Army of the Potomac, January 17, 1862, General Orders and Circulars, Army of the Potomac. RG 109, NA. Also see Geo. W. Lay to General, January 25, 1862, J.B. Walton Papers, F5, Louisiana Historical Association Papers, Tulane University, New Orleans, La.

19. Otis D. Smith to Sir, February 8, 1862, Otis David Smith Papers, Alabama Department of Archives and History, Montgomery, Ala. (ALDAH). Also see Johnnie [Buchanan] to Mother, February 22, 1862, John Buchanan Papers, University of South Carolina, Columbia (USC); E.A. Davis to Sir, February 12, 1862, George W. Clower, ed., "Confederate Life at Home and in Camp," *Georgia Historical Quarterly* 40, no. 3 (1956): 304.

20. Theodore [Fogle] to Father & Mother, June 30, 1861, Theodore T. Fogle Papers, Emory University, Atlanta, Ga. Also see Benj. F. White to Dear Young Friend, January 5, 1862, James J. Phillips Papers, NCDAH; *Richmond Examiner,* October 2, 1861.

21. L.M. Blackford to Mother, January 11, 1862, Launcelot Minor Blackford Papers, UVA.

22. Milton Barrett Diary, November 1, 1861, J. Roderick Hiller and Carolynn Ayers Heller, eds., *The Confederacy Is on Her Way Up the Spout: Letters to South Carolina, 1861–1864* (Athens, Ga.: University of Georgia Press, 1992), 31; James W. Bacon to Friend, January 26, 1862, Hugh Conway Browning Papers, Duke; W.B. Young to Aunt, July 29, 1861, William Dunlap Simpson Papers, Duke. Also see James P. Williams to Aunt Mary, October 14, 1861, James P. Williams Papers, UVA; Beauregard to Davis, August 23, 1861, P.G.T. Beauregard Papers, LC; Joseph E. Johnston to Jefferson Davis, August 23, 1861, C.C. Jones Papers, Duke; Thomas H. Williams to Sir, November 19, 1861, and January 22, 1862, Letters Sent, Medical Director's Office, RG 109, NA.

23. See Lloyd Powell to Father, June 30, 1861, Powell Family Papers, Col-

lege of William & Mary, Williamsburg, Va.; J.R. McCutchan to Kate, n.d. [1861], Rockbridge Historical Society Papers, Washington & Lee University, Lexington, Va. (W&L).

24. See General Order No. 11, Head Quarters, Virginia Forces, May 5, 1861, Virginia Forces, Entry 64, Marked Box 87, RG 109, NA; W.P. Hefflin, *Blind Man "on the Warpath"* (n.p.: 190-), 17; Hussen to Darly, [June or July 1861], James A. Davidson Papers, ALDAH; S.P. Hilthouse to Wife, Children, and Friends, June 29 and July 12, 1861, Civil War Miscellaneous Collection, USAMHI; W.P.S. to Brother, August 21, 1861, Atlanta, *Southern Confederacy*, August 29, 1861.

25. R. Fairfax to Mama, January 31, 1862, Fairfax Brothers Papers, MC; Theodore [Fogle] to Sister, October 26, 1861, Theodore T. Fogle Papers, Emory University.

26. See Robert H. Miller to Mother, February 20, 1862, Forrest P. Connor, ed., "Letters of Lieutenant Robert H. Miller to His Family, 1861–1862," *Virginia Magazine of History and Biography* (*VAMHB*) 70, no. 1 (1962), 73–74; General Order No. 61, Army of the Potomac, November 20, 1861, General and Special Orders and Circulars Issued, Army of Northern Virginia, M921, F30–5, RG 109, NA; Charges and Specifications against Lieutenant Colonel C.M. Bradford, Benjamin Huger Papers, MC; Lafayette McLaws to Wife, August 18, 1861, Lafayette McLaws Papers, SHC, UNC; W.G. Kisling to Cousin Ginnie, January 5, 1862, W.G. Kisling Papers, MC; Price Channing Diary, December 25 and 27, 1861, R. Price Channing Papers, SHC, UNC; Thomas S. Preston to Wife, March 15, 1862, Preston-Davis Papers, UVA.

27. James F. Cameron to Father and Mother, December 21, 1861, James F. Cameron Papers, ALDAH. Also see Joseph E. Embry Diary, August 21, 23, and 26, 1861, Joseph W. Embry Papers, UVA; Longstreet to Colonel Thomas Jordan, September 6 and August 1, 1861, Compiled Military Service Record of James Longstreet, NA; General Orders, No. 68. Head Quarters, Army of the Potomac, November 27, 1861, General and Special Orders and Circulars Issued, Army of Northern Virginia, M921, F41–5, RG 109, NA.

28. [Daniel Hileman] to Rate, September 22, 1861, Daniel Hileman Folder, Rockbridge Historical Society Manuscripts, W&L; F.P. Johnson to Father & Mother, September 22, 1861, CWTIC, USAMHI. Also see J.H. Newman Diary, August 11, 1861, J.H. Newman Papers, VASL.

29. R.T. Scott to Family, February 4, 1862. Keith Family Papers, VAHS; Special Orders, No.—, Head Quarters, Department of Fredericksburg, August 20, 1861, Orders, 1861–65, John B. Brown Papers, NCDAH; R.A. Bryant to Eugenia, October 20, 1861, Bryant Family Papers, VASL. Also see R. Fairfax to Jenny, November 12, 1861, Fairfax Brothers Papers, MC; John T. Thornton to [Wife], October 1, 1861, John T. Thornton Papers, UVA.

30. Thomas S. Preston to Wife, March 13, 1862, Preston-Davis Papers, UVA. Also see John W. Daniel to Father, January 13, 1862, John Warwick Daniel Papers, UVA; W.G. Kisling to Cousin Ginnie, January 5, 1862, W.G. Kisling Papers, MC; J.H. Everett to Wife, July 9, 1861, John A. Everett Papers, Emory University; C.C. Blacknall to Jinny, May 18, 1862, Oscar W. Blacknall Papers, NCDAH; J.A. Cotton to Uncle, September 16, 1861, Martin, ed., *VAMHB* 37 no. 1, 21; R. Fairfax to Mama, August 22, [1861], R. &. E. Fairfax Papers, MC; John M. Tilley to Wife, September 11, 1861, John M. Tilley Papers, Georgia Department of Archives and History, Atlanta, Ga.

31. Will [Critcher] to Wife, November 2, 1861, E.R. Crockett Papers, CAH.

32. Charles Kerrison to Etta, July 19, 1862, Kerrison Family Papers, USC.

33. J.T. Thompson to Mother and Sisters, March 26, 1862, Aurelia Austin, ed., "A Georgia Boy with 'Stonewall' Jackson: The Letters of James Thomas Thompson," *VAMHB* 70, no. 3 (1962), 322; R.E. Lee to Son, February 23, 1862, Markham Papers, MC; Thomas S. Garnett to Emma, December 5, 1861, Garnett Family Papers, VASL.

"A Navy Department, Hitherto Unknown to Our State Organization"

John M. Coski

Governor John Letcher had opposed secession, and embraced it only after the state convention voted on the evening of April 17, 1861, to take Virginia out of the Union. Within hours, the reluctant governor was a commander in chief, confronting the challenge of saving the state's two most important military assets: the federal armory and arsenal at Harpers Ferry and the Gosport Navy Yard in Portsmouth directly across the Elizabeth River from the vital port of Norfolk. Officials in Norfolk were particularly anxious about the fate of the yard. They informed Letcher on April 17 that they had sunk three light boats to obstruct the channel and removed the buoys to thwart U.S. Navy warships going in or out of the river and pleaded with the governor to demand the surrender of the yard.[1] "For god's sake put some body in command," telegraphed Thomas T. Cropper on April 18. "Norfolk will be taken unless reinforcements are sent[;] authorize me to seize & sink any vessel in Port not enough vessels sunk[;] order company to sustain me."[2]

Letcher ordered Maj. Gen. William B. Taliaferro, commander of the state's militia, to rescue the facilities at Norfolk and Portsmouth. Ordered to accompany and cooperate with Taliaferro was Cdr. Robert Baker Pegram, one of the first two naval officers to offer his services to the state. He was to proceed to Norfolk "with authority to organize naval defences, enrol & enlist seamen and Marines . . . and do and perform whatever may be necessary to preserve and protect the property of the Commonwealth and citizens of Virginia."[3] With only three hundred local troops and no ships or heavy guns available, Taliaferro concluded that he could not take the yard by force

65

and instead requested men and heavy guns sufficient to demand the yard's surrender.[4]

The situation grew more ominous on the evening of April 20. The steam sloop USS *Pawnee* arrived in Hampton Roads, picked up a regiment of Massachusetts troops from Fort Monroe, and steamed past the ineffective obstructions into Norfolk harbor, reportedly carrying on board 240 gallons of turpentine and other combustibles.[5] In the predawn hours of April 21, the men from the *Pawnee* and other Federal forces began firing on the ships and the buildings at the yard and endeavored to blow up the stone dry dock—one of only two in the United States. The alarmist Cropper sent another telegram to Letcher in desperation: "Oh, for god's sake. . . . Send us a commander[.] [T]he Pawnee has just brought a large number of troops to the Navy Yard[.] I now hear the black Republican cheers at the Navy Yard[.]"[6] Virginia troops marched in on the morning of April 21 to find the navy yard an inferno and feared the worst. If the ships, heavy guns, and facilities at Gosport were destroyed, then Virginia had virtually no naval resources to defend her coastline and rivers.

Anticipating this prospect, Letcher ordered the seizure and detention of commercial vessels that might prove useful as warships. Particularly promising were the two New York–based steamships owned by the Old Dominion Steamship Company, *Jamestown* and *Yorktown*, then fortuitously in the James River.[7] From points along the commonwealth's navigable rivers came reports of other vessels about to leave for points north. The schooner *Nelly Day* was about to sail from Port Walthall on the Appomattox for Connecticut with a load of coal. Should she be detained? Letcher's secretary, George W. Munford, replied: "You will cause Schooner Nelly to be stopped. Detain her for the State." A vessel in the Rappahannock River was about to leave Fredericksburg for Boston with a load of corn. Should she be stopped? Letcher's order: "Stop the corn."[8]

While Virginia troops could not stop the destruction of the navy yard, a small party under command of naval captain George T. Sinclair seized a large, undefended supply of gunpowder at old Fort Norfolk.[9] Virginia troops loaded about half the 2,800 pounds of powder on small vessels and sent them upriver to Richmond.[10]

Even these small victories seemed fated to evaporate. Navy lieutenant William H. Parker wired Letcher from Norfolk: "Pawnee gone up James River supposed after the steamers Yorktown & Jamestown."[11] A militia officer stationed along the James reported that the seized U.S. Navy light-house tender *James Buchanan*, carrying five hundred pounds of the captured powder, had run aground below City Point and appealed to Letcher to send a steam tug. Letcher's secretary contacted Richmond ship chandler R.O. Haskins and arranged for the tug *Sea Board* to rescue *Buchanan*.[12] The powder was transferred to lighters and routed to Petersburg by way of the Appomattox River, "fearing Pawnee may capture it going up James river."[13]

By the end of the day, it was clear that *Pawnee* was not steaming up the James River, but was in fact headed back up the Chesapeake Bay to Washington, D.C., and that things were not all that bleak at Norfolk. "Perfect quiet has taken the place of the wild excitement that prevailed here during Saturday and Sunday last," wrote a newspaper correspondent from Norfolk on Tuesday, April 23.[14] George Sinclair reported from the shipyard that while the fleeing Federals had spiked the cannon, the nails were "easily removed" and the guns still serviceable. Governor Letcher assured Confederate president Jefferson Davis and South Carolina governor Francis W. Pickens that the navy yard buildings were burned but that the ordnance was not destroyed.[15] In fact, Virginia authorities found at Gosport 1,198 heavy guns, most of them without carriages, along with stocks of small arms and other weapons. Within days, Virginia authorities began sending heavy guns to defensive points throughout the commonwealth and to the military forces of other Southern states.

With the Gosport yard and its rich ordnance stores secured, Virginia had the foundation for a viable state navy. The state began immediately to build upon this foundation. Two months later, after turning over the state navy to the Confederate Navy, Letcher boasted that, within a week of the state's secession, "a navy department, hitherto unknown to our state organization," was fully and effectively organized.[16] The new department was not to be permanent. According to a convention signed between Virginia and the Confederacy on April 25, Virginia's military forces were to be transferred to the Confederacy after the voters had a chance to ratify the ordinance of secession on May 23. In the meantime, Virginia's forces would cooperate with Confederate forces, but remain administratively separate.[17]

Virginia's naval defense preparations actually began months before the state seceded from the Union. Virginia had increased its orders of weapons and ammunition in the months after John Brown's raid on Harpers Ferry in late 1859. The South's primary supplier of ordnance lay within the boundaries of Virginia's capital: the Tredegar Iron Works owned by Joseph Reid Anderson.[18] Virginia's General Assembly in January 1861 authorized $200,000 to plan and construct coast, harbor, and river defenses.[19] Immediately after voting Virginia out of the Union on April 17, the state's secession convention invited Virginians in the U.S. Navy and Army to enter the state service.[20] Within days, a flood of U.S. Navy veterans had tendered their services to the state. On April 20, the convention created a three-member Advisory Council and charged it with coordinating the state's defensive preparations. Among the council's members was Cdr. Matthew Fontaine Maury, the internationally celebrated naval scientist. Finally, on April 27, the convention formally created a state navy consisting of two thousand seamen and marines, which was to be governed by the same rules prevailing in the U.S. Navy.[21]

The Advisory Council appointed Capt. Samuel Barron, Capt. Sidney Smith Lee, and Cdr. Robert Pegram to a joint commission of army and navy officers. The commission's assignment was "to name all efficient and worthy Virginians and Residents of Virginia in the Army and Navy of the United States; for the purpose of inviting them into the service of Virginia."[22] There was no shortage of such officers, and in the brief life of the Virginia Navy the challenge was to find suitable duties for all of them and to accommodate the statutory respect for the rank order that existed in the old navy.

The three officers on the commission exemplified the wealth of experience available to the state navy. Barron was the fourth generation of a bona fide Virginia naval dynasty. His uncle, Capt. James Barron, had risen to the command of the U.S. Navy's Mediterranean Squadron, but saw his career tarnished when he surrendered his ship, *Chesapeake*, to the British warship *Leopard* in 1807, and ruined when he killed naval hero Stephen Decatur in a duel in 1820. In contrast, James Barron's brother, Cdr. Samuel Barron, was commandant of the Gosport Navy Yard when he died suddenly in 1810; he was so well regarded that the navy commissioned his two-year-old son, Samuel, as midshipman in 1812. At age six, Samuel Barron reported for duty at Gosport and was sailing the seas at age ten. Forty-three years on the ladder finally brought Barron a captaincy in 1855.[23] "Smith" Lee (1805–1869) entered the navy in 1819 and commanded a ship in Comdr. Matthew C. Perry's historic expedition to Japan in 1853. Lee was the older brother of Gen. Robert E. Lee and was commandant of the U.S. Naval Academy at the same time that his brother was superintendent of the U.S. Military Academy.[24]

The youngest of the three officers, Robert Pegram was Virginia's most celebrated naval hero on the eve of the war. In 1855, then-lieutenant Pegram was in Hong Kong as executive officer of the USS *Powhatan* when an English vessel escorting a convoy of merchant ships in the South China Sea requested help against Chinese pirates. Pegram commanded a two-ship rescue operation that captured ten pirate ships, liberated six of their prizes, and won the admiration and gratitude of the English officers. Three years later, the Commonwealth of Virginia passed an official resolution commending Pegram for his "brilliant courage and admirable conduct" and presented him with a sword.[25]

The de facto commanding officer of the Virginia Navy was Barron, who was chief of the Office of Orders and Detail—traditionally the most powerful of the navy's administrative departments. Mirroring the U.S. Navy's organization, the Virginia Navy Department also included an Office of Provisions and Clothing, commanded by paymaster John DeBree; the Office of Ordnance and Hydrography, commanded by Cdr. George Minor; the Bureau of Medicine and Surgery, headed by surgeon William F. Patton; the Bureau of Yards and Docks, commanded by Capt. Hugh N. Page; and the Bureau of Construction.[26]

On May 2, the Advisory Council approved the joint army and navy board's list of nominations for appointments in the Virginia Navy. It was an impressive list of men who had answered Governor Letcher's appeal to resign their hard-won positions in the U.S. Navy to cast their lots with their native or adopted state. For all his experience and seniority, Samuel Barron was not the ranking officer. That honor—and the grade of flag officer—belonged to sixty-five-year-old French Forrest. Appointed midshipman in the U.S. Navy in 1811 at the more traditional age of fifteen, Forrest reached captain in 1844. By 1861, Forrest had a dazzling résumé along with a Prince Valiant haircut and a chiseled face that made him look like an old salt from romantic fiction. He had once been in command briefly of the Washington Navy Yard, and the Advisory Council placed him in command of the Gosport Navy Yard.[27] Barron and Smith Lee shared the grade of captain with George Allen Magruder, William Francis Lynch, and William Conway Whittle. The older brother of Confederate Gen. John Bankhead Magruder, George Magruder was chief of the U.S. Navy's Bureau of Ordnance when he resigned from the service on April 22. His seniority in the Virginia Navy did not translate into an important assignment, however, and he did not even receive a commission in the Confederate Navy.[28] The Norfolk-born Lynch was raised an orphan and entered the service relatively late in life at age eighteen. By 1851, his career had taken him around the world and given the erudite Virginian enough adventures that he had written and published a book of "Observations Afloat and On Shore" and a narrative of an expedition to the Holy Land.[29]

His mere thirty-two years in the U.S. Navy landed Robert Pegram at the bottom of the list of fifteen commanders. Senior to him were the Advisory Council's naval representative Matthew Fontaine Maury and Ordnance Bureau chief George Minor. Also appointed commanders were Arthur Sinclair (scion of yet another Virginia naval dynasty), John Randolph Tucker, Thomas Jefferson Page, Thomas R.R. Rootes, Thomas T. Hunter, and William L. Maury. Tucker, Page, Rootes, and Hunter were destined to command ironclad warships in the Confederate Navy, while William Maury commanded the commerce raider CSS *Georgia.*

Perhaps the most remarkable men in the Virginia and, subsequently, in the Confederate Navy, were among the twenty officers appointed lieutenants. Catesby Ap Roger Jones, a native of Clarke County, entered the service in 1836 and won the admiration of Cdr. John A. Dahlgren, the commandant at the Washington Navy Yard and the U.S. Navy's acknowledged ordnance expert. Three younger lieutenants who entered the U.S. Navy in 1841 and graduated in the first class at the U.S. Naval Academy in 1846, John Mercer Brooke, Robert Dabney Minor, and Hunter Davidson, received tutelage in naval science at the feet of Matthew Fontaine Maury at the U.S. Naval Observatory. All three officers, along with Catesby Jones, employed their expertise in ordnance and emerging naval technologies for the benefit of the Confederate Navy. Considered among the most brilliant men in the service, John Brooke was a pensive, brooding man destined to make his mark in the Civil War for his relentless research and development in naval armor and weaponry.[30] The future U.S. Navy hero David Dixon Porter later observed that in 1861 there were two men whose service the Union could not afford to lose: Catesby Jones and John Brooke.[31] Also on that list of talented lieutenants were H.H. Lewis, George W. Harrison, John Wilkinson, John S. Maury, Charles C. Simms, William H. Parker, James Henry Rochelle, William Sharp, Robert Randolph Carter, and William C. Whittle Jr.

In the patriotic fervor of 1861, men deemed too young and too old for active command volunteered. Midshipmen at the U.S. Naval Academy re-signed their commissions and offered their services to their native states. To continue their training, Capt. Richard L. Page, who was naval aide-de-camp to Letcher, suggested establishing a temporary school ship at Nor-folk. The old frigate USS *United States*—later the CSS *Confederate States*—was pressed into service as that school ship.[32] The state created a short "reserve list" for the most senior officers, on which they were not in line for promotion. Being put on the "reserve list" was a slight to officers with ambition or fragile egos. Cdr. Murray Mason was "mortified" to learn that his rank in state service was lower than that which he held in the old navy. Lt. John S. Taylor protested being placed in "the equivocal and invidi-ous category of the 'Reserve List.'" Joseph Myers, in contrast, thanked the governor effusively for "the *unexpected* honor" of his appointment as com-mander on the reserve list.[33]

Along with the Navy Department, Virginia created a small Marine Corps. Following naval tradition, these men were to serve as a fighting force aboard the warships or in landing parties against shore positions. Bvt. Mjr. George H. Terrett, a thirty-two-year U.S. Marine Corps veteran, was the ranking marine officer. Commodore Forrest charged Lt. Adam N. Baker with organizing the marine rendezvous, and he also oversaw the distribu-tion of men to Virginia's warships. Son, brother, and nephew of U.S. mili-tary officers, the Pennsylvania-born Baker entered the U.S. Marines in 1853. Late in 1861 he apparently deserted the Confederate Marine Corps.[34]

All the competent and experienced officers were of little use without sailors, ships, and weapons for those ships. There was no shortage of men living or working in the commonwealth who had experience on ship crews. To recruit these men, the state followed the traditional custom of establish-ing naval rendezvous—or recruiting stations—in metropolitan areas.[35]

Befitting a formally organized fighting force, the state navy issued uni-forms to the sailors and marines. Consistent with the universally accepted Western naval custom, the uniforms were blue. The uniform for officers, seamen, and marines of the state navy was to "correspond in all respects to that of the United States Navy" except for the substitution of Virginia state buttons.[36] The Virginia Navy distributed blue cloth pea jackets, blue flannel jumpers, blue cloth trousers, blue satinet trousers, blue flannel overcoats, undershorts, and drawers, blue cloth caps, and calf skin shoes and woolen socks.[37]

Thanks to the state's considerable maritime resources and decisive action after April 17, the fledgling navy was not without warships. The most promising vessels were those that the U.S. Navy had tried to scuttle at the Gosport Yard. Ten warships were at Gosport when the Federals abandoned it. Six of them were beyond salvage. Another, the frigate *United States*, was among the oldest in the service and was so decrepit that the Federals had sunk, but did not even attempt to burn, her. Gosport commandant French Forrest ordered master shipbuilder Joseph Pierce to pump her out and Cdr. Thomas R. Rootes to take command of her. By mid-May, *United States* was the first commissioned ship in the Virginia Navy. She served as the receiving ship for sailors entering the state navy and as a school ship for drilling officers and men. And while she was not seaworthy, she was outfitted with a nineteen-gun battery for harbor defense.[38]

Virginia authorities contracted with the salvage company of B. & J. Baker for $15,000 to raise three ships: the twenty-gun sailing sloops *Germantown* and *Plymouth*, and the steam frigate *Merrimack*. The Bakers raised *Germantown* and *Plymouth* just before the end of the Virginia Navy's short life, and neither vessel was commissioned as a Virginia or Confederate warship.[39] In contrast, Gosport Comdt. French Forrest pressed the Bakers to raise the new forty-gun frigate *Merrimack*, which the Federals had burned to the water line. "The greatest expedition is required," Forrest wrote on May 18.[40] By the end of May, the Bakers had raised *Merrimack*, and she lay in Gosport's stone dry dock awaiting a decision on her fate. Some authorities wondered about the value of the "burned and blackened hulk," and the Virginia Navy did nothing with her.[41] In Confederate hands, *Merrimack* would achieve immortality as the ironclad *Virginia*.

In the hectic first few weeks of Virginia's putative independence, the commonwealth seized and leased dozens of small vessels and borrowed vessels from the state's revenue service.[42] Authorities employed most of them for transporting ordnance and other supplies. Norfolk officials authorized B.M. William H. Face to charter the steamer *Thomas Reaney* for use in his effort to obstruct the channel.[43] The steamers *Empire* and *Harmony* remained in service at Norfolk for the duration of the Virginia Navy. Commanded by Lt. James Milligan of the state's Virginia Revenue Service, *Empire* was primarily a transport ship. *Harmony* was on "ordnance duty," under the "exclusive control" of Cdr. Archibald Blair Fairfax of the Navy's Ordnance Bureau. Neither ship was commissioned in the Virginia Navy, but the crews of both ships received their provisions from the navy, and the *Empire*'s eighteen men received pay and clothing from the navy.[44]

Several ships initially leased proved valuable enough to be commissioned into the state navy. On April 21, the state leased the steamer *Northampton* from the Norfolk and Chesapeake Steamboat Company for $100 per day.[45] Built in 1860, she was 180 feet long, with a shallow draft of four feet, and capable of steaming at seventeen miles per hour. A board of officers inspected her and found that she was "admirably adapted for River service and we recommend that she be purchased by the state." With a capacity of eight hundred men and their baggage, *Northampton* was, Barron informed the Advisory Council, "probably the largest steamer in operation on the James River." The governor authorized her purchase for $45,000.[46] The state paid $6,000 in three installments to a Norfolk salvage firm for *Teaser*, a Philadelphia-built tugboat. Equipped with two thirty-two-pounder guns, the *Teaser* became one of the first ships in the Confederate Navy's James River Squadron.[47]

Within a week of the state's secession, Governor Letcher announced that the state would return all but two of the detained ships and compensate their owners for damage and their crews for their pay.[48] Two wooden side-wheel steamers were exempt from the terms of this proclamation. *Yorktown* was seized at the Richmond wharf as she prepared to leave for New York "with a large amount of merchandize." *Jamestown* was seized at City Point reportedly loaded with $50,000 in ordnance and military stores.[49] Captain Barron believed that *Jamestown* was "unfit for the service of the State." A committee of Richmond citizens disagreed, and the Advisory Council agreed to let a board of naval officers decide whether she could be of service for river defenses or for transportation.[50] The Confederate Navy later decided to fit her out with a two-gun battery and assign her to the James River Squadron. No one had any doubts about the value of *Jamestown*'s sister ship, *Yorktown*. Built in 1859, *Yorktown* was 250 feet long and 34 feet wide at beam. She was, wrote her former executive officer, Lt. James H. Rochelle, in 1865, "a side-wheel steamer of beautiful model. . . . She was considered a fast boat, and deserved the reputation."[51] Barron assigned Capt. John Randolph Tucker to command the ship and supervise her fitting out "with as heavy a battery as she will bear." She would be, Barron reported, "a valuable auxiliary to the defenses of James River."[52]

It was not only for Hampton Roads and the James River that the state outfitted warships. On the York River, authorities hired the schooner *David Vannam* to transport ordnance to erect batteries at West Point.[53] For $2,000 a month the state leased the steamer *Logan* from the Baltimore & Fredericksburg Steam Boat Company, but did not fit her out as a warship.[54] On the Rappahannock, Lt. Henry H. Lewis chartered the steamer *Virginia* from Old Dominion Steamboat Company for $2,000 per month; the company paid for the crew's wages and supplies.[55] On the Potomac in early May, Lt. Charles Simms captured the side-wheel steam transport *George Page* (known also as the *City of Richmond*), which the U.S. Army Quartermaster Department had used; though lightly armed, *George Page* under Simms's command was enough of a presence to instill caution in the U.S. Navy forces operating on the Potomac.

Vital to the work of salvaging, converting, fitting out, and supplying the navy's new warships were the resources of the state's shipyards and shipping industry. Not surprisingly, those resources were concentrated in the Norfolk area, especially in the Gosport Navy Yard in Portsmouth. The yard's commandant, French Forrest, refused an assignment to command the naval defenses on the Potomac, which he believed was "of secondary consideration" to Gosport. Forrest described the yard as "the great fountain from which the Navy of the Commonwealth must draw its supplies."[56] It had not only the stone dry dock and other facilities, but a skilled and experienced workforce. Twenty-four hours after Virginia seized the yard, Forrest appointed men to fill the positions of dockmaster, master caulker, clerk of the yard, master block maker, master mechanic, master cooper, civil engineer, and secretary to the commandant.[57] Through navy agent George Loyall, the state purchased hardware, muslin, marine glass, and flags from civilian firms. The navy also paid Norfolk area women for hand work.[58]

More surprising was the importance of the naval resources in Virginia's capital city. Although one hundred miles up the James River from Norfolk, Richmond was a port city, accessible to oceangoing vessels via the port of Rocketts located just east of the city line. Along Richmond's waterfront were facilities and businesses that serviced the city's substantial waterborne commerce and transportation. The Virginia State Navy took full advantage of those businesses. Joseph R. Anderson's Tredegar Iron Works, which was destined to provide iron plate, heavy guns, and ordnance for the Confederacy's ironclad warships, provided guns, gun carriages, and ordnance for *Yorktown, Jamestown, Northampton, Logan,* and several of the land batteries erected by the Virginia Navy.[59] Richard O. Haskins's Rocketts shipping supply business leased several vessels to the state navy and sold large quantities of small stores and provisions for the vessels stationed at Richmond. Other smaller merchants sold coal, lumber, beef, and supplies for those vessels.[60]

The most important service provided by Richmond's naval facilities was the conversion of *Yorktown* from a passenger vessel into a warship. On May 15, Commandant Forrest ordered master ship carpenter Joseph Pierce to report to Barron in Richmond and ordered that the yard send specific guns, carriages, and ordnance to Richmond for *Yorktown*.[61] Over the next two months, Pierce supervised the work of ship carpenters, caulkers, joiners, laborers, and painters as they converted *Yorktown* into not only a warship, but a partially ironclad warship. Powered by a vulnerable side-paddle wheel instead of by the newly developed and invulnerable screw propeller, *Yorktown* required a layer of armor plate over her boilers. Pierce reported later that he had spent $11,514.49 for labor and material to convert *Yorktown*.[62]

Ships make a navy, but the most important and urgent work for the Virginia State Navy was erecting river defenses, not fitting out warships. The fires at Gosport had hardly cooled when the state's new military establishment began sending heavy guns by rail to Southern states and by water to key defensive points around the commonwealth. By the time that the Confederacy assumed control of the state's military forces, Virginia had mounted 320 of the 1,198 captured guns in defensive positions.[63] Along with guns, the Virginia Navy contributed the cream of its officers, many of whom commanded the newly erected batteries.

The challenges facing the fledgling navy were immense. All of the state's one thousand miles of coastline and navigable rivers were vulnerable to naval attack. From the Chesapeake Bay inland as far as one hundred miles to their fall lines, the Potomac, Rappahannock, York, and James rivers were navigable for oceangoing vessels and were like watery daggers poised at the state's interior. Andrew Talcott, the engineer who conducted the inspection of coastal and river defenses, reported on April 15 that because the York River was undefended, Richmond was vulnerable to enemy attack. An enemy force, he warned, could approach by water to within thirty-five miles of the capital, disembark, and threaten Richmond by land. Erecting defenses at Gloucester Point and Yorktown should be the state's first priority.

After the York was secure, the state should strengthen the James River defenses.[64] Talcott received Letcher's approval to implement his defense plan, and he started immediately for Yorktown. By May 12, the batteries at Yorktown, Gloucester, and West Point (where the Pamunkey and Mattaponi joined to form the York) were operational.[65] Capt. William C. Whittle, a fifty-six-year-old Norfolk native with forty-one years of experience in the U.S. Navy, was in command of the York River defenses.[66]

Whatever Talcott's opinion, the most alarming reports in the Virginia Navy's first days and weeks came out of Norfolk. On May 1, Lt. George T. Sinclair, an ordnance officer with the Confederate Navy, advised Maury and Letcher that Norfolk's defenses could not repel the enemy. It was widely assumed that Federal forces would try to complete the destructive work that they had failed to do on April 21, and that an attack over land would circumvent the existing defenses. The Gosport Navy Yard and the ordnance stored there represented a vital asset not only for Virginia, but for the Confederacy. "Do look at a chart," he urged Maury, "remember the value of this vast arsenal & then devote your strong mind to its preservation."[67] A few weeks later, a correspondent calling himself "Norfolk" echoed Sinclair's insistence that there should be at least ten thousand men defending Norfolk and Portsmouth. "Why are there not more of the large bodies of troops collected at Richmond sent to this much exposed point, where *so much* is at stake?" Along with more troops, Richmond ought to send "an experienced Military Commander who has *seen service.*"[68]

The command situation at Norfolk was the source of much concern and frustration. In overall command of forces around Norfolk was Brig. Gen. Walter Gwynn. Although he was a graduate of the U.S. Military Academy, he had left the service in 1832 to become a successful civil engineer and apparently did not inspire confidence in his military abilities.[69] Flag officer French Forrest was in command at the Navy Yard and over all naval forces in the Norfolk area. Typical of interservice commands, disputes erupted between Gwynn and Forrest, specifically over naval munitions and stores. Gen. Robert E. Lee wrote sternly to remind both men of the necessity of getting along.[70] Gwynn assured Lee that there was "the most cordial co-operation in all measures intended for the common defense, not only between Commodore Forrest and myself, but between all the officers of the Army and Navy in this command."[71] On May 24—the day after Virginia voters overwhelmingly ratified the state's secession—an order from the headquarters of Virginia forces relieved Gwynn from command and replaced him with Brig. Gen. Benjamin Huger.[72]

As Sinclair and others recommended, Virginia authorities began work on new fortifications around the natural harbor that lay between Norfolk and Portsmouth. Of particular importance were batteries at Sewell's Point, Craney Island, and Pig Point, each of which jutted out from the south bank into Hampton Roads. Ten days after the convention passed the secession ordinance, Virginia forces had more than seventy-five guns trained on the entrance to Norfolk harbor.[73]

Command problems also plagued the construction of defenses on the James River. In overall command on the James was sixty-eight-year-old captain Harrison Henry Cocke, a veteran of the War of 1812.[74] Not age, but apparent localism, put Cocke at odds with Virginia naval authorities. Cocke's home "Evergreen" lay on the south bank of the James River just east of City Point, where the Appomattox flowed into the James. He recommended the location of an earthen fortification at Hoods, a few miles downriver from "Evergreen," to be built on the foundations of old Fort Powhatan. Captain Barron approved the recommendation, and Cocke set immediately to work, monopolizing the equipment sent from Richmond that was necessary to transport and mount heavy guns.[75]

The following day, Col. Andrew Talcott of the army engineers turned his attention to the James River defenses and recommended that a major work be erected on Jamestown Island near the site of the ruins of the old church that marked the oldest English settlement in North America. The Jamestown fortifications were the easternmost line of defense on the James. Talcott charged navy lieutenant Catesby Ap Roger Jones with supervising the work.[76] Within two days, the work was underway and Jones had secured four thirty-two-pound guns for the battery. Jones, however, found himself without sufficient tackle to mount the guns or troops to protect the work in progress. A frustrated Jones wrote to Captain Barron: "It would appear that the fort above is considered of much greater importance than this. . . . It would appear that they consider themselves at liberty to supply themselves without reference to our wants, though we are more exposed to attack and more remote from the source of supply."[77] Barron replied to Jones: "I wish it were in my power to settle things in such a manner as to give you less trouble and more entire control." He and General Lee "sympathized" with his "annoyance," praised Jones's effort, and made it clear that they considered the work at Jamestown more important than Cocke's at Fort Powhatan, assuring Jones that he would have the resources necessary to advance his work.[78] By early June, the Jamestown batteries boasted twenty heavy guns. Fort Powhatan was outfitted with eight lighter guns; within a few months Confederate authorities abandoned the fort and transferred its guns to Mulberry Island.[79]

As it was for the opposing armies, the region just south of the Potomac River was the front line for the naval war in Virginia. Vital to the Confederate presence in northern Virginia was control of the Richmond, Fredericksburg & Potomac Railroad, which terminated at Aquia Creek, a tributary of the Potomac. The railhead was vulnerable to incursions by Union Navy warships, and Capt. William F. Lynch, the commander of the Virginia Navy's defenses on the Potomac, decided that defending the railhead was his first priority. In late April, Lt. Hunter H. Lewis of the Virginia Navy accompanied army engineers to find the best place for a battery to defend the railhead.[80] Lynch was also aware that Confederate batteries on the south bank of the Potomac could control the river and effectively blockade Washington, D.C. The Confederates searched for points that could control the river and also be defended against enemy attack. The most promising position was Mathias Point, but as early as June 4 Lynch suggested Evansport, near the site of the modern-day U.S. Marine base at Quantico.[81] The Virginia Navy did not succeed in erecting offensive batteries on the Potomac, in large part because the U.S. Navy was not sitting by idly and letting the Virginians dominate the state's waterways.

The force that the U.S. Navy had to challenge the Virginia Navy was not impressive. Delay, miscalculation, and sheer incompetence had prompted the U.S. naval officers in Norfolk to destroy the strongest ships in the area. As a result, the strongest vessel in Virginia waters was the new twin-screw steam sloop *Pawnee*, armed with a ten-gun battery. Despite superiority on paper, the U.S. Navy faced a shortage of active vessels; it resorted to the same kind of measures that the Southern navies did, particularly the chartering of civilian vessels. Among the vessels pressed into service in Virginia waters was the *Harriet Lane,* a side-wheel steamer that was the only steamer in the U.S. Revenue Cutter Service and known best as the ship used by H.R.H. the Prince of Wales during his 1860 visit to America.[82]

To rectify this situation, Cdr. James H. Ward on April 22 suggested the creation of a "flying flotilla" of fast and lightly armed warships. The flotilla would operate on the Chesapeake and its tributaries "to interrupt the enemy's communications; assuredly keep open our own; drive from those waters every hostile bottom; threaten all the points of a shore line accessible to such a force exceeding 1,000 miles in extent; protect loyal citizens; convoy, tow, transport troops or intelligence with dispatch; be generally useful; threaten at all points, and to attack any desired or important one."[83] The navy consented, and made available to Ward the side-wheel steamer *Thomas Freeborn*, carrying two thirty-two-pounders, and two small screw vessels, *Resolute* and *Reliance*, each carrying one or two guns.[84]

The only naval engagements that occurred during the life of the Virginia State Navy resulted from U.S. ships testing the emerging land batteries. Ward's "Potomac Flotilla" kept a close eye on the Potomac and Rappahannock river defenses. Between May 29 and June 1 the *Thomas Freeborn*, along with the *Pawnee*, attacked the Virginia forces at Mathias Point. Lynch reported that the *Pawnee* fired 392 shots and the *Freeborn* 207 on June 1 alone. The heavy Union fire inflicted no casualties and minimal damage. "Nobody hurt at Aquia Creek, notwithstanding Yankee Ward's lying report," Samuel Barron assured Catesby Jones. Ward reported that he silenced the batteries, while Lynch claimed that his guns fired only sporadically.[85] Ward was determined not to let the Southerners perfect batteries along the Potomac, and on June 27, 1861, led a landing party at Mathias Point. He was killed by a sharpshooter, the first U.S. Navy officer to die in action.[86]

Union naval forces attacked other points along the York River and Hampton Roads. On May 7, Lt. Thomas O. Selfridge steamed up the York in the side-wheel steamer *Yankee*. He reported that two thousand yards shy of Gloucester Point, a shot across the bow "first apprised me that the enemy had guns mounted." Selfridge exchanged a dozen shots with the batteries, then withdrew.[87] Federal warships also tested Norfolk's new defenses. On May 18–19, the *Monticello* opened fire on the unfinished batteries on Sewell's Point. Land forces managed to mount three guns and returned fire. On June 5, the *Harriet Lane* reconnoitered up Hampton Roads past Sewell's Point to Pig Point and opened fire on the Confederate batteries. Cdr. Robert Pegram, in charge of the Pig Point batteries, reported that during the fifteen- to twenty-minute engagement, the *Harriet Lane* fired thirty-three shots and inflicted no casualties or damage, while his batteries fired twenty-three shots in return.[88]

Much of the work perfecting the defenses was still in progress when it came time to transfer control of Virginia's navy to the Confederacy on June 10, 1861. Troops from Confederate states had arrived to help defend Virginia and, in turn, the Confederate Navy Department had access to the state's resources, most notably ordnance and ordnance stores. As early as mid-May, Confederate Navy secretary Stephen R. Mallory told Letcher that the Confederacy could assume control of the Gosport Yard immediately should Letcher wish to transfer it. Mallory informed Letcher that "in obtaining ordnance and ordnance stores from the yard, the officer charged with the necessary orders reports that, notwithstanding your Excellency's orders to the contrary, delays and obstacles injurious to the interests of the confederacy are imposed by those in command of the yard."[89]

The work on converting the passenger ship *Yorktown* into a warship extended a month beyond the formal transfer to the Confederacy. The state agreed to pay the bills for the work until Cdr. John Randolph Tucker transferred his flag to the newly christened *Patrick Henry.* This finally occurred on July 11.[90] Once the Confederate Navy assumed full control of *Patrick Henry*, the only remnant of the state navy apparatus was the Bureau of Yards and Docks commanded by Capt. Hugh N. Page. The state continued to appropriate money for Page and the bureau well into 1862, though their duties are not clear.[91]

The transfer proceeded smoothly save for the issue of rank. Governor Letcher and the Advisory Council protested when the Confederate Navy failed to offer commissions to all of the state's officers, but ultimately capitulated, since all but a few officers received ranks in the Confederate Navy commensurate with those held in the state navy.[92] Among those left off was Joseph Myers, whose effusive gratitude turned to enduring bitterness. Early 1862 found Myers still writing the governor's office asking about his commission.[93]

The accomplishments of the naval officers transferred to the Confederate Navy proved to be the Virginia Navy's most remarkable legacy. Samuel Barron continued his duties as chief of the Office of Orders and Detail for the Confederate Navy, succeeded in that office by other Virginians William F. Lynch, French Forrest, John Kirkwood Mitchell, and Sidney Smith Lee. Paymaster John DeBree similarly headed the Confederate Navy's Office of Provisions and Clothing, while Virginians George Minor and John M. Brooke made the Office of Ordnance and Hydrography an important center for technological experimentation and innovation. Predictably, senior Virginia officers commanded the Confederacy's James River Squadron for all but the last months of the war. Men who entered the Confederate Navy from the Virginia Navy, including commanders Robert B. Pegram, John R. Tucker, and Thomas R. Rootes, commanded many of the ironclad warships commissioned in the James River Squadron and throughout the South. Adoptive Virginian William H. Parker founded and superintended the Confederate States Naval Academy—an institution that was housed on board the converted warship *Patrick Henry.*

Patrick Henry, which underwent a second conversion into a school ship at Rocketts, was the only one of the Virginia State Navy vessels that survived the entire life of the James River Squadron. Her sister ship *Jamestown* served a year as a light warship, but was intentionally sunk in May 1862 to obstruct the channel against an enemy squadron at Drewry's Bluff. That was also the fate of the transport ship *Northampton.* Like *Jamestown* and *Patrick Henry*, *Teaser* participated in the historic battle of Hampton Roads on March 8, 1862. *Teaser* achieved historical distinction in her own right as the floating headquarters of the Confederacy's Submarine Battery Service and as the Confederacy's first "aircraft carrier"—the launch deck for a hot air observation balloon. This career was short-lived, as she was captured by the enemy on July 4, 1862. The small converted warships helping to protect the York, Rappahannock, and Potomac rivers, *Logan, Virginia,* and *George Page*, were scuttled and burned in the spring of 1862 when the evacuation of Confederate shore defenses left them vulnerable to Federal warships.[94]

This strategic retreat also resulted in the evacuation of the fortifications that the Virginia Navy had erected along the state's rivers and harbors. On May 10, 1862, Confederate forces evacuated Norfolk and, along with it, the Gosport Navy Yard. The abandonment of Norfolk in turn doomed the one vessel from the Virginia State Navy that had made an epochal contribution to the Confederacy and to the history of naval warfare.

At the end of May 1861, the Bakers succeeded in raising the frigate *Merrimack.* Two weeks after her badly burned hulk was transferred to the Confederate Navy, secretary Stephen Mallory summoned to Richmond three former Virginia officers—constructor John L. Porter, chief engineer William P. Williamson, and future Ordnance Office head lieutenant John Brooke—to discuss transforming *Merrimack* into an ironclad warship. The work was performed at Gosport's Dry Dock No. 1 by several hundred skilled and unskilled laborers and consumed enormous quantities of materials, including more than seven hundred tons of iron plate produced by Tredegar Iron Works. Under the watchful eye of the man who would serve as her executive officer, Lt. Catesby Jones, the CSS *Virginia* took shape. She was commissioned on February 24, 1862, and made her maiden voyage on March 8— nearly wrecking the Union Navy's blockading fleet in Hampton Roads and rendering obsolete wooden warships all over the world.[95]

While Samuel Barron expressed understandable pride in the accomplishments of the Virginia State Navy in June 1861, most of those accomplishments were lost with the evacuation of the Virginia Tidewater in the spring of 1862. Frustrating and disillusioning as this was, the experience was typical. The Virginia State Navy served a function similar to that of the navies established and passed on to the Confederacy by other coastal states— as an interim force that bought time for the construction of stronger vessels and fortifications. Other states hurriedly transformed passenger vessels, transports, and tugs into warships, assembling "mosquito fleets" that fared badly in contests against U.S. warships.[96] The Virginia experience transcended the typical. The 1,200 guns from Gosport Navy Yard armed the shore batteries of Virginia and the entire Confederacy. Gosport's dry dock allowed the construction of the Confederacy's prototype ironclad warship. Thanks to its military and industrial assets, Virginia's navy was able to endow the Confederacy with more than a few weak warships and a wealth of competent officers. Time would tell how these assets would serve the Confederate war effort.

Notes

1. H.B. Cooke to John Letcher, telegram, April 17, 1861, Governor John Letcher Executive Papers, Library of Virginia, Richmond (henceforth Letcher Papers); receipts for charter of *Thomas Reaney,* April 16, 1861 and ca. May 9, 1861 and receipt for *Henry Reed,* May 14, 1861, Virginia Navy Department Records, Library of Virginia; W.H. Face to John Letcher, April 23, 1861, Letcher Papers. The author would like to thank Vince Brooks of the Library of Virginia for assistance with newly processed Naval Department records.

2. T.T. Cropper to John Letcher, April 18, 1861, Letcher Papers.

3. John Letcher to Robert Pegram, April 18, 1861, Letcher Papers.

4. U.S. Navy Department, *Official Records of the Union and Confederate*

Navies in the War of the Rebellion (Washington, D.C.: Government Printing Office, 1894–1922), series I, vol. 4, 306–7 (henceforth *ORN*). For a narrative of events in Norfolk, see J.H. Robertson, "War Comes to Norfolk Harbor, 1861," *Virginia Cavalcade* (Spring 2001): 64–75.

5. *ORN*, series I, vol. 4, 292–93; R.M. Smith to John Letcher, April 20, 1861, Letcher Papers.

6. T.T. Cropper to John Letcher, April 20, 1861, Letcher Papers.

7. *Richmond Enquirer*, April 20, 1861; J.V. Scott to John Letcher, April 18, 1861, Letcher Papers.

8. W.B. [Barton?] to John Letcher, April 20, 1861, Letcher Papers.

9. *ORN*, series I, vol. 4, 308.

10. Ibid., 274; W.B. Taliaferro to John Letcher, telegram, April 20, 1861, Letcher Papers.

11. William Parker to John Letcher, telegram, April 21, 1861, Letcher Papers.

12. E.L. Brockett to John Letcher, telegram, April 21, 1861, Letcher Papers; Invoice for payment of R.O. Haskins for services of *Sea Board*, April 21, 1861, with message from George Munford to R.O. Haskins, Virginia Navy Department Records, Library of Virginia, Richmond.

13. E.L. Brockett to John Letcher, April 20[?], 1861, Letcher Papers.

14. *Richmond Enquirer*, April 25, 1861.

15. G.T. Sinclair to George Munford, telegram, April 21, 1861; John Letcher to Francis Pickens, telegram, April 22, 1861; George Munford to Jeff Davis, telegram, April 22, 1861, Letcher Papers.

16. John Letcher's message to Convention, June 17, 1861, Letcher Papers.

17. The text of the military convention between Virginia and the Confederacy is printed in U.S. War Department, *War of the Rebellion: A Compilation of Official Records of the Union and Confederate Armies* (Washington, D.C.: Government Printing Office 1880–1901), series IV, vol. 1, 243–44 (hereinafter cited as *OR*).

18. See Charles B. Dew, *Ironmaker to the Confederacy: Joseph R. Anderson and Tredegar Iron Works* (New Haven, Conn.: Yale University Press, 1966).

19. *Acts of the General Assembly of the State of Virginia passed in 1861* (Richmond: William F. Ritchie, 1861), 28.

20. *Ordinances Adopted by the Convention of Virginia in Secret Session*, appendix to *Acts*, 8.

21. Ibid., 11–12.

22. James I. Robertson Jr., *Proceedings of the Advisory Council of the State of Virginia, April 21–June 19, 1861* (Richmond: Virginia State Library, 1977), 13, 16.

23. Brent Tarter, "The Barron Family: A Virginia Naval Dynasty," *Virginia Cavalcade* (August 1998): 170–72.

24. J. Thomas Scharf, *History of the Confederate States Navy: From Its Organization to the Surrender of Its Last Vessel* (New York: Rogers & Sherwood, 1887), 710–711.

25. Resolution, April 6, 1858, Eleanor S. Brockenbrough Library, The Museum of the Confederacy, Navy Collection, Richmond, Va.; Edward F. Heite, "Captain Robert B. Pegram: Hero under Four Flags," *Virginia Cavalcade* 14 (Autumn 1965): 38–43.

26. Virginia Navy Department Records; Robertson, *Proceedings,* 46.

27. Entry for French Forrest in Allen Johnson and Dumas Malone, eds., *Dictionary of American Biography* (New York: Charles Scribner's Sons, 1943), VI, 531–32; George W. Munford to French Forrest, April 19, 1861, and R.L. Page to French Forrest, May 2, 1861, French Forrest Papers, Virginia Historical Society, Richmond, Va., confirm Forrest's position as "Senior officer in the State Navy of Virginia" and flag officer.

28. *ORN,* series I, vol. 4, 270; Paul D. Casdorph, *Prince John Magruder: His Life and Campaigns* (New York: John Wiley & Sons, 1996), 112.

29. W.F. Lynch, *Naval Life: Observations Afloat and On Shore* (New York: Charles Scribner, 1851) and W.F. Lynch, *Narrative of the United States' Expedition to the River Jordan and Dead Sea* (Philadelphia: Lee and Blanchard, 1850); Jack P. Lewis, "William Francis Lynch, Explorer of the Dead Sea," *Near East Archaeological Society Bulletin* (Fall 1992): 2–9.

30. George M. Brooke Jr., *John M. Brooke: Naval Scientist and Educator* (Charlottesville: University Press of Virginia, 1980).

31. Quoted in William N. Still Jr., *Iron Afloat: The Story of the Confederate Armorclads* (Nashville: Vanderbilt University Press, 1971), 21.

32. Robertson, *Proceedings,* 28; *ORN,* series I, vol. 5, 808.

33. Murray Mason to John Letcher, May 8, 1861, and John Taylor to John Letcher, May 5, 1861, and Joseph Myers to John Letcher, May 10, 1861, Letcher Papers.

34. Robertson, *Proceedings,* 41, 49; Ralph W. Donnelly, *Biographical Sketches of the Commissioned Officers of the Confederate States Marine Corps* (Privately printed, 1973), 2, 45–46; French Forrest to Adam Baker, April 22, 1861, Gosport Order Book, 1, Virginia Navy Department Records.

35. French Forrest to Lt. G.W. Harrison, Naval Rendezvous, Norfolk, May 1, 1861, in Gosport Order Book, Virginia Navy Department Records; lease of building from Ann B. Lacoste for $25 per month, April 22, 1861, Virginia Navy Department Records.

36. General Order No. 2, April 25, 1861, in *Richmond Enquirer,* May 2, 1861.

37. Clothing requisitions and returns of clothing issued, May and June 1861, Virginia Navy Department Records.

38. French Forrest to Joseph Pierce, April 25, 1861, and French Forrest to Thomas Rootes, May 14, 1861, Gosport Order Book, 21, 74, Virginia Navy Department Records; *ORN*, series I, vol. 5, 806.

39. Accounts of George Loyall, Navy agents, undated, Virginia Navy Department Records.

40. French Forrest to Messrs. Baker, May 18, 1861, Gosport Order Book, 84, Virginia Navy Department Records.

41. Quoted in John V. Quarstein, *The Battle of the Ironclads* (Charleston, S.C.: Arcadia Publishers, 1999), 26.

42. French Forrest to Capt. James Milligan, May 17, 1861, Gosport Order Book, 56, Virginia Navy Department Records.

43. Invoices in Virginia Navy Department Records.

44. Gosport Order Book, May 5, 7, 11, 1861, pp. 48, 56, 67; Gosport Order Book, April 24, 1861, p. 16; payroll of *Empire*, May 2–July 1, 1861, Virginia Navy Department Records. On July 1, *Empire* was stripped of her crew; the state asked the owner of *Harmony* on July 12 about extending the charter.

45. Virginia Navy Department Records.

46. Robertson, *Proceedings*, 64, 67; Report of board of inspection to John Letcher, May 1, 1861, Letcher Papers.

47. Payment dated September 27, 1861, in Virginia Navy Department Records.

48. Advisory Council to Letcher, April 23, 1861, Letcher Papers; Draft of Governor's Proclamation, April 24, 1861, and modifying order, April 23, Letcher Papers; published proclamation in *Richmond Enquirer*, April 25, 1861; records of payment made to the crew of *James Buchanan* are in Virginia Navy Department Records; Certificate of release of *City of Richmond*, signed by R.B. Pegram, April 25, 1861, and B.F. Hallett to John Letcher, May 2, 1861, regarding detained schooner *W.H. Farnham*, Letcher Papers.

49. *Richmond Enquirer*, April 20, 1861.

50. Robertson, *Proceedings*, 29, 51–52; John Robertson to John Letcher, May 3, 1861, Letcher Papers.

51. James H. Rochelle, "The Confederate Steamship 'Patrick Henry,'" *Southern Historical Society Papers* 14 (1886): 127–28.

52. *ORN*, series I, vol. 5, 803.

53. Virginia Navy Department Records.

54. *ORN*, series I, vol. 5, 809; Robertson, *Proceedings*, 147.

55. Virginia Navy Department Records.

56. French Forrest to John Letcher, April 25, 1861, Letcher Papers.

57. Gosport Order Book, April 22, 1861, pp. 4–7, Virginia Navy Department Records. Note that the Confederate Navy "dispensed with" or redefined most of these positions. Gosport Order Book, July 3, 1861.

58. Accounts of George Loyall, Navy Agent, Virginia Navy Department Records; Vouchers of William H. Peters, paymaster, Virginia Navy Department Records.

59. Virginia Navy Department Records. See John M. Coski, *Capital Navy: The Men, Ships, and Operations of the James River Squadron* (Campbell, Ca.: Savas Woodbury Publishers, 1996) for details on Richmond's naval resources.

60. Receipts in Virginia Navy Department Records.

61. Gosport Order Book, May 15, 1861, Virginia Navy Department Records.

62. Pierce's itemized account, July 22, 1861, ibid.

63. Letcher's message to the Convention, June 17, 1861, [draft of Document XXXV], Letcher Papers.

64. Andrew Talcott to John Letcher, April 15, 1861, Letcher Papers.

65. Andrew Talcott Diary, entries of April 16, 17, 1861, Virginia Historical Society, Richmond, Va.; *ORN*, series I, vol. 6, 704. Lt. John Brooke expressed dismay that the state had delayed for months in implementing Talcott's plan. George M. Brooke Jr., ed., *Ironclads and Big Guns of the Confederacy: The Journal and Letters of John M. Brooke* (Columbia: S.C.: University of South Carolina Press, 2002), 18.

66. Scharf, *History*, 300.

67. George T. Sinclair to M.F. Maury and George T. Sinclair telegram to John Letcher, May 1, 1861, Letcher Papers; also A.B. McLean to Robert E. Lee, May 3, 1861, Letcher Papers.

68. "Norfolk" to John Letcher, Letcher Papers.

69. Robertson, *Proceedings*, 6; *Register of the Graduates of the United States Military Academy* (West Point: U.S. Military Academy, 1970), 212.

70. Robert E. Lee to Walter Gwynn, May 4, 1861, Letcher Papers.

71. Walter Gwynn to Robert E. Lee, May 6, 1861, *OR*, series I, vol. 2, 809.

72. *OR*, series I, vol. 2, 867

73. John W.H. Porter, *A Record of Events in Norfolk County, Virginia, from April 19th, 1861 to May 10th, 1862* . . . (Portsmouth, Va.: W.A. Fiske, 1892), 24.

74. "Commodore Harrison Henry Cocke," *Confederate Veteran* 14 (February 1906): 76–77.

75. S. Barron to Harrison Cocke, May 2, 1861, Cocke Papers, Virginia Historical Society, Richmond, Va.

76. David F. Riggs, *Embattled Shrine: Jamestown in the Civil War* (Shippensburg, Pa.: White Mane Publishing Company, 1997), 19–23.

77. Roger Jones to S. Barron, May 6, 1861, *ORN*, series I, vol. 6, 700–701.

78. S. Barron to Roger Jones, May 11, 12, and 27, 1861, *ORN*, series I, vol. 6, 703–5.

79. *ORN*, series I, vol. 5, 804, and *ORN*, series I, vol. 7, 437, 461.

80. Mary Alice Wills, *The Confederate Blockade of Washington, D.C., 1861–1862* (Parsons, W.V.: McClain Printing Company, 1975; reprint: Shippensburg, Pa.: Burd Street Press, 1998), 21–22.

81. Ibid., 33–34, 64.

82. *ORN,* series II, vol. 1, 99; U.S. Navy Department, Naval History Division, *Civil War Naval Chronology* (Washington, D.C.: Government Printing Office, 1961–1965).

83. J.H. Ward to Gideon Welles, April 22, 1861, in *ORN,* series I, vol. 4, 420.

84. *ORN,* series I, vol. 4, 458.

85. *ORN,* series I, vol. 4, 495; *ORN,* series I, vol. 6, 709; Wills, *Blockade,* 29–30.

86. Wills, *Blockade,* 37–39.

87. *ORN,* series I, vol. 4, 380–81.

88. *ORN,* series I, vol. 5, 646–47, 699–700.

89. Stephen Mallory to John Letcher, May 14, 1861, and Stephen Mallory to John Letcher, telegram, May 14, 1861, Letcher Papers.

90. Payment to R.O. Haskins, July 19, 1861, with note from W.L. Powell to Paymaster John DeBree, August 29, 1861, Virginia Navy Department Records.

91. Payments to Capt. Hugh N. Page, Bureau of Yards and Docks, Virginia Navy Department Records.

92. Robertson, *Proceedings,* 154–56; *ORN,* series I, vol. 6, 708–9.

93. Joseph Myers to George W. Munford, February 17, 1862, Virginia Navy Department Records.

94. See Coski, *Capital Navy* for details of James River Squadron after June 1861.

95. John V. Quarstein, *C.S.S. Virginia: Mistress of Hampton Roads* (Appomattox, Va.: H.E. Howard, 2000); William C. Davis, *Duel between the First Ironclads* (Garden City, N.Y.: Doubleday, 1975).

96. For details on these state navies, see Scharf, *History,* and Raimondo Luraghi, *A History of the Confederate Navy* (Annapolis, Md.: Naval Institute Press, 1996).

Afro-Virginians' Attitudes on Secession and Civil War, 1861

Ervin L. Jordan Jr.

Virginia in 1861 was a biracial commonwealth of more than half a million blacks and slightly more than a million nervous whites (1,047,411 whites; 548,907 blacks, of which 490,865 were slaves and 58,042 were free blacks). In one sense, the Old Dominion personified black America because it had more black inhabitants than anywhere else in North America and the most enslaved blacks in the Western Hemisphere except Brazil. One of every six of the Confederacy's 3.7 million blacks lived in Virginia.[1]

Regardless of their numbers, there are inherent difficulties in discerning black Virginians' true feelings about secession during the first months of the war. Insofar as black self-documentation is concerned, they lacked a voice or active participation in public and civic affairs and overall left little first-hand documentation. Much of the war's surviving record consists of whites' biased accounts of black activities. The nature of antebellum and wartime events and race relations North and South makes this more of a research challenge than most due to the lack of wartime African American newspapers and scarcity of diaries, letters, and similar writings by free blacks. As for slaves, in many instances only contemporary fragmentary anecdotes and remarks in their oral and written testimonies exist, and when quoted it is usually with pro-Confederate sentiments for obvious reasons.

Those whose opinions about the war were directly solicited by tense whites took great care to answer guardedly, like Culpeper Court House free black barber Ira Field: "I don't know . . . this war . . . is the worse thing that could ever be settled." In another part of the state an elderly slave answered, "I'm on the Lord's side." But most kept a tight-lipped and enigmatic low profile; seventy years later many ex-slaves were afraid to talk about "reb times" and risk offending white Southerners and ex-Confederates by inadvertently saying the wrong thing. "I ain't telling white folks nothing," Petersburg octogenarian and old folks' home resident Ishrael Massie told an interviewer in 1937, "'cause I'm scared to make enemies."[2]

Black Virginians habitually expressed one sentiment to whites while secretly holding the opposite; one historian has characterized them as wearing "inscrutable masks [and] watermelon smiles" while feigning disinterest about the war. African American history is often the story of what blacks have done in America and what white Americans have done to them. Any analysis of black Virginians' attitudes toward secession and civil war must take into consideration that their words and deeds were often filtered by contemporary whites' power over them. Possibly the best means of ascertaining black Virginians' collective and individual perspectives about the times is to examine their words and deeds concerning slavery, free blacks, and Afro-Confederates; their surreptitious longings for freedom as manifested by running away; their relations with the Union army; and limited attempts to rise up against their racial oppressors.

As the national clouds of Civil War darkened over Virginia, many slaves believed the dawn of their freedom was at hand. They saw portents in a multitude of prophetic visions based on Christianity and superstition. "A prevalent opinion among them is that this war is a fulfillment of the eleventh chapter of Daniel," a Northern periodical reported in early 1861. This chapter (Daniel 11:15, 25, 40) contained an allegorical reference to war between North and South: "The king of the north shall come, and cast up a mount, and take the most fenced cities: and the arms of the south shall not withstand, neither his chosen people, neither shall there be any strength to withstand. . . . And he shall stir up his power and his courage against the king of the south with a great army; and the king of the south shall be stirred up to battle with a very great and mighty army; but he shall not stand." In the privacy of their ramshackle cabins and covert churches they also found hope in the mysticism of Luke 21:9 and 15: "But when ye shall hear of wars and commotions, be not terrified: for these things must first come to pass; but the end is not by and by. . . . For I will give you a mouth and wisdom, which all your adversaries shall not be able to gainsay or resist." Slaves had long identified themselves with Old Testament Israelites who, after centuries of bitter bondage, had been delivered from slavery to the Promised Land. They also believed the increase in several natural phenomena such as shooting stars and an unusual profusion of insects were omens of an apocalyptic war during which God would finally set them free.[3]

On November 5, 1860, the day before Lincoln's election, Richard Hackley, a slave at the University of Virginia, wrote his master: "I hope that Mr. Lincoln or no such man may ever take his seat in the presidential chair." From Wheeling in the north, Danville in the south, Bluefield in the west, and Norfolk in the east, urban and rural whites, slaveholders and non-slaveholders, feared the black presence in their midst despite such loyalty pronouncements. On the face of it, they cared little about what blacks wanted. Yet before and after the war came to Virginia, more than ever before blacks were watched for signs of discontent or assertiveness, reading of Northern newspapers, and contacts with Republicans, Yankees, or abolitionists.

After John Brown's abortive attempt at Harpers Ferry the Old Dominion joined other Southern states in requesting more arms from the federal government. The state adjutant general addressed a letter in November to Secretary of War John B. Floyd, a former Virginia governor, claiming that the commonwealth was daily facing increasing insecurity and dangers manifested by "domestic insubordination." He added the governor's request that the federal government immediately send seven hundred muskets to defend against the threat. These and other conspiracy concerns would obsess white Virginians throughout the war. In September 1861 a young ex-slave employed by Union officers at Fort Monroe recounted how Virginia slaves often spoke of John Brown as a good man who had given his life to free them.[4]

Aware of the coming strife, Afro-Virginians prepared themselves as best they could. A Petersburg slave and Underground Railroad agent code-named "Ham and Eggs," though characterizing "the politics of the day in a high-rage" in the Old Dominion, nevertheless informed his Northern contacts that he wanted to continue to send them "some very good hams"—runaways. Elizabeth "Lizzie" Keckley, a former Dinwiddie County slave who had purchased her freedom, found employment in Washington as a seamstress for the family of Mississippi senator Jefferson Davis. She would later write in her memoirs that Varina Davis had predicted to her that the South would secede and win the coming war, and the North would blame blacks for the national strife and treat them harshly. Keckley declined Varina Davis's offer of continued employment in the South and in early 1861 became a dressmaker and confidante to Mary Todd Lincoln, first lady of the United States.[5]

When Virginia seceded on April 17, 1861, and joined the fledgling Confederacy in May, this evoked demonstrative patriotism. Richmond citizens celebrated by hoisting a raggedy, barefooted grinning black man upon the shoulders of Houdon's statue of George Washington in the state capitol building. Meanwhile, Richard Gill Forrester, a fourteen-year-old slave whose task it was to raise and lower United States and Virginia flags at the state capitol, rescued the national flag after secessionists tossed it in the trash. He secreted the Stars and Stripes under his bed for the duration of the war, hoping for a Union victory and his freedom.[6]

Notwithstanding vainglorious public displays of unity and Confederate nationalism, Virginia remained a state divided by geography and race. Unionist whites in the western counties opposed secession as treason and rebellion and would eventually secede to become West Virginia. But a Rockingham County poem predicted unity among all Virginians regardless of race, gender, or status:

> Shoulder to shoulder, son and sire!
> All, call all! To the feast of fire!
> Mother and maiden, children and slave,
> A common triumph or a single grave!

Confederate Virginians expected swiftly to whip Yankeedom and return home to a South where slavery and black inferiority would be forever perpetuated. Robert Snead, an Amherst County soldier, wrote a letter in July 1861 that was both an appeal and a warning: "I commit to you my servants the safe keeping of My dear wife and children . . . you will take care of them . . . and conduct yourselves so as not [to] get in any trouble or difficulty while I am gone." The *Richmond Dispatch* opined that slavery would prove an asset of strength for the South as it had during pervious American wars and at Harpers Ferry. Not all whites were as sanguine. "Virginia is to be the principal seat of war and bear the brunt of its great battles," a University of Virginia professor grimly predicted two weeks before Virginians ratified secession. Legislators and newspaper editors voiced their constituents' fears: "What will happen to our cause if a few Nat Turners crawl out? Can we really expect the Negroes to stand with us?" A worried Powhatan County farmer wrote Jefferson Davis that "ours are envenomed deadly foes, ready for any dirty work," and claimed their agents were already at work inciting slaves to attack whites.[7]

The new and uncertain times caused almost immediate hardship among slave families as panicked owners relocated them to other states like Texas and Missouri (so many Virginians had emigrated to Missouri with their slaves during antebellum times that the central part of the state had become known as "Little Dixie"); by evacuating they hoped to hold onto their slaves a while longer. Former Lynchburg slave Adeline Henderson told how her master ordered his hundred slaves to start packing for Missouri. "We didn't know what it was all about," she reminisced nearly sixty-five years later, "but we had to do what we were told." It took her and the others three months to walk to Missouri. This practice, which increased as the war expanded across the South, became known as "running the negroes" or "refugeeing." Still, as typified in a poem published in Richmond about a slave named Jerry, slaveholders engaged in quasi-bargains with their slaves, promising all would be well if they continued their lawful servitude:

> If poverty's cup I am sentenced to drain,
> I'll part with you—last of them all;
> Your kindness, old Jerry! would double my pain,
> And your sorrows embitter my fall.
> If fate or misfortune should cause us to part,
> There's a God will unite us once more!
> So drink my good health, and console your old heart,
> And love me and serve, as before.

As the war became prolonged times got hard for whites; but for blacks, especially slaves, hard times had never been a stranger. Lorenzo Ivy, a twelve-year-old plantation slave, claimed he was often not fed for several days at a time and when he did receive food it consisted of little more than a tin cup of buttermilk and some cornbread. To add to his misery, his overseer became meaner the longer the war continued.[8]

By necessity or choice, enslaved Virginians knew what the war might signify to them, but at the outset they could do little outright to impede the Confederate war effort or to support the Union. "When I was still a child," ex-Franklin County slave Booker T. Washington wrote in his memoirs, "I could hear the slaves in our quarters whispering in subdued tones that something unusual 'the war' was about to take place, and that it meant their freedom." According to Washington, this renewed hope had begun a year before the war:

> During the campaign when Lincoln was first a candidate for the Presidency, the slaves on our far-off plantation, miles from any railroad or large city or daily newspaper, knew what the issues were. When the war was begun between North and South, every slave on our plantation felt and knew that, though other issues were discussed, the primal one was that of slavery. Even the most ignorant members of my race . . . felt in their hearts, with a certainty that admitted no doubt, that the freedom of the slaves would be the one great result of the war, if the Northern armies conquered.[9]

Confederate Virginians generally regarded slavery and white supremacy as a fundamentally natural order and divinely ordained way of life. They and other white Southerners identified themselves as "the master race" (a phrase chillingly echoed by Nazi Germany less than a century later). Confederate vice president Alexander H. Stephens, who had already declared slavery as the South's cornerstone, disparaged Northerners as blacks' oppressors and Southerners as their true protectors: "This is a war against reason in every sense of the term. In the first place, many of those engaged in it are engaged in a crusade nominally to ameliorate the condition of a portion of our population. They are in a crusade to make things better than the Creator made them, or to make things equal which he made unequal. . . . These very people would do, as some are reported to be doing in Virginia, capture the black population and send them off to Cuba." Yet slaveholders feared destruction of slavery regardless of the war's outcome. Whites on both sides of the Mason-Dixon Line openly speculated that slaves might hold the balance of power between North and South.[10]

Slaves knew they were human and wanted their freedom yet also understood the constraints of their condition and tried to bear up as best they could. For their own individual and collective physical and emotional self-preservation they developed a camouflaged reticence and stoicism about themselves. One antislavery journal claimed: "They have their revolutionary and patriotic songs, which they sing in private. They hold secret religious meetings, the burthen of their prayers being that the Lord will help the North, and hasten the day of their emancipation." A Northerner expelled from the state early in the war reported: "It was interesting to notice the assumed ignorance and indifference of the slaves while in the presence of their masters, and that the moment they believed themselves safe, and near a Northern man, or one whom they could trust, they brightened with intelligence, and spoke of passing events with wonderful accuracy and feeling . . . greedily devouring every fact and opinion, and then going forth to spread among their fellows that which they had acquired."[11]

Sometimes their sphinx-like masks were briefly unveiled to reveal their innermost feelings as some displayed unprecedented assertiveness, resulting in traditional punishments, especially when caught discussing the war among themselves. A Fairfax slave overheard by whites telling other slaves "the Yankees would fight" received a severe whipping. Shortly thereafter he fled to the sanctuary of Federal lines near Falls Church where he displayed his lacerated back to horrified officers as proof that he had "served under the stripes, before he sought the protection of the stars." While standing in the streets of Richmond one slave began complaining to his fellows about his master's harshness. "Never mind," replied one his companions, "Massa Lincoln will be here soon and, and then it will be all right." But their conversation was overheard, the blacks arrested, and each given thirty-nine lashes.[12] For the moment, whites—especially slave owners—dominated blacks economically, legally, politically, socially, and racially. And the majority of white Virginians agreed with the righteousness of slavery whether they owned slaves or not.

As a distrusted minority within a distinctive ethnic minority that was 90 percent enslaved, free blacks already had enough indigenous troubles without causing additional ones for themselves by challenging white supremacy. White Virginians' antebellum intolerant vigilantism and perceptions of free blacks as potential adversaries had made them circumspect. Free blacks' cultural self-protectiveness was heightened because they were treated as racial outsiders who lived in the shadows of slavery. Accordingly, they tended to be law-abiding and kept low profiles as war tensions increased. Regardless of their racial fears, whites insisted free blacks would not be permitted idleness or to shirk their responsibilities to the Confederate cause. Before the end of the summer it was suggested to President Davis that working without pay in hospitals to care for sick and wounded soldiers be compulsory for free blacks. They were also subject to unfair arrests and punishments as forced laborers for unionists. After hearing rumors that Confederates planned to force free blacks to fight as soldiers, Albemarle County farmer John Aleslock fled to Washington where he was arrested in May 1861 and told he would be held indefinitely unless he agreed to work for the Yankees. Seven months later he was still confined.[13]

State legislators were also determined that free blacks would contribute to the cause one way or another. In July 1861, all able-bodied free black males between eighteen and fifty were ordered to serve as military laborers or on public works. Those who did not comply were subject to fines, imprisonment, or enslavement. That same month Richmond's mayor, espousing the carrot-or-stick approach, summoned a group of free blacks to his office and verbally bullied them by reminding them that "it was no less their duty than that of white people to do something for the good of the country" since they were not permitted to enroll as soldiers. The next day nearly two hundred free blacks showed up at City Hall to volunteer their services as military laborers.[14]

Approximately 25 percent of the state's 59,000 free blacks were loyal to Virginia, the Confederacy, or both. With public-spirited alacrity they hastened to volunteer their services to the Confederacy, though most were pragmatic patriots hoping to protect their property, jobs, and status as the South's privileged black caste. As to restrictions on black enrollment in Southern troops, some exceptions were made. George Price and Austin Dix enrolled in the Eighteenth Virginia Infantry in June 1861. Dix, a drummer, would serve honorably for two years; the fifty-nine-year-old Price was honorably discharged in 1862. Mortimer Raymond, a Richmond police informer who reported on black offenders, was greatly astonished when sent to the whipping post for having "associated with a white woman upon terms of closer familiarity than the law permitted." He erroneously presumed his demonstrated loyalty to whites meant he could exercise prerogatives not normally granted to blacks.

Across the Confederate South, more often than not, free black hopes for special privileges and favoritism because of their supposed loyalty were dashed as they were compelled to "stay in their place." Bowman Seals, an Alabamian describing himself as an excellent marksman and a "practical mechanic," wrote Jefferson Davis offering his services because he believed Northerners were blacks' greatest enemies. John Jones, a black New York

City resident, delivered an impromptu public speech on behalf of the Confederacy in the autumn of 1861 insisting that the rebels could not be defeated and that he would help the South whip the Yankees. Seals's offer was ignored and Jones was thrown into a local lunatic asylum.

Free blacks navigated a paradoxical relationship between themselves and a commonwealth that seemed unable to decide whether it trusted them or not, whether it wanted them to stay or leave. If there was any natural alliance between slaves and free blacks the war threatened to tear apart this tenuous bond. Several free blacks also owned slaves and occasionally jealousies caused by status and caste tensions were brought out into the open. A visiting South Carolina slave maid indignantly complained to her mistress that Richmond slaves were claiming Virginian soldiers had won the battle of First Manassas. At Harpers Ferry a slave who had escaped to a Union camp near Charleston was advised by a free black servant employed in the camp to return to his master to be better off than Northern free blacks. The slave tartly replied, "If that free man thinks I am better off than he is, let him trade places with me for a little while."[15]

Afro-Confederates' scruples were either coerced, feigned, or sincere. Although they sought to contribute to the Confederate war effort on their own terms, they were riddles to the war's contending groups. Confederate whites did not completely trust them, the Yankees considered them aberrations, and fellow blacks despised them as racial traitors—"skillet heads." Like the proverbial crabs in a basket trying to pull each other back from escape, slaves and free blacks did not care to see members of their own race getting above themselves. They accused Afro-Confederates of standing behind falsehoods out of fear or self-centered convenience to save themselves from enslavement if free or to win manumission if they were slaves. Afro-Confederates never claimed to represent collectively all blacks but shrewdly claimed that blacks should think and act as they did. During the Union's occupation of Alexandria a visiting *New York Examiner* journalist asked Joe, a recently freed slave, why Virginia blacks were supporting the Confederacy. Joe denounced the Confederacy: "We know what's going on. Darkeys not so blind as white folks think." When the New Yorker pointed out that many slaves had said they would stand by their masters, Joe scoffed that "Darkeys talks to suit his master, don't like to be strung up. Darkey say anything, depends on who he talks to. . . . Black people knows what they're about, these times."[16]

Afro-Confederates were exploited for propaganda purposes though occasionally publicly praised and welcomed into the Confederate cause as civilian and military volunteers. As a reward for their slaves' unselfish heroism in battling a fire, Christiansburg whites held a large banquet and dance in their honor at the local courthouse. "Let the North look upon this picture," a local newspaper smugly reported, "and then upon the miserable, sordid starving condition of the [free] negro among them, and be satisfied that slavery is [their] true status." During the spring of 1861 efforts to enlist companies of black soldiers, "to refute with bullets the stale slanders of the abolitionists," were begun in several communities like Lynchburg, albeit temporarily. A young woman wrote her aunt in May 1861 that Lynchburg free blacks were patriotically enlisting at such a rate that grateful white residents no longer doubted their fidelity. About sixty Amelia County blacks volunteered to perform any service required of them; in April another sixty blacks, marching behind a Confederate flag, went to Richmond to volunteer as soldiers but were politely thanked and sent home. Frederick Douglass, black America's leading spokesman, alleged the Confederacy was actively enrolling black soldiers and worried this might spread suspicion of blacks in the North and thwart efforts to turn the war into an antislavery crusade.[17]

The first of the war's battles fought on Virginia soil provided Afro-Confederates the opportunity to prove their loyalty. Allegedly, the first Union officer killed in battle, Maj. Theodore Winthrop of Massachusetts, was shot dead on June 10, 1861, by a black member of the Wythe Rifles during the Battle of Big Bethel. James Humbles, a bugler with the First Virginia Cavalry, single-handedly killed a Union soldier during a skirmish at Falling Waters on July 2, 1861. After the First Battle of Bull Run on July 21, 1861, on their own initiative, local slaves rounded up lost Union soldiers and turned them over to Confederate authorities. The congregation of a black Richmond Methodist church were thanked by their white pastor, a Reverend Nolly, for their prayers for the safety of the Washington Artillery of New Orleans. Nolly claimed that because of their piety the six-hundred-man regiment had only suffered the loss of one man killed in battle.[18]

Union officers acknowledged blacks' contributions to the Confederate war effort, especially in building fortifications and defensive works that seemed unconquerable. "We can whip you," Yankee pickets told their Confederate counterparts, "if you keep your Negroes out of your army." During a December 1861 reconnaissance near Newport News, members of the Twentieth New York Infantry were attacked by Confederate cavalry accompanied by "negro infantry." Regimental officers fumed afterward: "This is, indeed, a new feature of the war. We have heard of a regiment of negroes at Manassas, and another at Memphis, and still another at New Orleans, but did not believe it till it came so near home, and attacked our men. There is no mistake about it. [We] were actually attacked and fired on, and wounded by negroes. . . . If they fight us with negroes, why should we not fight them with negroes, too?" Some of the wounded New Yorkers, angered by what they considered an uncivilized stratagem, vowed thereafter to kill every black on sight.[19]

By the fall of 1861 Afro-Confederates' enthusiasm for volunteering had somewhat cooled due to harsh treatment and promises broken by their Confederate taskmasters, and as compulsory labor became the norm. After First Manassas, more urban blacks were rounded up and delivered to the front as military laborers, often with little or no pay, poor food, and harsh working conditions. A few whites condemned such abuses. The president of the James River and Kanawha Canal was among those conceding that blacks were not always given full credit and praise for their unpretentious zeal and efficiency as the sinews of the commonwealth's war economy.[20]

When asked by a Northerner if she had run away from her master, one slave laughingly replied, "Golly no, Massa run away from me!" Seeking to escape to Union-held areas of the state did not necessarily mean that slaves— and some free blacks—sided with the North, but rather it evinced clear-sightedness in taking advantage of chaotic conditions. Not all such attempts were successful. Shortly after Lincoln's inauguration seventeen slaves on a Petersburg plantation politely informed their owner that they were now free and going north. He did not try to stop them but managed eventually to have them recaptured and sold further south.

On rare occasions a few slaves escaped to Africa. Henry Jarvis fled Northampton County in 1861 from an owner whom he characterized as "the meanest man on the Eastern Shore," after being shot at several times without cause. He went to Fort Monroe where Gen. Benjamin Butler informed him the war was not a black man's war. Jarvis boldly predicted it would become one before it ended. From there he made his way to Liberia by way of Cuba but returned to America after two years. During an 1872 interview, when asked why he did not stay in Africa, Jarvis replied, "I went to shore in Liberia an' looked about, but I 'cluded I'd rudder come home." Other runaways used the war as an opportunity to reunite with their loved ones. Shortly after Westmoreland County slave Samuel Ballton and his wife, Rebecca, were married in 1861, they were separated when his owner hired him out as a laborer at Confederate fortifications near Richmond. He bided his time and a year later escaped by posing as a loyal slave who had escaped from the Yankees and was returning home to "massa." He rescued his wife and mother-in-law and eventually settled in Alexandria. Ballton later enlisted with the Fifth Massachusetts Cavalry and was among the first black Union occupation soldiers to enter Richmond in April 1865.[21]

When field hands Frank Baker, Shepard Mallory, and James Townshend reached Fort Monroe in May 1861 they were the first of thousands of slave refugees designated "contrabands" and by turns protected, employed, or exploited by Mr. Lincoln's soldiers. Washington and Richmond legislators passed laws in the summer of 1861 to regulate runaways to their military and pecuniary advantage. The Confiscation Acts of August 6, 1861, freed slaves employed or used, with the consent of their owners, by Confederate authorities, against the federal government; under this act slaves who reached Fort Monroe, which they termed "the Freedom Fort" and "Freedom's Fortress," were deemed free. The Confederate Congress responded on August 30 by ordering the keeping of judicial records of slaves "abducted, or harbored" by persons acting under the authority of the United Sates government for filing in the Confederate State Department's archives in order to obtain financial compensation after the war. One Northern newspaper estimated that if only half of Virginia's slaves fell under Union control, nearly $150 million would be realized, more than enough to pay the costs of waging the war; any postwar settlement requiring the return of these slaves could be accomplished at half-price and still realize $75 million for Washington's coffers.[22]

Slaves knew little about such schemes and continued to flee to the nearest Union outposts. An estimated five hundred fugitive slaves reached Fort Monroe by June 1861; in October, two thousand. Such were their numbers that by September the American Missionary Association, a Christian radical abolitionist organization founded in 1846 to promote the Gospel and educate African Americans, opened a school in Hampton headed by Virginia-born free black Mary S. Peake, and another at Fort Monroe, teaching children by day and adults at night. By the end of the first year of the war, thousands of Virginia slaves were living in contraband camps in Tidewater, Hampton Roads, and the outskirts of Washington, D.C. On the question of slavery or freedom, and loyalty to the North or the South, Virginia slaves voted with their feet.[23]

In Stephen Vincent Benét's epic poetic homage to the war, "John Brown's Body," Spade, a runaway slave who reaches Union lines only to be forced to work as an unpaid laborer, resentfully declares, "I ain't honin' to go an' fight in no white folks war." Interrelationships between Southern blacks and white Northerners during the course of the war were forged and tested in the Old Dominion. Blacks, particularly slaves, considered Yankees as their allies. During the Battle of Big Bethel in June 1861, several Hampton blacks were seen anxiously milling in the streets awaiting news of the outcome. When asked what it would mean for them if "the Unioners" won, they answered they would be free; but if not "De Seceshers" would make things worse for them. After the battle, and no longer believing Fort Monroe a safe haven, many sought the assistance of Northern missionaries to go to Canada. Confederate authorities, despising Hampton as a "harbor of runaway slaves and traitors," burned the town on August 7, 1861, to deny its becoming a black colony under the protection of a federal fort where blacks had supported themselves—the women as laundresses and their menfolk on Uncle Sam's payroll as fortifications laborers.[24]

However, as Northern armies occupied parts of the state, black Virginians would quickly learn that not all Yankees were trustworthy, sympathetic, or antislavery. In Hampton, Union authorities decided to revive a custom long loathed by free blacks and slaves, namely the ringing of a curfew bell at the local courthouse upon which all blacks were required to be in their homes with interior lights extinguished. Although black Hamptonians felt this custom interfered with their new rights as free men and women, they complied grudgingly when the necessity of this measure in preventing Confederates from using lights at night to communicate with spies behind Union lines was explained to them. And black Hampton schoolteachers gratefully acknowledged that "many of the poor soldiers, who are suffering from wounds and exposure to weather," helped teach black children in church and school. Even so, Alexandria slaves complained of sexual harassment of female slaves when the city was occupied by Union troops in May 1861, accusing white soldiers of abusing "dose women most shameful, violating them promiscuously."[25]

Slaves were not always welcomed to Union lines. After his troops occupied Accomac County, Gen. John A. Dix issued a proclamation to its residents promising to respect their personal and property rights, especially where slaves were concerned, and instructed his regimental and corps commanders to deny sanctuary to runaways. Nevertheless, a group of thirty Accomac slaves arrived in Philadelphia the following month after having walked from the county and being supplied with financial donations from Wisconsin troops for their journey. At this stage of the war some Union officers seemed to relish returning runaways to Confederate authorities. Six runaway slaves in a boat were captured by the USS *Quaker City* off Cape Henry in May 1861 and returned to their Norfolk owner after he made a formal request for their return by flag of truce. The Federal naval officer in charge of the transfer blithely noted afterward, "we are glad to get rid of them . . . we don't wish to be stigmatized as negro-stealers." In August a senior officer commenting on the escape of three Virginia slaves to Baltimore, expressed his personal ambivalence on the "contraband issue," and said that soldiers would not meddle with runaways except to return them to their owners. These and similar incidents caused black Virginians to distrust white Union soldiers; slaves who had hoped the Yankees would free them became so embittered they accused them of wearing Uncle Sam's uniforms but having Jeff Davis hearts.[26]

A runaway named Charles could barely restrain his emotions as his employer absentmindedly whistled "Dixie" one evening in camp. "We've stopped singing that song," he grumbled, "and I don't wish I was in Dixie." When asked where Dixie was, Charles retorted, "Norfolk, that's where its at; kills the blacks in Dixie like sheep, while working on the batteries." Numerous blacks discovered the fortunes of war meant they had exchanged Confederate masters for Union ones. Suffolk resident Tom Hester, assigned to care for the horses of a Confederate regiment, was shot through the jaw at First Manassas and captured by Union forces "whilst I was runnin' roundst dere spittin out blood an' teeth." Taken to Alexandria where his wound was treated, Hester was unhappily employed as a Federal teamster for the rest of the war.

Such situations were somewhat ameliorated as Union military commanders learned that fugitive slaves possessed intelligence and information that might save their soldiers and lead to victory. "Our black friends down south," as they were characterized, were the only allies Union soldiers trusted as they pushed into the South: "These poor creatures realize plainly enough that we are their friends, and they have never let slip an opportunity of showing us that their friendship is worth having." But blacks had their own opinions. "Slaves will fight for those who fight for them," one Richmond slave secretly told a sympathetic white New Yorker shortly before the state's secession.[27]

One of the most vivid examples of black Virginians' attitudes toward the war was the increased number of slave rebellions, in particular those allegedly and directly supported by abolitionist extremists and Union arms. The state had been the bloodstained ground of some of the South's fiercest and most audacious antebellum slave revolts including the one led by Gabriel Prosser, a would-be revolutionary liberator who studied French military manuals and plotted in 1800 to establish a black republic with Richmond as its capital; Nat Turner, a Southampton County slave whose 1831 uprising killed more whites than any other in American history; and John Brown, a white Northerner who presumptuously plotted in 1859 to arm slaves from a federal arsenal and carve out a black guerrilla base in Virginia's mountains from which to launch all-out war against slaveholders. "Virginia Fugitive," a Northerner compelled to flee Richmond because of his neighbors' animosity, told a reporter: "To the Southern mind, there is nothing so terrible as the fear of servile insurrection." It was widely believed that if a slave insurrection occurred in Virginia, it would be known to Louisiana slaves within a few days.[28]

The siege mentality, and what historian Armistead Robinson labeled "insurrection anxiety" among white Virginians, was contrary to their public racial bravado; they feared blacks collectively and individually as personal and internal security threats. Any malcontent black could be another Nat Turner. During the next four years, in an effort to tighten controls and prevent any militaristic alliances between slaves and the Yankees, the General Assembly enacted nearly forty laws concerning blacks, including free black voluntary enslavement, labor conscription, special wartime taxes on free black males, transportation of convict slaves, and official pronouncements calling for the perpetuation of slavery.[29]

Despite laws and lynchings, Afro-Virginians defied whites in the name of vengeance and liberty. When a Staunton slave woman became unmanageable her owner decided to sell her, but she cut off three of her fingers in January 1861, thus preventing her sale and showing continued rebelliousness. Throughout the spring and summer of 1861 there were attempted slave uprisings and rumors of insurrections that emboldened other blacks and unnerved whites. In May sixteen blacks and a Massachusetts white man were arrested by Confederate troops for plotting a slave uprising in Winchester; later that month another slave conspiracy was exposed and foiled in King and Queen County. The Prince George County sheriff publicly flogged several slaves who had plotted a rebellion in August based on rumors of an anticipated arrival of Union troops at City Point. Yet slaves were not completely cowed by the increased presence of Confederate and state troops and paper laws. Crime, insolence, and pugnacity increased, leading some whites to believe they were at the mercy of warlike slaves. "The white man rule de day / De negro rule de night," was the catchphrase repeated among gleeful Richmond blacks.[30]

African American scholars maintain that the Confederacy was little more than white supremacy cloaked in grandiose Southern nationalistic dogma articulated by pseudo-aristocratic race elites who exploited poor whites, hoodwinked the bourgeois, and oppressed blacks—all to perpetuate and substantiate a racially biased socio-political-economic system ostensibly inherited from and ordained by America's Founding Fathers. More than sixty years after the war, African American historian and sociologist W.E.B. DuBois was convinced that "the South cared only for States Rights as a weapon to defend slavery. People do not go to war for abstract theories of government. They fight for property and privilege and that was what Virginia fought for in the Civil War." As the first year of the war came to a close, Virginia seemed firmly ensconced in the Confederate nation, and Afro-Virginians—as did their fellow black Southerners—took a wait and see attitude during 1861 while treading a dangerous middle ground in a time of national upheaval. They publicly remained silent unless to ostensibly support the South while praying for the Confederacy's defeat and the end of slavery. They knew the war would change things, bringing with it new demands and challenges; that it would, perhaps, become a war for freedom. They could not know that the whites' fratricidal war and the rise of a nationalized slaveholders' regime was the harbinger of the worst and best of times. The morning star of liberty seemed tantalizingly near as they looked toward the dawning of the day of liberation. "It is a great thing to have your liberty," replied Aunt Molly, a Richmond slave, when asked what she would do if "the wicked Abolitionists" came to Virginia.

As slavery increasingly became a difficult boulder to push up the hill of democracy, Molly and other Afro-Virginians faced the war—and the future—with pragmatic hope.[31]

Notes

1. Ervin L. Jordan Jr., *Black Confederates and Afro-Yankees in Civil War Virginia* (Charlottesville and London: University Press of Virginia, 1995), 13, 21; Peter M. Bergman, *The Chronological History of the Negro in America* (New York: Harper & Row, 1969), 221–22, 228; Robert Conrad, *The Destruction of Brazilian Slavery, 1850–1888* (Berkeley: University of California Press, 1972), 283. Cuba had a higher black population, 603,046, than Virginia's but fewer slaves. Accordingly, the highest-ranking areas in slave population were Brazil (1,715,000), Virginia (490,865), Georgia (462,198), Mississippi (436,631), Alabama (435,080), South Carolina (402,406), Cuba, (370,553), and Louisiana (331,726).

2. Daniel E. Sutherland, *Seasons of War: The Ordeal of a Confederate Community, 1861–1865* (New York: Free Press, 1995), 54–55 (Field quote); "On The Safe Side," *London (England) Times,* October 20, 1863; Charles L. Perdue Jr., Thomas E. Barden, and Robert K. Phillips, eds., *Weevils in the Wheat: Interviews with Virginia Ex-Slaves* (Charlottesville: University Press of Virginia, 1976), 205 (Massie quote).

3. "The End of Slavery," New York, *National Anti-Slavery Standard,* May 25, 1861; Perdue, *Weevils in the Wheat,* 115 (Charles Grandy interview), 241 (Sister Robinson interviews); Jordan, *Black Confederates,* 106–7, 332n44. There is another New Testament commentary similar to Luke's—Mark 13:7: "When ye shall hear of wars and rumors of wars, be ye not troubled: for such things must needs be; but the end shall not be yet." White Christians were not above superstition either; whenever a thunderstorm approached, one Fauquier County slaveholder, believing blacks immune from God's thunderbolts, would nervously order a group of his slaves to stand in a circle around him as protection. Jordan, *Black Confederates,* 111.

4. Carter G. Woodson, *The Mind of the Negro as Reflected in Letters Written during the Crisis 1800–1860* (Washington, D.C.: Association for the Study of Negro Life and History, 1926), 536–37 (Hackley quote); William R. Richardson to John B. Floyd, November 1, 1860, U.S. War Department, *War of the Rebellion: A Compilation of the Official Records of the Union and Confederate Armies* (Washington, D.C.: Government Printing Office, 1880–1901), series III, vol. 1, 2–3 (hereafter cited as *OR*); John Hope Franklin, *The Militant South, 1800–*

1861 (Boston: Belknap Press of Harvard University Press, 1956), 235–38, 240–42; "A Story of Fortress Monroe," New York, *Principia,* September 14, 1861, p. 767.

5. Ham & Eggs to Mr. W. Still, October 17, 1860, quoted in William Still, *The Underground Rail Road: A Record of Facts, Authentic Narratives, Letters, &c.* (Philadelphia: Porter & Coates, 1872; reprint, Chicago: Johnson Publishing Company, 1970), 23; Elizabeth Keckley, *Behind the Scenes, or, Thirty Years a Slave and Four Years in the White House* (New York: G.W. Carleton & Company, 1868), 69–74, 80–90.

6. "Desecration of the Statue of Washington at Richmond, Virginia," New York, *Harper's Weekly,* May 18, 1861, p. 311, as cited in Jordan, *Black Confederates,* 22, 332n46; Theresa Guzman-Stokes, "A Flag and a Family: Richard Gill Forrester, 1847–1906," *Virginia Cavalcade* 47 (Spring 1998): 56.

7. Frank Moore, *Rebel Rhymes and Rhapsodies* (New York: G.P. Putnam, 1864), 13–17, as cited in Jordan, *Black Confederates,* 16, 331n35, 22 (Snead quote); *Richmond Dispatch,* April 2, 1861, as cited in Robert F. Durden, *The Gray and the Black: The Confederate Debate on Emancipation* (Baton Rouge: Louisiana State University Press, 1972), 14; A.T. Bledsoe to Jefferson Davis, May 10, 1861, Lynda Lasswell Crist and Mary Seaton Dix, eds., *The Papers of Jefferson Davis* (Baton Rouge and London: Louisiana State University Press, 1992), VII, 160; Charles W. White, *The Hidden and the Forgotten: Contributions of Buckingham Blacks to American History* (Marceline, Mo.: C.W. White, 1985), 48; James Finch to Jefferson Davis, August 12, 1861 (Powhatan County), Crist and Dix, *Papers of Jefferson Davis,* VII, 281.

8. John W. Blassingame, ed., *Slave Testimony: Two Centuries of Letters, Speeches, Interviews, and Autobiographies* (Baton Rouge: Louisiana State University Press, 1977), 563–64; David Hackett Fischer and James C. Kelly, *Bound Away: Virginia and the Westward Movement* (Charlottesville and London: University Press of Virginia, 2000), 178–80; Jordan, *Black Confederates,* 22, 254–55; Randolph B. Campbell, *An Empire for Slavery: The Peculiar Institution in Texas, 1821–1865* (Baton Rouge: Louisiana State University Press, 1989), 243–46; Clarence L. Mohr, *On the Threshold of Freedom: Masters and Slaves in Civil War Georgia* (Athens and London: University of Georgia Press, 1986), 99–105, 110–19; Bohemian [William G. Shepperson], ed., *War Songs of the South* (Richmond: West & Johnson, 1862), 183 (slave Jerry); Blassingame, *Slave Testimony,* 737 (Lorenzo Ivy).

9. Booker T. Washington, *The Story of My Life and Work* (Toronto: J.L. Nichols & Company, 1900), 37; Booker T. Washington, *Up From Slavery* (New York: A.L. Burt Company, 1901), 8. As a slave among slaves, the five-year-old Booker (so characterized because of his precocious fascination with books and

learning) was appraised at $400 in December 1861. Louis R. Harlan, ed., *The Booker T. Washington Papers* (Urbana: University of Illinois Press, 1972–1989), II, 11.

10. "Master race" quote, *Lynchburg (Va.) Virginian,* November 3, 1864, as cited in Durden, *Gray and the Black,* 79; "The Plans and Hopes of the Rebels: Speech of Alexander Stephens," New York, *National Anti-Slavery Standard,* August 3, 1861 (this, perhaps the Confederacy's most widely known speech, was delivered March 21, 1861, in Savannah, Georgia. In it, Stephens declared slavery the cornerstone of the Confederacy); see Durden, *Gray and the Black,* 7–8; "May God Protect the Slave," New York, *Principia,* August 3, 1861, p. 790.

11. "The End of Slavery," New York, *National Anti-Slavery Standard,* May 25, 1861 (slaves' secret gatherings); "Sable Clouds: The Slaves Wide Awake," New York, *National Anti-Slavery Standard,* June 29, 1861 (expelled Northerner's quote).

12. "Sable Clouds: Slaves Mustn't Express an Opinion about the War" and "Prefers the North to Dixie's Land," New York, *National Anti-Slavery Standard,* August 10, 1861 (whipped Fairfax slave); "Sable Clouds: Disaffected Slaves," New York, *National Anti-Slavery Standard,* August 17, 1861 (whipped Richmond slaves).

13. Jesse Watson to Jefferson Davis, August 2, 1861 (free blacks as hospital workers); Crist and Dix, *Papers of Jefferson Davis,* VII, 272; "The Contrabands in Washington Jail," New York, *Principia,* December 21, 1861, pp. 873–74. "Ailstork/Aleslock/Alestork/Hailstock/Hailstork" were common free black family surnames in antebellum Albemarle County; see Ervin L. Jordan Jr., "A Just and True Account: Two 1833 Parish Censuses of Albemarle County Free Blacks," *The Magazine of Albemarle County History* 53 (1995): 120, 134, and, Perdue, *Weevils in the Wheat,* 285.

14. June Purcell Guild, *Black Laws of Virginia: A Summary of the Legislative Acts of Virginia Concerning Negroes from Earliest Times to the Present* (Richmond: Whittet & Shepperson, 1936; New York: Negro University Press, 1969), 194; James H. Brewer, *The Confederate Negro: Virginia's Craftsmen and Military Laborers, 1861–1865* (Durham, N.C.: Duke University Press, 1969), 138–39.

15. Jordan, *Black Confederates,* 201–2, 209, 214; H.C. Blackerby, *Blacks in Blue and Gray: Afro-American Service in the Civil War* (Tuscaloosa, Ala.: Portals Press, 1979), 16; James I. Robertson, *18th Virginia Infantry* (Lynchburg, Va.: H.E. Howard, 1984), 50, 74; "City Intelligence: Mayor's Court," *Richmond Daily Enquirer,* December 2, 1861; Bowman Seals to Jefferson Davis, March 27, 1861, Crist and Dix, *Papers of Jefferson Davis,* VII, 82; "A Negro Preaching

Secession Doctrine," *New York Herald,* October 5, 1861; C. Vann Woodward, ed., *Mary Chesnut's Civil War* (New Haven and London: Yale University Press, 1981), 106 (South Carolina slave); "Slave-Catching in the Army," New York, *National Anti-Slavery Standard,* August 3, 1861 (Harpers Ferry slave). Virginia had a long history of black informers; see Robert S. Starobin, ed., *Blacks in Bondage: Letters of American Slaves* (New York: New Viewpoints, 1974; New York: Marcus Weiner, 1998), 137–40.

16. Jordan, *Black Confederates,* 231; "Secesh, Massa, All Secesh," New York, *Principia,* January 18, 1862, p. 912 (slave Joe).

17. "A Nut for Abolitionists," *Christiansburg (Va.) New Star,* February 16, 1861; George Morris and Susan Foutz, *Lynchburg in the Civil War* (Lynchburg, Va.: H.E. Howard, 1984), 10; Miss M.M. Brown to "My Dear Aunt Elle," Lynchburg, May 18, 1861, Papers of William Daniel Cabell and the Cabell and Ellet Families, #276 & 276-A, Box 1, folder "Correspondence," Special Collections Department, University of Virginia Library, Charlottesville; Charles Kelly Barrow, J.H. Segars, and R.B. Rosenburg, comps. and eds., *Black Confederates* (Gretna, La.: Pelican Press, 2002), 9, 10n9, 20.

18. Hubert Blackerby, *Blacks in Blue and Gray* (New Orleans: Portals Press, 1979), 1; Robert J. Driver, *1st Virginia Cavalry* (Lynchburg, Va.: H.E. Howard, 1991), 188; Robert J. Trout, *With Pen and Saber: The Letters and Diaries of J. E. B. Stuart's Staff Officers* (Mechanicsburg, Pa.: Stackpole Books, 1995), 14, 276n33; Woodward, *Mary Chesnut,* 113; "Sable Clouds: A Slave Saving a Whole Regiment by Prayer," New York, *National Anti-Slavery Standard,* September 7, 1861. William, a slave eyewitness to the battle, later told a New York audience that two hundred Confederate officers' body servants were put to work after the battle burying the dead every day until the stench became intolerable; a visiting South Carolinian woman noted in her diary that as they returned to Richmond "the negroes come in loaded like mules." See "Sable Clouds: A Slave's View of the Bull Run Fight," New York, *National Anti-Slavery Standard,* September 28, 1861; Woodward, *Mary Chesnut,* 119.

19. Joseph T. Wilson, *The Black Phalanx: A History of the Negro Soldiers of the United States in the War of 1775–1812, 1861–'65* (Hartford: American Publishing Company, 1888), 103; "Attack on Our Soldiers by Armed Negroes," New York, *Principia,* January 23, 1862, p. 915; "Attack on Our Soldiers by Armed Negroes," New York, *National Anti-Slavery Standard,* January 18, 1862; Jordan, *Black Confederates,* 222, 371n20. The Twentieth New York, identified in the *Principia* article as the "German Rifles," was actually the "United Turner Rifles." "Turner" derived from the German word "turnen" meaning "gymnast" and "turnverein," the athletic clubs where they exercised; see C. Eugene Miller and Forrest F. Steinlage, *Der Turner Soldat: A Turner Soldier*

in the American Civil War: Germany to Antietam: A Biographical Narrative of a German Immigrant Who Served as a Private in the 20th Regiment, New York Volunteers, the United Turner Rifles (Louisville, Ky.: Calmar Publications, 1988).

20. Brig. Gen. John Bankhead Magruder to Col. George Deas, August 9, 1861, *OR,* series II, vol. 1, 763; Brewer, *Confederate Negro,* 7, 76. After First Manassas some white males cited slave labor shortages as an excuse for avoiding military duty. Wright Gatewood to Jefferson Davis, August 12, 1861, and Virginia officers to Davis, August 23, 1861, Crist and Dix, *Papers of Jefferson Davis,* VII, 281, 307–8.

21. "Sable Clouds: The Slaves in Western Virginia," New York, *National Anti-Slavery Standard,* August 17, 1861; "The End of Slavery," New York, *National Anti-Slavery Standard,* May 25, 1861 (Petersburg incident); Blassingame, *Slave Testimony,* 544–47 (Ballton), 606–11 (Jarvis). Jarvis later enlisted in the Union army and served with the Fifty-fifth Massachusetts Infantry (Colored).

22. Jordan, *Black Confederates,* 83–85; "The News/Wednesday, June 4," New York, *Principia,* June 12, 1862, p. 979; 37th Congress, 1st session, "An Act to perpetuate testimony in cases of slaves abducted or harbored by the enemy, and of other property seized, wasted, or destroyed by them," August 30, 1861, *OR,* series IV, vol. 1, 593; "Negro Slaves as Contraband of War—An Element of Immense Strength to the Government," *New York Herald,* May 30, 1861.

23. "Negroes Taking Refuge At Fort Monroe," New York, *Frank Leslie's Illustrated Newspaper,* June 8, 1861, p. 55; see also illustrations "Stampede among the Negroes in Virginia—Their Arrival at Fort Monroe," June 6, 1861, pp. 56–57; "Gen. Wool and the Contraband Negroes," *Charleston (S.C.) Mercury,* October 1, 1861; Dorothy Sterling, ed., *We Are Your Sisters: Black Women in the Nineteenth Century* (New York: W.W. Norton, 1984), 166, 261–63; Lewis C. Lockwood and Charlotte L. Forten, *Two Black Teachers during the Civil War: Mary Peake, the Colored Teacher at Fortress Monroe [by] Rev. Lewis C. Lockwood, and, Life on the Sea Islands [by] Charlotte Forten* (1863 & 1864; reprint, New York: Arno Press, 1969), 5–6, 15–16, 30–36, 44–45; Rayford W. Logan and Michael R. Winston, *Dictionary of American Negro Biography* (New York: Norton, 1982), 486.

24. Stephen Vincent Benét, *John Brown's Body* (Garden City, N.Y.: Doubleday, Doran, and Company, 1928), 228; "Sable Clouds: Negro Patriotism," New York, *National Anti-Slavery Standard,* August 24, 1861; "The Evacuation of Hampton," Richmond, *Semi-Weekly Examiner,* August 9, 1861; "A Story of Fortress Monroe," New York, *Principia,* September 14, 1861, p. 767; Jordan,

Black Confederates, 85, 100; Brig. Gen. John Bankhead Magruder to Col. George Deas, August 9, 1861, *OR,* series II, vol. 1, 764.

25. "The Curfew Bell At Hampton Court House, Virginia," New York, *Frank Leslie's Illustrated Newspaper,* August 10, 1861; Sterling, *We Are Your Sisters,* 262; "Important from the South: Our Naval Correspondence," *New York Herald,* November 29, 1861(Alexandria complaints).

26. "Chronicles of the War: Eastern Shore of Virginia," New York, *National Anti-Slavery Standard,* November 23, 1861; "[Thirty-seven Contraband Negroes]," Rochester, N.Y., *Douglass' Monthly,* December 1861, p. 573; "Sable Clouds: Catching Fugitive Slaves," New York, *National Anti-Slavery Standard,* May 25, 1861; Maj. Gen. John A. Dix to Simon Cameron, August 8, 1861, *OR,* series II, vol. 1, 763; Blassingame, *Slave Testimony,* 737–38 ("Jeff Davis hearts" quote).

27. "Sable Clouds: Negro Patriotism," New York, *National Anti-Slavery Standard,* August 24, 1861 (Charles quote); Perdue, *Weevils in the Wheat,* 137–38 (Tom Hester); "Our Black Friends Down South," New York, *Harper's Weekly,* June 14, 1862; "The End of Slavery," New York, *National Anti-Slavery Standard,* May 25, 1861 (Richmond slave comment).

28. Ervin L. Jordan Jr., "Slave Insurrections," *Encyclopedia of the United States in the Nineteenth Century, Volume 3: Printing Technology–Zoos,* Paul Finkelman, ed. (New York: Charles Scribner's Sons, 2001), 162–64; "The End of Slavery," New York, *National Anti-Slavery Standard,* May 25, 1861 ("Virginia Fugitive"); "Sable Clouds: Apprehended Slave Insurrections," New York, *National Anti-Slavery Standard,* August 31, 1861.

29. Armistead L. Robinson, "In the Shadow of Old John Brown: Insurrection Anxiety and Confederate Mobilization, 1861–1863," *Journal of Negro History* 65 (Fall 1980): 279–97; Guild, *Black Laws,* 91–92, 121–22, 140–41, 169–70, 193–97, 217–18; Philip J. Schwarz, *Slave Laws in Virginia* (Athens, Ga.: University of Georgia Press, 1996), 114–15.

30. "Desperate Negro Woman," Staunton, Va., *Vindicator,* January 11, 1861; "Sable Clouds: Hundreds of Fugitive Slaves," New York, *National Anti-Slavery Standard,* June 8, 1861 (Winchester); Jordan, *Black Confederates,* 177 (King and Queen County); Rebecca Meade to John Meade, August 22, 1861, Ruffin and Meade to John Meade, August 22, 1861, Ruffin and Meade Family Papers (no. 642), Kenneth M. Stampp, ed., *Records of Ante-Bellum Southern Plantations from the Revolution through the Civil War, Series J, Selections from the Southern Historical Collection, Manuscripts Department, Library of the University of North Carolina at Chapel Hill, Part 9: Virginia* (Frederick, Md.: University Publications of America, 1985–), reel 29, series 1, subseries 1.5, folder 14, frames 0586–0589 (Prince George County); E. Merton Coulter, *The Confeder-*

ate States of America 1861–1865 (Baton Rouge: Louisiana State University Press, 1950), 258 (Richmond quote).

31. W.E.B. DuBois, "Robert E. Lee," New York, *Crisis* 35 (March 1928): 97; "Sable Clouds: Trying the Slave Pulse," New York, *National Anti-Slavery Standard,* May 25, 1861 (Aunt Molly).

Richmond Becomes the Capital

William C. Davis

When the Deep South states began their careers in secession, there was virtually no coordination or even much cooperation among them. Each acted independently. Indeed, previous attempts among a few ardent disunionists to bring about a coordinated movement had been rebuffed indignantly by secession men in several states like Mississippi and Georgia, because they perceived it as outside interference in their "state sovereignty." Thus when South Carolina passed its ordinance of secession in December 1860, there was no prearranged next step. The Palmetto State was simply out on a limb by itself. Nevertheless, secession leaders there and elsewhere naturally assumed that if or when more states joined South Carolina in attempting to leave the Union, then they would naturally have to enter into discussions among themselves about their mutual interests in defense, trade, and all the other considerations that went with being "independent." They may not have admired Yankees like Benjamin Franklin, but they all remembered what he had said to their own revolutionary forefathers during an earlier crisis for the colonies: If they did not hang together, they would all most assuredly hang separately.

Consequently, even the day before the actual declaration of secession, South Carolina issued a call to other states contemplating secession to meet with her delegates in a convention to discuss the possibility of forming a new confederation. They had a seventy-five-day head start on the Union before Abraham Lincoln took office on March 4, 1861, and it was precious time that they could use to determine what they were to be and how they were to meet whatever response Lincoln chose to make to disunion. Many did not necessarily expect war, but they all saw as self-evident that a united front posed a greater potential deterrent to any precipitate action from the North than the prospect of several isolated and independent states.

Just as secession leaders did not make prior plans for unity in leaving the Union, neither had they held any serious discussions on whether or how to unify themselves afterward. Part of that lack of preparation included no thought to where they should locate their center of political power. After all, if they did not know in advance if they were to have a new nation, or on what basis, it would have been a bit premature to start making plans for a capital. Days after sending out the invitations to the other slave states that might secede to hold a convention to decide the issues confronting them, South Carolina also issued a call for the meeting to be held at Montgomery, Alabama, then the geographical center of the Deep South states. As one South Carolinian declared to a delegate from Georgia three weeks before the convention, the representatives of the states then seceded must "weld them together while they are hot."[1] On February 4, 1861, the convention assembled with six states represented, and within a few days produced a Provisional Constitution, created a government, and chose Jefferson Davis as its provisional president.

Montgomery, which had been a quiet city of about eight thousand, jumped to over twenty thousand almost overnight as volunteers, lobbyists, journalists, and opportunists all flocked to the presumed new power center of the new Confederacy. Civic leaders began to make plans for an indefinite career as capital of the Confederate States of America. They would improve the city streets and sidewalks, clean out the artesian wells in the downtown area, erect fences, pass ordinances to control loose dogs and animals, tighten the rein on movements of free and slave blacks, and undertake civil beautification to make it a city worthy of its status. Private citizens commissioned plans for building a huge new hotel that would be the grandest in the South, while others began refurnishing the wharves on the Alabama River.[2] Not everyone was pleased at the prospect, of course. Society doyens of Montgomery predicted that being a national capital would "demoralize the society beyond purification."[3] Others saw the matter in a more positive light. "Let Alabama have the Capital," declared a Montgomery editor, "and let Montgomery be the city."[4] It was even suggested that the area around the city be ceded to the new government like the District of Columbia, and called the District of Davis.

It was not to be that easy, however. Nothing in the call for the convention, or in the actions of the new Provisional Congress, made any move toward the official establishment of a permanent capital. After all, by its application of the adjective "provisional" to itself, its constitution, and its president, the Congress made it clear that all of its actions were stopgaps to get the government going pending longer and more measured deliberations—which could produce a more perfect permanent constitution, and with it a system of government designed to last. That made Montgomery by definition a "provisional" capital, which to Montgomery and to other cities throughout the seceded states suggested that there was an opportunity to fill a vacuum and thereby profit for themselves.

There was no shortage of self-nominated candidates. From Georgia, Atlanta, Macon, and Augusta all threw their names into the hat. Other Alabama cities decided to vie with Montgomery for consideration as well, among them Tuscaloosa, Huntsville, Selma, and even tiny Wetumpka and Spring Hill. Surprisingly, given its role as seedbed of secession, Charleston, South Carolina, made no concerted bid for consideration, but the state's capital at Columbia did, and so did tiny Pendleton.[5] Even more surprising, Nashville and Memphis both had lobbyists pleading their cases as ideal Confederate capitals, despite the fact that Tennessee had not yet seceded, and would not for months yet. Their boosters offered all manner of inducements: high heat, low heat, freedom from fevers, good rail connections, telegraphic service, and access to the seacoast. Atlanta's anxiety was so great to get the honor that its supporters even pointed out that the legislators would have steady access to an abundance of Georgia peanuts.[6]

The choice depended very much on political and geographical realities. When the provisional government formed itself, there were just six seceded states represented: South Carolina, Mississippi, Florida, Georgia, Louisiana, and Alabama. Texas seceded on the eve of the convention and soon had delegates in Montgomery as well. Obviously if no more states left the Union, then the capital must be located in one of those seven states. But there were eight other slave states along the border between the Deep South and the North: Missouri, Arkansas, Kentucky, Tennessee, Maryland, North Carolina, Delaware, and Virginia. At least some of them were expected to secede, too, though they were more conservative and conflicted over disunion, and would not act hastily. With the exception of tiny Delaware, the secession of any one of them would shift the geographic center of the new Confederacy. Indeed, any one of those states would carry enhanced importance in Confederate affairs thanks to its position on the border. If war came and Lincoln sought to invade the Confederacy to put down the rebellion, his armies would first have to be met on that border. Particularly vital were Kentucky, Tennessee, North Carolina, and Virginia. Should they or any two or three of them secede, then all or part of the northeastern frontier of the Confederacy would sit behind the barriers of the Potomac and/ or Ohio rivers. In time of war any separatist government by definition lives chiefly on the bayonets of its armed forces. If they fail, then the movement fails with them. Hence if Virginia or Kentucky were to secede, then a capital at faraway Montgomery or Wetumpka, or even a peanut-fed government in Atlanta, could be too far from the front to manage the defense effectively. Inevitably, the larger the Confederacy became after its foundation, the more its political center had to shift northward from Montgomery.

In fact, by late March some in the new Confederacy asserted that if Maryland and Virginia both seceded, then the Confederacy would automatically come into possession of the District of Columbia by virtue of having it surrounded, and therefore ought to install its new regime in the marbled halls of Washington.[7] While no one as yet lobbied for Richmond as a capital, it was commonly assumed that if Virginia seceded, then its capital would be a strong and logical candidate. However, by early April the Old Dominion had already three times rejected secession, though disunion sentiment was gradually growing. Then came the firing on Fort Sumter on April 12. Lincoln, now installed as president, responded by declaring a state of insurrection and calling on all the states, including Virginia, for volunteers to put down the uprising. It was clear that force would be used against fellow Southerners, and that Virginia could not avoid choosing a side, for either way the armies of the North would be marching across her soil.

In Montgomery, President Davis and his cabinet immediately renewed efforts to bring the border states across the line to join them, with Virginia being most important of all. Virginians were not unaware of Confederate hopes of making her a sister in the new Confederacy. On February 5, just the day after the original convention first met, one South Carolinian wrote to her senator R.M.T. Hunter that if only she would secede, "Virginia shall have things exactly as she wants them capital included."[8] At the news of Lincoln's call for volunteers the Old Dominion's special convention finally acted, and on April 17 voted to secede. President Davis was meeting with Vice President Alexander H. Stephens when the telegram reached Montgomery later that day with the glorious news. The usually pessimistic vice president predicted privately that it meant the end of the war even before it began.[9] In Montgomery the word of Virginia's secession created almost as great an outpouring of enthusiasm as the fall of Fort Sumter a few days before. Indeed, it became almost a drunken revelry. Virginians in town were feted, and more arrived the following day with the latest intelligence. The cabinet got word that Governor John Letcher intended to occupy the Norfolk Navy Yard and the arsenal at Harpers Ferry with Virginia state forces. He needed help before Lincoln could send troops across the Potomac, for Virginia's brave act had now put her first in line in front of Northern guns. Letcher also wanted to start negotiations right away for an alliance with the Confederacy as an interim measure pending the formal ratification of the Confederate Constitution necessary for her to apply for statehood.

Sensitive to the importance of the moment, Davis and the cabinet sent Stephens to Virginia as head of a commission to meet with Letcher and his legislature and convention. Time could be blood now, and the vice president left within hours on an evening train on April 18. No sooner had Stephens left than his embassy became what one reporter called "food for the speculative."[10] Rumors began to spread in Montgomery that the capital would be shifted to Richmond, and that Davis would have Stephens run the government there while he led Confederate armies personally.[11] Unfortunately, the people would get little substantive information for several days yet. Stephens reached Richmond on April 22 and immediately closeted himself with Letcher. The next day he appeared before a closed session of the state convention where he urged them immediately to adopt a treaty with the Confederacy, and then as soon as possible follow that with adoption of the Confederate Constitution and an application for statehood.

He said something more in closing, though whether it was spontaneous or the result of discussions with Davis and the cabinet he never said. "The enemy is now on your border—almost at your door—he must be met," warned the vice president. The best way to stop Lincoln at the Potomac was for all Southern forces to be coordinated by one head at Montgomery. But then Stephens added that perhaps that head ought to be in Richmond. "While I have no authority to speak on that subject," he went on coyly, "I feel at perfect liberty to say, that it is quite within the range of probability that, if such an alliance is made as seems to me ought to be made, the seat of our government will, within a few weeks, be moved to this place." Congress had not declared Montgomery to be a permanent capital, and the inevitability that Virginia would be the first scene of conflict almost demanded that "the whole may be transferred here."[12]

While he put a good public face on his dealing with them, privately the ever-gloomy vice president did not feel sure of the convention. He did sign a draft treaty with a designated special committee of the convention, but was not sanguine that the body as a whole would accept it. "The Virginians will debate & speak though war be at the gates of their city," he complained privately.[13] The imagery he used in his complaint, combined with what may have been an off-the-cuff remark in his speech, may have given him an idea. If "their city"—Richmond—were of such importance that the enemy really would march to its gates, then perhaps the inducement of making that city the Confederate capital would be sufficient bait to stop the debating and get a favorable vote. Stephens quickly followed up on his remarks of April 23 by speaking with members of the convention and dropping hints that if Virginia seceded, then the president would back legislation in the Provisional Congress to establish the Confederacy's permanent capital in Richmond.

It was a move that served everyone's purpose. By seceding, Virginians knew they made themselves the primary target of any invasion, and there was no better way to guarantee that they got special attention to their defense than to have the capital in the Old Dominion. They were also close enough to Washington to know without being told of the economic benefits that accrued to a national capital. Davis would gain a base in what was politically the most important of the border slave states, and thereby send a message to other wavering border states that they could expect the Confederacy to serve their interests, too. In fact, in the weeks ahead three more would secede—Arkansas, North Carolina, and Tennessee—though Missouri, Kentucky, and Maryland could never be lured away from the Union. Virginia gave Davis a defensible border along the Potomac and extending to the Ohio along the northwestern counties, and making Richmond the capital put him within minutes by telegraph of most of the armed forces that would have to be arrayed to defend that line. Being just one hundred miles from Washington, Richmond would be at high risk as a prime symbolic and strategic target for Lincoln. But the trade-off in speed of communications in coordinating defense, vital for an underdog, made the hazard worthwhile; and Richmond also gave the Confederacy use of a major rail center at adjacent Petersburg, as well as the outstanding military and civilian manufacturing facilities in the city. A capital at Richmond would be at a distant remove from the Confederate interior in Georgia, Alabama, and Mississippi, not to mention the areas west of the Mississippi, but everyone knew without asking, North and South alike, that the focus of any major military campaigns were going to be in Virginia east of the Appalachians, and down the Mississippi to the west.

In fact, Stephens's hints, like his pessimism, were probably unnecessary. He may or may not have come to Richmond authorized by Davis to suggest moving the capital, but the subject was all but implicit in the very act of Virginia's seceding. Virginians were going to insist on it anyhow, and Davis was quite ready to meet their demand, since it accorded with his own strategic ideas for defense. And while the state convention was prone to talking for its own sake, there was never any doubt of its approving the treaty and taking the next steps for statehood. On April 25 the convention adopted the treaty.[14] Then the next day delegate John Goode rose to propose a new resolution:

> Resolved, That the President of the Confederate States and the constituted authorities of the Confederacy be, and they are hereby cordially and respectfully invited, whenever, in their opinion, the public interest or convenience may require it, to make the city of Richmond, or some other place in this State, the seat of the Government of the Confederacy.

Surprisingly, Goode's resolution did not meet with unanimous approval. Indeed the first voice following him was a delegate from the southwestern part of the state who tried to get the resolution tabled. He failed, but then voices of caution and uncertainty dominated the brief debate. J.G. Holladay of Norfolk expressed concern at the appearance of such a resolution. They had only just the day before adopted and ratified a treaty with the Confederacy. "It seems to me that we no sooner enter into that Southern Confederacy, than we seek to reap pecuniary advantages by the location of the capital within the State of Virginia," he complained. "To do this, as the first act of this Convention after it has placed the State within the Southern Confederacy, would seem to indicate a purpose to clutch the spoils, and thus inaugurate the system which rendered Washington politics so infamous in the eyes of the world." The resolution, if adopted, would put the state in a humiliating posture, and he argued that "for the honor of Virginia," he hoped the convention would defeat the resolution.

Jeremiah Morton rose in response to observe that Georgia's convention had already passed a similar resolution, meaning that Virginia would hardly stand alone in seeking the capital. Moreover, without naming Stephens or revealing that there had been discussions on this very subject with him, Morton added that he was certain that the vice president actually expected this invitation from Virginia, and it was implicit that he spoke for Davis and the government. Forget matters of "spoils" for the moment, Morton argued. "Look at what is the condition of the country." They faced a mortal threat, and it was imperative to have the president as close to the scene of conflict as possible. Virginia had no money in its treasury, while the new Confederacy did have several million dollars in hand. It could fund Virginia's defense; the Old Dominion could not. If inviting the capital to relocate to Richmond brought that treasury with it, and the ability to save the state from Lincoln, then he would risk epithets about spoils once their safety was secured.

Another delegate rose to add that Stephens had stated openly his wish to have the capital move to Richmond, and had gone beyond that to assert that it might be necessary to do so. How could Virginia seem grasping if it merely did what the Confederate government wanted and expected? Still, to soften the appearance of self-serving, he proposed to amend the resolution with a preamble stating that since Stephens had told the convention that it might be necessary to relocate to Richmond, therefore, the convention issued Goode's invitation. "This," said Wood Bouldin, "is designed to show that we are not asking for any advantage, but meeting an overture that was made by the Commissioner." Goode, to whom Stephens seems not to have spoken beforehand, confessed that he was unaware of such overtures by the vice president, but found the amendment acceptable. But then Bouldin immediately withdrew it anyhow, only to be followed by William C. Wickham of Richmond itself who asked if it was not rather premature to ask Davis to make the city his headquarters when, as yet, the ordinance of secession had not yet been put before the people of the state for ratification. How embarrassing would it be to have the government accept the invitation, only to have Virginians reject secession and statehood in the Confederacy subsequently! Morton did not like the way the debate was going, and so rose to cut it off by calling for the previous question. A vote sustained his call, and then they voted on Goode's original resolution. The balloting ended sixty-three for and thirteen against, an overwhelming majority. Those voting against included Wickham and even the convention's president, John Janney, but not Holladay, who abstained. Many others abstained, too, or simply were not present, for there were not enough total votes to make a quorum. Seeing that they could not do further business without a voting quorum present, the convention adjourned.[15]

They reconvened the next day and when the resolution came up again as unfinished business, this time a quorum was present and it passed without further debate, seventy-six to sixteen. Janney, Wickham, and this time Holladay opposed it, but their voices were futile. Goode immediately moved that the convention send a telegram to Montgomery, and Morton successfully proposed that the cloak of secrecy be lifted from this act so that the public could know what they had done. Now the decision lay with the Congress in Alabama.[16] The reaction in the city streets was mixed.

Davis was delighted at the news, though now that Virginia had seceded he faced the fact that he could not unilaterally deliver the capital to the Old Dominion. That lay within the gift of the Congress, not the executive, and Davis was already experiencing the first of years of difficulties he would undergo with a small but vocal opposition centered around some in the Georgia and South Carolina delegations, particularly the old "fire-eating" secessionist Robert Barnwell Rhett, and Thomas R.R. Cobb, brother of the presiding officer of the Congress, Howell Cobb of Georgia.

The hard-line secessionists did not trust Virginia. Some did not even want her in the Confederacy, fearing that her location so close to the North tainted her with unionist and possibly even antislavery ideas, while her slow progress to secession gave them reason to question her commitment to the new cause. "We fear they come to us for no good purposes and with strong hopes for reconstruction," grumbled Georgia's Thomas R.R. Cobb. "Our Congress look with suspicion on this Virginia delegation."[17] Meanwhile, Alabama could be expected to oppose giving up the capital, and there were still those strong lobbies in favor of Atlanta and other cities. From the outset, the only doubt about making Richmond the capital lay not with the Virginia convention, but with the Congress in Montgomery. No wonder that when Stephens arrived back in Montgomery on May 4 he found some legislators inclined "to give Va. the cold shoulder." Still he believed that by the summer the Confederacy would shift its government out of necessity of being closer to the scene of conflict, and possibly but not certainly to Richmond.[18]

The Congress approved the treaty with Virginia on May 6, and the next day admitted her to statehood. That boded well, and already one reporter wrote that "if there is anything in signs, I shall not be surprised to learn that the Congress will adjourn in a few weeks to meet at Richmond."[19] Once more Richmond was all the gossip. Now much depended on the arrival of that delegation that Cobb seemed inclined to distrust. They started to trickle in the same day the treaty was adopted, and within a few days four of them were there, led by R.M.T. Hunter, of whose devotion to secession no one was in doubt. Indeed, some already spoke of him as a successor to Davis as president when the permanent government was installed in February 1862, and no one thought him more suitable for the job than Hunter himself. Small though its numbers might be, the Virginia delegation—which grew slowly as more members finally arrived—exerted disproportionate influence from the first, which in some quarters only served to add resentment to suspicion. It did not help that almost immediately Governor Letcher became difficult to deal with. He drank too much, refused to communicate with proper authorities, and began to resist Confederate authority in his state. His antics hardly helped the cause of moving the capital to his city, and Davis had already spent so much of his time wooing the Old Dominion that one angry Alabamian told the chief executive bluntly that he was ignoring the original seceded states that created the Confederacy: "You were elected President of them, not of Virginia."[20]

Davis, Stephens, and the Virginia delegates had a task before them to secure sufficient support for relocation, and all knew its urgency, and not just for strategic reasons. A failure would have been a severe humiliation for Davis—which his opponents anticipated—and a blow to the prestige of the new government itself. Certainly the Virginia delegates lobbied hard, not least because they all disliked Montgomery, especially the obese Hunter, who feared the daily walk up the hill to the statehouse would kill him.[21] Indeed, Hunter came with only two lines on his agendum: promoting himself for the presidency, and moving the seat of government to Richmond. If he could help achieve the latter, it would only rebound to the encouragement of the former.[22]

The Permanent Constitution framed and adopted in March authorized the Congress to create a federal district akin to the District of Columbia, at a place of its choosing, and there establish a permanent capital. Several states had already submitted memorials to Congress proposing themselves as hosts, and offering to provide suitable land. Virginia did the same when its convention invited the government to come to Richmond on April 26. No sooner did the Congress reconvene on April 29 than the concerted drive to move to Virginia commenced. Interestingly, it was one of the sensible South Carolinians, W.W. Boyce, who first introduced the subject on the floor by presenting a resolution for relocation on May 1. At that moment, in fact, it seemed to be taken for granted that the move to Richmond would be made since Davis and a majority of the cabinet and delegates supported the idea. Alabama, understandably, resisted the move, and a few others in the "opposition" ridiculed the proposition, with Cobb saying it was all because the wives of the congressmen wanted to be closer to the hot springs and spas of the Virginia mountains.[23]

With the arrival of Virginia's delegates a genuine campaign to win approval of the relocation commenced, and ironically, it was the work of the Virginians themselves that raised a more vocal opposition, reflective of that old suspicion and resentment of their motives. Not unaware of that dynamic, the Virginians enlisted sympathetic delegates from other states to manage the matter in the Congress, so as to reduce the appearance of self-service on their part. But there was no doubt that Hunter and his colleagues pulled the strings. Within a week Stephens thought they would be successful, and on May 11 a new resolution went onto the floor calling for the assembly to adjourn on May 23 and then reconvene at Richmond or wherever else the president designated on July 20. However, the resolution only covered the Congress itself, and did not address relocation of the government's executive departments. Since some assumed that Davis might actually take personal command of the growing army in Virginia, the resolution simply envisioned a move of convenience to have Congress close to the president.

After some debate it passed, and a partial victory appeared to be won. Stephens confidently told his brother on May 13 that they would be adjourning to reconvene in Virginia, most probably at Richmond, though he urged him to keep quiet on the subject until a public announcement.[24] All the bill had to do was secure approval from the Judiciary Committee, and it could be on Davis's desk for signature.[25]

Judiciary gave its assent to the bill on May 15 and it went to Davis's office. But meanwhile an outcry against the act began to emerge. Journalists accused the Congress of having a secret intent of occupying Washington itself as a permanent capital, and charged that the Richmond move was only one step on the journey. Worse, once in Washington, the government would then find a compromise with the North and reconstruct the old Union. With a natural self-interest, one Atlanta editor protested: "What? Call this little *itinerating* concern a *permanent* government?" He likened them instead to a traveling grocery. "Who bids for the next squat," he spat contemptuously.[26]

Then the president surprised them all, for when the bill came to him on May 17 he handed it back with his veto, and wisely so. The bill simply did not accomplish enough. It appeared to him to be folly to move the president and the Congress but to leave all the other branches of the government in Montgomery. "Great embarrassment and possible detriment to the public service must result," he said in his veto message. Moreover there was a practical problem. Three of his cabinet members were concurrently members of the Congress—Secretary of State Robert Toombs, Secretary of the Treasury Christopher G. Memminger, and Postmaster General John H. Reagan. Such men could hardly fulfill both their cabinet and congressional duties at desks six hundred miles apart! He clearly wanted a bill that moved the entire government and all of its departments. Despite the logic of his arguments, the veto stung a few, chiefly in the opposition, for they supported the resolution on the assumption that it really did not move the permanent government and Congress could always be relocated back to Montgomery after the emergency in Virginia was passed. Moreover, the opposition did not like this president handing down vetoes so early in his administration. Some like Rhett and Cobb feared already that Davis was too hungry for personal power. They tried to mount an override, but it became quickly apparent that they did not have the votes.[27]

That same afternoon a Louisiana delegate submitted a revised bill that addressed Davis's concerns, but when the house adjourned for the day without taking action, a renewed speculation swept the city. Perhaps Montgomery would not lose the capital after all. Proponents of other places like Huntsville and Opelika, Alabama, suddenly found hope, and even Nashville—which still was in a state that had not left the Union—renewed its bid. With the initial fervor of the potential move blunted by the veto, some like Howell Cobb began to think that perhaps there would be no move anywhere. Backers of relocation were not so easily discouraged, however. The next day three of them from three different states all introduced new resolutions, and Congress appointed May 20 as a day for debate and discussion. When they convened in secret session that day, they wrangled for over four hours. First they considered another resolution that moved only the Congress, but it died without gaining a single vote. Then they went on to two others that called for moving the entire government, and on a permanent rather than ad hoc basis. Debate and amendment reduced them to a single bill providing for adjournment on May 21, the very next day, and then the relocation of the whole government to Richmond with Congress reconvening July 20.

And now the Congress came up against a peculiarity in its rules of order drafted by Stephens back on February 4 when it first convened. Whatever his failings—and he would before long be a prominent member of Davis's opposition—the vice president had an incisive mind. He understood that in those formative days the delegates could not afford to waste time, for time was about the only advantage they had over Lincoln before he took office. They could not risk deadlocks in tied votes, nor could they hazard being delayed by parliamentary tricks such as delegates finding themselves in the minority on an issue and unable to vote it down, but still being able to delay its passage by absenting themselves from the hall and thus destroying a quorum. In a crisis, every time they voted they needed to achieve a decision.

Stephens's solution was simple and effective. States would vote as blocs, one state, one vote. That gave the states an equal voice regardless of their size. In any vote on a bill, a tie defeated a measure. Moreover, on any vote within a delegation as to how that state's vote ought to be cast, a tie meant that state cast no vote. And on the critical issue of a quorum, Stephens provided that but a single member of any delegation being present was sufficient to constitute a quorum from his state, and he could cast its vote. The provision presented an interesting theoretical possibility. Originally there were fifty delegates from seven states. Virginia's secession made it eight states. Arkansas, the ninth state to secede, brought her delegates into Congress on May 18—just in time to help decide the location of the capital. Thus five states now constituted a majority. Yet the quorum rule made it technically possible that only five men, one from each of those states, could pass legislation even if all of the other states had full delegations voting. No one envisioned such an eventuality actually happening, but now it nearly did.

At the end of the debate on relocating to Richmond on May 20, there was a call for a voice vote. Arkansas, Georgia, Texas, and naturally Virginia, all voted for the move to Richmond. Alabama understandably voted against, as did Florida, Mississippi, and South Carolina, all of them Deep South states still harboring suspicion and some resentment and envy of the Old Dominion. Louisiana's delegation had the decision, but their four delegates present split, two for and two against. That tie gave them no vote, leaving an even vote on the bill, and that by the rules meant its defeat. It was 2:00 P.M., and the Congress adjourned for the afternoon to reconvene that evening. The session itself would close the following day, and there seemed little chance of resurrecting the move to Richmond now.

But then seemingly unrelated events took control. With the relocation bill dead, the Congress finished other last minute business that evening. Yet a number of delegates left before they convened to pack their cases or catch an afternoon train for Atlanta and parts east. As the day's session approached its end just three states, Alabama, Virginia, and Texas, still had full delegations present, and the others were dwindling. But those absentees changed the equation in the hall. Little Florida had only three delegates, two of whom had opposed the move, but now friends of the measure pressured one of them into changing his vote. That put Florida in favor of Richmond. Then another Louisiana delegate who had missed the earlier balloting arrived late in the day and he was for the bill. His vote broke the tie in his delegation and Louisiana suddenly stood for Richmond. Those two men made the difference. Then, ironically, a delegate from South Carolina who favored the move in spite of his delegation's majority opposition, moved that they reconsider the vote on the measure. In another voice vote six states stood for the move and only three against, and it passed, even though the actual delegate vote was much closer: twenty-four to twenty. That was all it took. The capital of the Confederacy would be moved to Richmond.[28] Bitter opponents of the move like Rhett, who was among those who left the hall in the afternoon and did not return for the decisive evening session, thought it all reeked of corruption.[29]

Almost overnight the government evaporated from Montgomery. Congress had until July 20 to meet again in the new capital, but the executive departments had to close down and move quickly to get back into operation, and Treasury was already packed in anticipation of the move even before the bill passed. Every train headed east took boxes of packed archives and cars loaded with bureaucrats and clerks. The president himself left on May 26 with no fanfare, no send-off. He simply boarded a car on an evening train, all but unseen by other passengers, and left. As his train sped east, already the speculation mounted as to the wisdom of the move. Some feared that it sent the wrong message to the Confederate public, who might lose confidence in an "itinerant" government. The impact on world opinion could be equally damaging, as critics charged that the move turned the government into a "portable pedlar's wagon." One journalist said it was mad luck. "I can't bear your traveling circus, or menageries, or cabinets of curiosities," he grumbled, "no more can I bear this going about of our political cabinet."[30]

When the trains began to bring the bureaucrats into Richmond, many breathed a sigh of relief. Letcher's erratic actions and his increasing lack of cooperation with Montgomery made many fear that without a firmer guiding hand in power in the Old Dominion, the state could slide back toward the Union. "No man but President Davis can save her," warned one Virginian. As soon as the telegraph brought definitive word of the vote to move, Confederate agents in the city began taking action on securing rented quarters for the government offices. On May 25 the city council called a special meeting to consider a resolution endorsing the relocation "with the liveliest satisfaction," and promising to do everything in its power to show its sense of the distinction thus bestowed in being made the first city of the Confederacy. They called on themselves and the mayor to show Davis every hospitality, including sending a special train to greet the president when he reached Petersburg, and to bring him thence to the new capital. A committee was appointed to look for suitable quarters to be provided on an interim basis until an executive mansion could be purchased. And when Davis actually reached the city on May 29 he moved into a suite of rooms at the Spotswood Hotel, where he would stay as the guest of the city until the city acquired the Brockenbrough mansion on Clay Street for his residence.[31] The hotel virtually shimmered with waving flags, while other residents hung bunting and waved banners from the windows on Davis's arrival.[32]

Meanwhile, a few blocks away the clerks began the task of unpacking the boxes of records and moving into their temporary quarters in what everyone hoped would be a permanent capital on the world map. Some of them found a surprise when they pried the tops from the wooden crates. Sitting atop the records in many of them were horseshoes, placed there by a superstitious well-wisher in Montgomery when they were packed. It was his way of trying to ensure that good fortune would attend this new capital in this new nation.[33]

Notes

1. William Trescott to Howell Cobb, January 14, 1861, William Trescott Papers, South Caroliniana Library, University of South Carolina, Columbia.

2. William C. Davis, *"A Government of Our Own"; The Making of the Confederacy* (New York: Free Press, 1994), 278–80.

3. Thomas F. De Leon, *Four Years in Rebel Capitals* (Mobile, Ala.: Gossip Printing Company, 1890), 76.

4. *Montgomery (Ala.) Daily Post,* February 13, 1861.

5. Davis, *Government,* 279–80.

6. Ibid., 146, 371–72.

7. *Natchez (Miss.) Daily Courier,* March 26, 1861.

8. W.W. Boyce to Hunter, February 5, 1861, R.M.T. Hunter Papers, University of Virginia, Charlottesville.

9. Alexander H. Stephens to Linton Stephens, April 18, 1861, Alexander H. Stephens Papers, Manhattanville College of the Sacred Heart, Purchase, N.Y.

10. *Columbus (Ga.) Daily Times,* April 23, 1861.

11. *Charleston Mercury,* April 25, 1861.

12. Speech before the Virginia Secession Convention, April 23, 1861, Henry Cleveland, *Alexander H. Stephens, In Public and Private. With Letters and Speeches, Before, During, and Since the War* (Philadelphia: National Publishing Company, 1866), 744.

13. Stephens to Linton Stephens, April 25, 1861, Stephens Papers.

14. Stephens to Jefferson Davis, April 25, 1861, U. S. War Department, *War of the Rebellion: A Compilation of the Official Records of the Union and Confederate Armies* (Washington, D.C.: Government Printing Office, 1880–1901), series I, vol. 51, part 2, 32–33; John Janney to Davis, April 27, 1861, Dunbar Rowland, comp., *Jefferson Davis, Constitutionalist: His Letters, Papers and Speeches* (Jackson, Miss.: Mississippi Department of Archives and History, 1923), V, 67.

15. George H. Reese, ed., *Proceedings of the Virginia State Convention of 1861, February 13–May 1* (Richmond: Virginia State Library, 1965), I, 546–48;

Journals and Papers of the Virginia State Convention of 1861 (Richmond: Virginia State Library, 1966), I, 205.

16. Reese, *Proceedings,* I, 566–67.

17. Thomas R.R. Cobb to Marion Cobb, May 4, 1861, "Correspondence of Thomas Reade Rootes Cobb, 1861–1862," *Publications of the Southern History Association* 11 (September–November 1907): 321.

18. Stephens to Linton Stephens, May 4, 1861, Stephens Papers.

19. *Augusta (Ga.) Daily Constitutionalist,* May 1, 1861.

20. Spencer Adams to Davis, May 1, 1861, Lynda Lasswell Crist and Mary Seaton Dix, eds., *The Papers of Jefferson Davis* (Baton Rouge: Louisiana State University Press, 1992), VII, 143.

21. John B. Jones, *A Rebel War Clerk's Diary at the Confederate States Capital* (Philadelphia: Lippincott, 1866), I, May 24, 1861, 41.

22. Ibid.

23. Davis, *Government,* 388.

24. Stephens to Linton Stephens, May 13, 14, 1861, Stephens Papers.

25. Ibid., 389.

26. Atlanta, *Southern Confederacy,* May 14, 1861.

27. U.S. Congress, *Journal of the Congress of the Confederate States of America* (Washington, D.C.: Government Printing Office, 1904), I, 225, 241–43.

28. *Journal,* I, 254–55.

29. William C. Davis, *Rhett: The Turbulent Life and Times of a Fire-Eater* (Columbia, S.C.: University of South Carolina Press, 2001), 473.

30. New York, *Citizen,* June 1, 1867.

31. Louis H. Manarin, ed., *Richmond at War: The Minutes of the City Council 1861–1865* (Chapel Hill, N.C.: University of North Carolina Press, 1966), 40.

32. Sallie Putnam, *Richmond during the War; Four Years of Personal Observation* (New York: G.W. Carleton & Company, 1867), 38.

33. New York, *Citizen,* June 1, 1867.

The Shenandoah Valley of Virginia

Michael Mahon

Nestled between the Blue Ridge Mountains on the east and the Allegheny Mountains on the west, the Shenandoah Valley of Virginia runs southwestward from Harpers Ferry for more than 160 miles to Lexington, Virginia. Although considerable in length, the Valley is not very wide, averaging thirty miles. A landscape of breathtaking splendor and fertility, the Valley for decades had been recognized as one of the most agriculturally productive regions of the state.

Yet at the start of 1861, the Valley's abundant fertility was not the prevailing thought in the minds of most Shenandoah inhabitants. Of greater concern was the secession crisis that was threatening to tear the nation apart. Opposed to secession as a way of resolving the differences between the North and South, the vast majority of Valley residents remained so in the aftermath of Lincoln's election in November 1860, and South Carolina's secession from the Union the following month.

In response to the escalating crisis, Virginia governor John Letcher, who still believed that the Union could be preserved, convened a special session of the state legislature. Speaking on January 7, 1861, Letcher called for a convention of all the states to see if a solution agreeable to all sides could be reached, denounced extremists both North and South, and stated in no uncertain terms that Virginia would oppose any use of force by the federal government to keep the Union together. He further maintained that a state convention was unwarranted, at least for the time being. The legislature agreed with Letcher in regard to the first three issues, but had a different viewpoint concerning the last, and after considerable argument, passed a bill that called for an election to be held on February 4 to send delegates to a state convention that would convene in Richmond on February 13. The bill also called for the decisions of the convention to be submitted to the people for ratification.[1]

In the Valley, most individuals viewed the decision to hold a state convention with skepticism, realizing that it would only be used as a tool by secessionists to usher Virginia out of the Union. In Harrisonburg, John T. Harris, representative of the Ninth Congressional District, stated that he would vote for any candidate who opposed secession and supported the initiative that called for the actions of the convention to be approved by the people. The *Lexington Gazette* also called upon its readers to protect their rights by voting to "have the action of the Convention . . . submitted to your judgment, for ratification or rejection." Since most Valley citizens opposed secession, it came as no surprise that the majority of delegates chosen were committed to Virginia remaining in the Union. On election day, of the nineteen delegates elected in the ten Valley counties, only the four representatives from Page, Shenandoah, and Warren counties entertained the view that Virginia should secede. The measure requiring the convention's action to be ratified by the people also passed by a large plurality.[2]

As expected, unionists were ecstatic over the results, but their victory was short lived. Using recent events—Lincoln's election, South Carolina's secession, and the Republicans' refusal to compromise on any of the issues—to bolster their argument, secessionists in the weeks following were able to persuade many who had previously thought otherwise that if the South was to preserve their rights and property, by which they meant slaves, it had no other recourse but to secede from the Union. One individual who agreed with this assessment was Augusta County resident John D. Imboden. From his perspective, the Union already was dissolved, the only question now left before the country being how the South would leave, peaceably or by force. Desiring the former but fearing it would be the latter, he had told a close friend a few months earlier: "I am afraid the die is cast—and that no power on earth can avert the impending ruin of anarchy & bloodshed."

Also working in favor of the secessionists was the fact that they knew that Virginia, despite its reservations, would never be able to walk away from the rest of the South. The *Winchester Virginian* had acknowledged this point in early December when it stated the South was "one family . . . and if South Carolina secedes, and thus inaugurates a final issue with the

North, we are necessarily forced to stand in defense of our homes, interests, and people." This assessment did not change with time. When asked in March which way Virginians would go if forced to decide, North or South, a Lexington unionist stated that he believed the people would respond "Southward."[3]

Unionists throughout the Valley were aware of the disadvantages they had to overcome, but they also knew the direction Virginia ultimately took would depend in large part on how Lincoln responded to the crisis once he took office. In his inaugural address on March 4, Lincoln informed the Southern states that he had no intention of interfering with the institution of slavery in the states where it currently existed, stating that he had no legal right to do so. But with equal clarity, he declared that no state had the constitutional right to withdraw from the Union, and any ordinances or resolutions to that effect were illegal. He stated further that he would, as bound by the Constitution, enforce the laws of the Union in all of the states.

Reaction to the president's speech in the Valley was swift and to the point. While a few individuals viewed it as conciliatory in tone, the vast majority maintained that it only exacerbated an already tense situation. In Augusta County the Reverend Francis McFarland voiced his displeasure with the address, stating that he doubted Lincoln's policy "would preserve the peace of the country." At the convention in Richmond, Frederick County delegate Robert Y. Conrad declared the impact of the speech was "like [that of] an earthquake." James Dorman, delegate from Rockbridge County, agreed with Conrad's assessment and noted that Herculean efforts were required to counteract its effect. The *Staunton Vindicator,* for the most part, equated the address as an act of war and stated that coercion by the North would be *"met by the stern resistance of a united South."*[4]

Not surprisingly, in the aftermath of Lincoln's address, secession sentiment gained throughout much of the Valley. In late March, the *Richmond Enquirer* stated that a majority of residents in Shenandoah County had come to embrace disunion, and that considerable segments of Rockingham and Augusta counties were becoming more receptive to the idea. Even more significant was the change of heart by the conservative *Lexington Valley Star.* Stating that the time had come for Virginia to leave the Union, the editor, in announcing the paper's new stance, declared: "The Old Dominion has done all that honor will allow to preserve the Union. Everything has failed, and the question now is shall we unite with the prosperous South—or shall we starve with the Black Republicans?"[5]

By this time, it was apparent to all unionists that the point had been reached where the slightest incident could be used to induce Virginia to secede from the Union. One who knew this better than most was Congressman Harris. "We are to some extent standing on a volcano which may burst at any moment," he said, writing to a close friend. "One imprudent act at Washington would cause an explosion in our midst which would overwhelm any Union man & plunge the state into disunion. . . . When men's heads are once turned to revolution, or distraction, they are past reason." In Richmond, Dorman professed the same instincts. Conversing with James D. Davidson in early April, he told his political confidant that he feared "business of a civil kind" was nearly at an end and he had grave misgivings about future events.[6]

Dorman was right; behavior of a civil nature was at an end. Less than a week after Dorman's conversation with Davidson, Confederate military forces opened fire on Fort Sumter in Charleston Harbor. Two days later the fort surrendered. In response to the attack, Lincoln issued a call on April 15 for seventy-five thousand troops to put down the rebellion.

The president's decision to use force doomed whatever chance there was of Virginia's remaining in the Union. Virginians would never agree to the use of force against a Southern state, and on April 17 the convention in Richmond voted eighty-eight to fifty-five to enact an ordinance of secession. Virginia had taken itself out of the Union, but of the nineteen Valley delegates, only seven voted in favor of the measure, and two of them, Dorman and Alford Barbour of Jefferson County, did so only after they knew that all hope of Virginia's remaining in the Union was gone.

As required by law, the ordinance had to be ratified by the people, but everyone knew that the election on May 23 was a formality. Lincoln's call for arms had produced a dramatic change in public opinion throughout the state. Immediately following Lincoln's announcement, James Davidson in Lexington stated that after conferring with thirty of the town's most prominent unionists, they all agreed that the time had come for Virginia to secede. In Winchester, resident James Marshall declared that in spite of the anger and dissatisfaction they felt with the actions of the convention, the people in the northern part of the Valley would fight before surrendering to Northern aggression. Farther south in Staunton, Alexander H.H. Stuart reluctantly bowed to the will of the people and accepted the fact that Virginia had seceded; but he also vented his anger at secessionists, who had played upon the emotions of the populace to achieve their ends. Writing to a friend, he said: "We have been duped, betrayed, & swindled. The best interests of the State, of humanity, & civil liberty, have been sacrificed to advance the interests of selfish conspirators. We have been taken out of the Union & into the Southern Confederacy in the most precipitate manner. But what can we do? . . . Our people have not changed their sentiments, but will acquiesce in the action of the convention."

Statewide, the citizens approved the measure by a vote of 125,950 to 20,373. In the Valley, the resolution also passed by an overwhelming margin in all of the counties except Berkeley, where the residents, still unwilling to accept the idea of Virginia's leaving the Union, rejected the ordinance by more than 750 votes.[7]

Once hostilities commenced, because of its strategic location, the Valley immediately became the scene of military operations. During the early morning hours of April 18, Virginia forces captured the U.S. arsenal at Harpers Ferry, seizing arms manufacturing machinery and small amounts of small arms and equipment. On April 27, Governor Letcher appointed Thomas J. Jackson colonel of Virginia volunteers and placed him in command at Harpers Ferry with orders to organize and train the volunteer recruits assembling there. A week later he received a directive authorizing him to seek volunteers in all the Valley counties as far south as Rockingham.[8]

Jackson was rewarded heartily for his efforts. Anxious to defend their homes and country, thousands of the Valley's fathers and sons answered the call for volunteers. Within days of its capture, more than 1,200 recruits had assembled at Harpers Ferry, and by early June the figure had swelled to over 6,500. Included in this number were the men of the Second, Fourth, Fifth, Twenty-seventh, and Thirty-third Virginia Infantry Regiments, which under Jackson's leadership would soon gain considerable fame and come to be known as the "Stonewall" Brigade.[9]

The Confederates clearly understood the importance of the Valley to the war effort and determined, despite its close proximity to the enemy, to do everything they could to defend the region. In Richmond Gen. Robert E. Lee notified Gen. Joseph E. Johnston, who assumed command at Harpers Ferry when Virginia became part of the Confederacy, that it was vital for the post to be defended because its loss would undermine public confidence. Another senior government military official also informed Johnston that it was crucial Harpers Ferry and the rest of the Lower Valley be held because their loss would effectively divide the state in half, prevent the Confederacy from taking advantage of its vast economic resources, and provide the enemy with an avenue to strike deep into the heart of Virginia.

Johnston agreed completely with those in Richmond that Harpers Ferry should be defended, but he also knew that militarily the position was indefensible. To retake the town and capture the Confederate forces stationed there, all the Federals had to do was cross the Potomac River at any point above or below Harpers Ferry, get behind their position, and cut off all means of escape. To prevent this possibility, Johnston on June 15 withdrew to Bunker Hill, twelve miles north of Winchester, where he would be beyond the reach of capture but still in position to confront the Federals if they advanced up the Valley. In camp above Winchester until mid-July, the troops under Johnston were then ordered to Manassas, where they took part in the first Battle of Bull Run.[10]

For the remainder of the year, military activity in the Valley was confined to minor Federal cavalry raids in the Lower Valley, Jefferson and Berkeley counties in particular. The Confederates did not squander this respite offered by their opponent. Aware that vast quantities of subsistence would be needed to sustain the military forces being assembled in Virginia, the Confederate military authorities scoured the countryside, sparing no effort to garner all possible subsistence from the region. When in command at Harpers Ferry, Jackson urged the War Department in Richmond to release the necessary funds so he could purchase supplies. Creative in his methods, Jackson even sold the stockpile of coal of the Baltimore & Ohio Railroad at Martinsburg and used the proceeds to obtain additional provisions from area farmers. Concerned that the Federals would advance up the Valley and deny the Confederates the resources of the region, Samuel Cooper, adjutant general of the Confederate Army, directed Johnston after he got back to Winchester to strip the countryside clean of all subsistence that would benefit the enemy, especially horses and beef cattle.[11]

Responsible in large measure for the Confederates' success in this endeavor was Wells J. Hawks. A lifelong resident of the Valley and at one time the mayor of Charlestown before the war, he enlisted in the Second Virginia Infantry when hostilities erupted. Even more significant, he was well acquainted with the Valley's resources, and to put his knowledge to good use for the Confederacy Jackson made him his chief commissary officer. In the ensuing weeks, Hawks and his subordinates purchased and transported substantial quantities of beef, pork, bacon, wheat, flour, corn, oats, and vegetables to the supply depot at Winchester—so much so that Johnston asked the War Department to assign at least a half dozen more commissary and quartermaster officers to his command so they could assist in its storage and distribution.[12]

The Confederates continued to look to the Valley as a chief source of supply for the army following the Battle of Bull Run. Unable to provide the troops stationed at Manassas with adequate rations solely from Richmond, Secretary of War Leroy P. Walker in September called upon the subsistence department to forward additional supplies from the Valley to alleviate the shortfall. With his headquarters at Winchester, Hawks continued to forward supplies to the army at Manassas following Jackson's return to the Valley in November. In a dispatch on December 9, Hawks notified Maj. Francis G. Ruffin of the Commissary Department in Richmond that he had "purchased 1,300 barrels of flour for the army since I have been here. . . . I could get 5,000 bls [barrels] of flour in as short a time as it could be sent here. I could if desirable purchase and send to Manassas, a large quantity of flour. The troops at this place cannot consume one third of the flour that can be purchased here. Wagons that bring over our supplies from Strasburg could take back loads of flour for Manassas. . . . It is very important that the flour should be removed from the border." The extent to which the Confederates depended upon subsistence from the Valley can also be seen in a dispatch Adjutant General Cooper sent to Maj. John Harman, Jackson's quartermaster, in Staunton at the start of December, in which the general informed Harman that the Virginia Central Railroad would be unable to comply with his request to transfer troops to Manassas because at present "all its means" were required for the transportation of supplies.[13]

The Confederate military authorities were not the only ones preoccupied with war preparations. Although not on the front lines, the civilian population also contributed to the Confederate cause in a significant manner. At the start of hostilities a number of local municipalities raised funds to help furnish the troops with arms, ammunition, and clothing. In Augusta County the people raised $50,000, and in Winchester the town council appropriated $10,000 for the same purpose. Rockbridge County citizens went one step farther and established separate committees to raise money, gather and manufacture clothes, and raise new volunteers. They even established their own commissary department to secure meat, flour, and vegetables to sustain the troops stationed in Lexington and other parts of the county.[14]

In addition to the actions by official authorities, the civilian populace also provided valuable assistance on their own. Aware that vast quantities of clothing would be needed, the Reverend Francis McFarland and volunteers from several of the local churches in Augusta County obtained several hundred yards of cloth and made over one thousand shirts for the troops. In Winchester, Harriet Griffith noted that many of the ladies banded together to form sewing circles and made hundreds of caps for the soldiers stationed in town. Farther south in Rockbridge County, longtime resident Robert Campbell traveled about the countryside obtaining provisions from friends and neighbors which he then forwarded to the army.[15]

The Valley's residents also gave invaluable help in taking care of the thousands of sick and wounded. During the opening stages of the conflict medical care in the army was extremely limited and until organized the people assisted in any way they could. Unaccustomed to military life, thousands of soldiers fell ill to a large number of diseases—mumps, measles, malaria, dysentery, and typhoid—to name a few. By July, in Winchester alone over two thousand men had become sick; to give them proper care most of the town's churches and public buildings were converted into hospitals. When they were filled to capacity, many individuals took the soldiers into their own homes. Soon after soldiers' aid societies were formed by residents in many of the towns throughout the Valley to help the military take care of the wounded and help relieve the overcrowding at the hospitals.[16]

During the opening stages of the conflict, Valley farmers and numerous business owners contributed their fair share to the war effort as well. It also did not take long for them to realize just how profitable a venture the war could be. Instead of shipping their excess quantities of meat and grain to Northern markets as before, farmers now sold them to the Confederate government. As a bonus, they increased their income even more by renting out their horses and wagons to the military to transport provisions and materials throughout the region.

Proprietors of businesses with products or services in current demand because of the war also experienced an economic windfall. Aaron Griffith, owner of Brookland Woolen Mills in Winchester, saw the demand for his products explode in the weeks following the outbreak of the conflict. He had so many new orders to fill that his daughter stated that he would have run two shifts if he had the workers to do it. Griffith was not alone in trying to meet increased demands. By summer's end, the twenty-one other woolen mills in the Valley were running at full production, turning out more than eight thousand yards of cloth daily, which were then made into a variety of products—shirts, pants, coats, and blankets—and shipped to the army for use. Artisans involved in the manufacture of shoes, boots, wagons, saddles, and harnesses, as well as blacksmiths and ironworkers, saw their business increase dramatically because of the demands of the military.[17]

This economic prosperity, however, was limited in scope. Merchants whose businesses did not have a direct tie to the military or war effort in many instances encountered hard times as individuals and families uncertain about the future were reluctant to make any nonessential purchases. Consequently, numerous business, such as clothing stores, jewelry shops, and furniture and cabinetmakers, suffered severe downturns.

In Lexington, one resident described economic conditions there as being "entirely prostrate" at the start of summer. Commenting on conditions in Winchester, one young lady stated that, except for taking care of the soldiers, business was at a perfect standstill, while prices for the most basic necessities were exorbitant and the goods even then hard to find.[18]

As the residents of the Shenandoah were about to discover, this was only one of many hardships they would have to endure as the war unfolded. Situated as they were at the border, the Confederates called upon the local militia several times over the year to help reinforce the army when threats arose. While loyal to the cause, the militia did not react kindly to having to report for duty. In Augusta County, Alexander H.H. Stuart expressed their sentiments perfectly when he told the government that "men go to the battle field with very little alacrity when they feel that they leave their wives and children exposed to horrors to which their own perils are as nothing." Consequently, they shirked their duties whenever possible and looked forward to the day they could return home.

While their behavior was less than honorable, the militia to a certain degree had just cause to be upset. With only women and children in many instances left at home to work the fields, they realized they could lose the summer harvest if they were not allowed to go back to their farms. Noting the lack of field hands, Sarah McKown of Gerrardstown in Berkeley County said: "The wheat fields will soon be ready for the scythes, but where are the reapers. . . . It is a sad tale to tell but they have gone to war."[19]

By August, the situation had reached the point where the citizens of Shenandoah County felt compelled to petition Governor Letcher to intervene on their behalf. Stating that there were less than two hundred adult male slaves in the entire county, the members of the county court requested the militia be released from service so they could return home and work their farms. If not, they told the governor, they would be hard-pressed to raise enough crops to support the local population, let alone produce any excess quantities for the army. Members of the Seventh Brigade, Virginia Militia, from Shenandoah County and currently stationed at Winchester, expressed the same sentiments in their own petition to the government. "The valley of Virginia is a wheat growing-country in which slave labor is scarce," they wrote in their appeal. "Consequently the larger proportion of the labor must be performed by white men between the ages of eighteen and forty-five years. The time for seeding the wheat crop has arrived, and unless at least a considerable proportion of the men now here can be returned to their homes to attend putting that crop in the ground we will be unable to raise supplies sufficient for our own subsistence."

The farmers' plight became even more acute when the army began impressing their teams and wagons to transport supplies and equipment. During the spring, they minded little when the military took advantage of their teams because there was not much work to be done on the farm and they welcomed the added income. But now at the height of the summer harvest, they could no longer afford that luxury. But the needs of the military took precedent over the needs of the farmers, and when they refused to release their teams and wagons, the army had no recourse but to impress them. This caused bitter resentment toward the military, and the local newspapers voiced their objection over the policy, stating that it prevented many farmers from planting and harvesting their crops at the appropriate time.[20]

With fear and anxiety now such an everyday aspect of their lives, many residents, especially those in the Lower Valley, opted to leave rather than stay and face an uncertain future. By the end of June, the majority of residents in Harpers Ferry had left for more peaceful surroundings, and the few who did remain had to contend with less than desirable living conditions—with businesses closed, private homes looted, public buildings abandoned or torn apart, and decaying animals lying in the streets. Soon afterward numerous individuals and families in Martinsburg, Shepherdstown, Charlestown, and Berryville also realized that circumstances dictated it would be best for them to leave. "The people are beginning to provide for themselves by flight in earnest," declared one resident in Shepherdstown after watching a steady stream of families and wagons packed with belongings heading farther up the Valley. This departure increased in numbers following Johnston's retirement to Winchester in June. Not wanting to be on the front lines when the fighting erupted, a considerable portion of Winchester's citizens also decided to depart when the army established defensive positions along the outskirts of their city. Yet for most Valley inhabitants leaving was not an option because, as they well knew, they had no place else to go. Faced with that reality, they accepted the fact that the war, like it or not, was now a burdensome part of their everyday lives and coped with its hardships as best they could.[21]

They soon found out just how gruesome it would be. On July 21, 1861, the Federal and Confederate armies fought at Manassas, Virginia. After a hard day of fighting, the Confederates had gained a major victory, driving the Federals from the field in complete disarray. Reports of the Confederates' success spread quickly throughout the South, where the people rejoiced over their victory, boasting that the South would never be conquered.

While they welcomed Confederate success on the battlefield, Valley residents were horrified by the casualty figures. With many of their husbands and sons involved in the fight, families throughout the region awaited with nervous anticipation the fate of loved ones. For most, in the days following they received the gratifying news that their family members had escaped unharmed. But a few were not so fortunate. Robert Conrad, former convention delegate from Winchester and Frederick County, lost his two sons, Tucker and Holmes Jr., both struck down by the same shell and found lying next to each other on the battlefield. In Lexington, James Davidson also had to cope with the loss of a son, and in Winchester and the surrounding countryside more than a half a dozen families lost a husband, son, or relative.[22]

The engagement at Manassas also enlightened the Valley's inhabitants to the harsh reality of war. Prior to this point, the conflict for all practical purposes had been one of words; fighting of a significant nature had yet to occur. That changed forever after the battle, and the Valley's residents quickly came to comprehend the element of death inherent in warfare. Confronted by this new reality in the days after the battle, Winchester resident Cornelia

McDonald sadly wrote in her diary: "We did not begin to realize the horrors of our victory till Tuesday evening when the wagons began to come in with their loads of wounded men; some came too with the dead."[23]

Valley residents also were disheartened to learn that not all of their fellow neighbors supported the Confederate cause. Although limited in numbers, unionists could be found throughout the entire region, though their presence was much more prevalent in the four counties—Berkeley, Clarke, Frederick, and Jefferson—of the Lower Valley. Opposed to secession before the war, they remained so after the outbreak of hostilities and most did little to disguise their feelings. In Winchester, a considerable unionist presence appeared early on and grew to several hundred by the end of the war.

Unionists even more vocal in their support could be found in Martinsburg and throughout all of Berkeley County. Even after it was clear that Virginia would secede, residents of Martinsburg held several mass rallies in support of the Union where they passed resolutions against secession and prevailed upon the people to reject the measure in the upcoming election. In fact, unionist feeling in this part of the Valley was so strong that the Confederate military thought it would be wise to send troops to the area immediately prior to the May 23 vote to subdue threats from individuals who were trying to suppress "the expression of southern feeling." The view of the townspeople did not change with the passage of time. Months later, when passing through the town, a Confederate soldier declared that Martinsburg deserved to be reduced to ashes because of its Northern sympathies.[24]

Two major factors were responsible for unionism being so widespread in this part of the Valley. One was that in Martinsburg and the rest of the county, many of the local community and political leaders took an active part in opposing secession. This was important because it emboldened many less prominent individuals, who under less supportive circumstances would have remained quiet, to come forward and voice their opposition. In leading the fight against secession in Martinsburg, no individual was more dedicated to the cause than Edmund Pendleton. As a delegate to the convention, he opposed any thought of Virginia's seceding and refused to sign the ordinance when it passed. After returning home, he continued to voice his opposition to secession at every opportunity. His unwavering dedication to the Union soon earned him the title of "Edmond, the Staunch and Steady," who "in the trial of terror and cajolery which subdued so many men of weaker mold," stood firm in face of adversity.[25]

The second factor was the presence of the Baltimore & Ohio Railroad. As the largest employer in the region, the company provided jobs to hundreds of local residents, many of whom were foreigners and fiercely loyal to the Union. When the conflict erupted and the people were forced to choose between the Confederacy and the Baltimore & Ohio, the majority opted for the railroad and their livelihood. A longtime resident of the region put the matter in perspective when he said, "We belong to the Baltimore and live, breathe and have our being on the B. & O. R.R. We want the whole state preserved in its integrity, but if it is to be divided between the U.S. and C.S., we must go with the party that holds the B. & O. R.R. & Baltimore." Also working against the Confederate cause was the decision to destroy the railroad. Although totally understandable from a military perspective—by doing so they would cut the North's most vital and direct line of communication and transportation of supplies to the western theater—in the eyes of the local population, the Confederates were only destroying the employees' means to make their living and support their families.[26]

The unionist presence in the Valley also caused problems for the Confederate military stationed in the region. With a sizeable number of the local inhabitants hostile to the Confederate cause, army commanders found it hard to collect information on Federal dispositions. Describing the adverse conditions his forces were operating under, Johnston told the War Department in late June: "The enemy's movements cannot be ascertained accurately. The population boarding the Potomac in Virginia is all hostile to us; they inform the enemy of every movement of ours, while we know nothing of his but what we see." Several months later, Alexander R. Boteler, former congressman from Jefferson County, expressed his outrage to Secretary of State R.M.T. Hunter about the unionist activity in the Lower Valley, informing the secretary that the counties were "infested with traitors" in daily contact with the enemy, and urging the government to empower the Confederate military forces with the authority to put an end to the situation.[27]

Still, as much as the two sides resented each other, they had no choice but to learn to live together. With much of the Lower Valley changing hands on a regular basis, neither side knew when it would need the other's assistance to survive. Helping a Yankee neighbor obtain supplies, receive medical attention, or back up something said when questioned by the provost marshal generally worked in one's favor later on when roles were reversed.[28]

Discouraging as well for Confederate and unionist alike as the war progressed was the spiraling cost of provisions. Within a few months, everyday items such as coffee, tea, sugar, and salt were in short supply and demanded a high price. Coffee that in August sold for twenty-five cents a pound, doubled in price within a month. During this same time period, the cost of a sack of salt increased from eight dollars to over thirty, and even then it was had to find. The uncertain conditions brought on by the war also caused a run on winter clothing as citizens, not wanting to be caught short, purchased whatever they could while it was still available. Aware that these conditions would only become worse in the months to come, Julia Chase of Winchester, in putting down her thoughts in Augusta wrote: "Our winter, I fear, will be rather a hard one. I hope we shall not have a severe one as regards to the weather."[29]

In the months since the firing on Fort Sumter, the lives of the Valley's citizens had undergone a major transformation. Prior to that day, their lives were ones of peace and prosperity; now they were filled with fear, uncertainty, and death, and they hoped for a swift end to the conflict. But as they well knew, it would continue for the foreseeable future, and as they were about to find out, it would not be long before they were caught up in the forefront of the fighting.

Notes

1. Henry T. Shanks, *The Secession Movement in Virginia, 1847–1861* (Richmond: Garrett and Massie, 1934), 123; Bruce Catton, *The Coming Fury* (Garden City, N.Y.: Doubleday, 1961), 196; Ralph A. Wooster, *The Secession Conventions of the South* (Princeton, N.J.: Princeton University Press, 1962), 140–41.

2. *Staunton* (Va.) *Spectator,* January 8, 15, 22, 1861; *Lexington* (Va.) *Gazette,* January 3, 31, 1861; Charlestown, *Virginia Free Press,* January 31, 1861; John T. Harris to Ben, January 15, 1861, John T. Harris Papers, Special Collections, Carrier Library, James Madison University, Harrisonburg, Va.; James D. Davidson to John Letcher, January 31,1861, James D. Davidson Papers, University Library, Washington and Lee University, Lexington, Va.; James D. Davidson to James B. Dorman, James B. Dorman Papers, Rockbridge Historical Society, University Library, Washington and Lee University.

3. John H. Miller to John T. Harris, January 19, 1861, Moses Walton to John T. Harris, January 29, 1861, James G. France to John T. Harris, January 29, 1861, Harris Papers; John D. Imboden to John H. McCue, December 3, 1860, McCue Family Papers, Special Collections, Alderman Library, University of Virginia, Charlottesville, Va.; *Winchester* (Va.) *Republican,* quoted in Shanks, *Secession Movement in Virginia;* James J. White to Colonel Reid, March 18, 1861, in Charles W. Turner, ed., *Old Zeus, Life and Letters (1860–1862) of James J. White* (Verona, Va.: McClure Press, 1983), 37.

4. Shelby Foote, *The Civil War: A Narrative* (New York: Random House, 1958), I, 38; Roy P. Basler, ed., *The Collected Works of Abraham Lincoln* (New Brunswick, N.J.: Rutgers University Press, 1953), IV, 262–71; James D. Davidson to James B. Dorman, March 6, 1861, Davidson Papers; David F. Riggs, "Robert Young Conrad and the Ordeal of Secession," *The Virginia Magazine of History and Biography* 86 (1978): 261; James B. Dorman to Cousin James, March 8, 1861, Dorman Papers; Staunton, *Vindicator,* quoted in Shanks, *Secession Movement in Virginia,* 176.

5. Edward H. Phillips, "The Lower Shenandoah Valley during the Civil War: The Impact of War upon the Civilian Population and upon Civil Institutions," (Ph.D. Dissertation, The University of North Carolina, Chapel Hill, 1958), 11; Shanks, *Secession Movement in Virginia,* 176.

6. John T. Harris to John B. Baldwin, March 16, 1861, Harris Papers; James B. Dorman to James D. Davidson, April 9, 1861, Dorman Papers.

7. Wooster, *Secession Conventions of the South,* 148–49; James D. Davidson to R.M.T. Hunter, May 2, 1861, Davidson Papers; James Marshall to Waitman T. Willey, May 11, 1861, Alexander H.H. Stuart to Waitman T. Willey, May 15, 1861, Waitman T. Willey Papers, West Virginia and Regional History Collection, West Virginia University Libraries, Morgantown; Staunton, *Spectator,* May 28, 1861; Phillips, "Lower Shenandoah," 102; *Richmond Examiner,* May 27, 28, 29, 1861.

8. Douglas Southall Freeman, *R.E. Lee: A Biography* (New York: Charles Scribner's Sons, 1934), I, 473; U.S. War Department, *War of the Rebellion: A Compilation of Official Records of the Union and Confederate Armies* (Washington, D.C.: Government Printing Office, 1880–1901), series I, vol. 2, 784, 802 (hereafter cited as *OR*).

9. John D. Imboden, "Jackson at Harper's Ferry in 1861," in Robert U. Johnson and Clarence C. Buel, eds., *Battles and Leaders of the Civil War* (reprint, New York: Thomas Yoseloff, 1956), I, 118; *OR,* series I, vol. 51, pt. 2, 135, 137; Robert G. Tanner, *Stonewall in the Valley: Thomas J. "Stonewall" Jackson's Shenandoah Valley Campaign, Spring 1862* (Garden City, N.Y.: Doubleday, 1976), 33.

10. *OR,* series I, vol. 2, 880–81, 889, 897, 901, 907–8, 923–24, 929–30.

11. Ibid., 814–15, 822, 824–25, 934, 940, 948–49.

12. Introduction to Wells J. Hawks Papers, part of the Thomas J. Jackson Collection, Special Collections, Duke University, Durham, N.C.; *OR,* series I, vol. 2, 967, 949.

13. *OR,* series I, vol. 5, 833, 835–36, 977; Wells J. Hawks to Maj. Francis G. Ruffin, December 9, 1861, Hawks Papers; Richard Goff, *Confederate Supply* (Durham, N.C.: Duke University Press, 1969), 55.

14. *Staunton Spectator,* April 23, 1861; *Winchester* (Va.) *Republican,* September 27, 1861; *Lexington* (Va.) *Gazette,* April 25, 1861.

15. Entry of May 19, 1861, in the Diary of Francis McFarland, Francis McFarland Collection, Special Collections, Alderman Library, University of Virginia, Charlottesville, Va.; entry for July 5, 1861, in the Diary of Harriet Griffith, from the Harriet Hollingsworth Griffith Collection, Winchester-Frederick County Historical Archives, Winchester, Va.; *Lexington* (Va.) *Gazette,* August 23, 1861.

16. Julia Chase Diary, July 2, 4, 7, 8, 1861, Handley Regional Library, Winchester, Va.; Rev. B.F. Brook Journal, June 16, 22, 29, July 12, 20, 1861, Winchester-Frederick County Historical Society Archives; Mary White to her father, October 19, 1861, Mary Louisa Reid-White Papers, Rockbridge Historical Society, The University Library, Washington and Lee University; *Lexington* (Va.) *Gazette,* October 24, 1861.

17. Phillips, "Lower Shenandoah," 326–27; U.S. Government, *Eighth Censes of the United States, Volume on Manufactures* (Washington, D.C.: Government Printing Office, 1861), 604–39; *OR,* series I, vol. 51, pt. 2, 587–88; Griffith Diary, 15.

18. James Reilly to William N. Pendleton, July 1, 1861, Pendleton Papers, Southern Historical Collection, Wilson Library, University of North Carolina at Chapel Hill, N.C.; Griffith Diary, June 9, 1861.

19. *OR,* series I, vol. 51, pt. 2, 180; Chase Dairy, July 6, September 16, 1861, Handley Regional Library; Mollie to Reuben, July 28, 1861, Margaret B. Burress Collection, Carrier Library, James Madison University, Harrisonburg, Va.; Sarah Morgan McKown Diary, June 19, 1861, Sarah Morgan McKown Papers, West Virginia and Regional Historical Collections, Morgantown, W.V.

20. *OR,* series I, vol. 5, 817–18, 820–21; *OR,* series I, vol. 51, pt. 2, 262–63; Mollie to Reuben, July 12, 1861, Burress Collection; *Lexington (Va.) Gazette,* September 19, 1861; McKown Diary, June 21, August 19, 1861.

21. Phillips, "Lower Shenandoah," 119–20; Joseph Barry, *The Annals of Harpers Ferry* (Martinsburg, W.V.: Berkeley Union, 1872), 69; Charles W. Andrews to his wife, May 17, 21, 24, June 1, 11, 1861, Charles Wesley Andrews

Papers, Special Collections, Duke University Library, Durham, N.C.; McKown Diary, June 29, July 7, 1861; Chase Diary, July 12, 15, 1861; McFarland Diary, July 2, 3, 4, 5, 8, 9, 1861.

22. McFarland Diary, July 24, 1861; Virginia Bedinger to her Mother, July 27, 1861, Bedinger-Dandridge Family Papers, Special Collections, Duke University Library; Bruce S. Greenwalt, ed., "Life behind Confederate Lines in Virginia: The Correspondence of James D. Davidson," *Civil War History* XVI (1970): 226; McKown Diary, July 26, 1861; Chase Diary, July 23, 1861; Griffith Diary, 26.

23. Virginia Bedinger to her Mother, July 27, 1861, Bedinger-Dandridge Papers; Tippie to Lizzie, July 23, 1861, Alexander R. Boteler Papers, Special Collections, Duke University Library; Cornelia McDonald, *A Diary with Reminiscences of the War and Refugee Life in the Shenandoah Valley, 1860–1865* (Nashville: Cullom & Ghertner Company, 1934), 29.

24. Phillips, "Lower Shenandoah," 93–94, 100; Charles W. Andrews to his wife, May 17, 1861, Andrews Papers; Edward Pendleton to Waitman T. Willey, May 3, 1861, Willey Papers; *OR*, series I, vol. 2, 863; Alexander Barclay to Hannah, December 23, 1861, Alexander T. Barclay Papers, The University Library, Washington and Lee University.

25. Phillips, "Lower Shenandoah," 96–99.

26. Ibid., 108–10.

27. *OR*, series I, vol. 51, pt. 2, 143; vol. 5, p. 919.

28. Phillips, "Lower Shenandoah," 149–50.

29. Mary White to her Father, October 19, 1861, Reid-White Papers; Chase Diary, August 15, 22, September 10, 22, November 17, 28, December 3, 14, 1861.

The Tarnished Thirty-fifth Star

C. Stuart McGehee

"I should like to show those traitors at Richmond . . . that we are not to be transferred like the cattle on the hills or the slaves on their plantations, without our knowledge and consent," wrote Chester Hubbard, delegate from Ohio County, after news of the Virginia 1861 Secession Ordinance reached the Ohio Valley. Hubbard's impassioned anti-secession rhetoric perfectly captured the fierce sentiments of those Ohio Valley unionists who created the state of West Virginia during the Civil War.[1]

West Virginia statehood is one of the most fascinating and controversial results of the Civil War, an event of constitutional ambiguity and fiercely disputed analyses. Although the events themselves are straightforward, their interpretation is enormously complex, and has come to reflect the origins, history, identity, and even the integrity of the Mountain State, the thirty-fifth star in Old Glory.[2]

Twenty thousand Union troops poured from Ohio into western Virginia in the late spring of 1861. President Lincoln knew that safeguarding the Baltimore & Ohio Railroad was a chief strategic aim; the B&O was the only east-west trunk line in the nation, and Union forces depended upon the railway for supplies and reinforcements in Virginia. In a brilliant series of engagements that summer, Maj. Gen. George B. McClellan earned his nickname of the "Young Napoleon" by defeating the scattered Southern detachments that threatened the railroad. In the battles at Philippi on June 3, Rich Mountain on July 11, and Carnifex Ferry on September 10, the Union troops completely destroyed Confederate defenses in western Virginia, securing the vital B&O for the Northern war effort. Although Confederate raids and counterthrusts repeatedly attempted to cut the railroad and reclaim trans-Allegheny Virginia, McClellan's 1861 campaign effectively won the war in the region and earned a call to Washington for its dashing com-

149

mander. Even senior Confederate military advisor Robert E. Lee admitted the futility of reversing the Southern disaster in northwestern Virginia.[3]

Safely behind Union lines, western Virginians opposed to secession and in general disillusioned with Richmond's perceived lack of revenue allocation and constitutional reform moved quickly. An assembly of self-appointed Ohio Valley leaders closely tied to the Baltimore & Ohio gathered in May in Wheeling and began the creation of the thirty-fifth state in the Union. They unilaterally declared themselves the "Restored Government of Virginia," were duly recognized as such by a wily Lincoln, and then promptly gave themselves permission to create a new state, whose boundaries were determined in a series of conventions and mass meetings. Many counties included in the new state, and all of those behind Confederate lines that remained in the Old Dominion, were not represented at either of the two "conventions" in Wheeling or in the subsequent irregular elections by which the process was at least partially legitimized. Moreover, many Virginia regions were similarly too occupied by war and turmoil to play a role in the movement to create the Mountain State, which culminated in the famous statehood ceremony in Wheeling on June 20, 1863.[4]

The state-makers certainly and sincerely expressed their political wishes, but some facts of the process deserve mention. The movement's leaders, John Carlile, Waitman Willey, Peter Van Winkle, Arthur Boreman, and Francis Pierpont, were not chosen by an enfranchised electorate, nor were they particularly exemplary of the political leadership in trans-Allegheny Virginia. In fact, the only governor of the commonwealth to come from what soon became West Virginia was Joseph Johnson of Harrison County, a strong secession supporter who chaired a "Southern Rights" convention in Clarksburg, four days after John Carlile's famous unionist rally at the Harrison County Courthouse in April 1861. The western counties had in fact voted strongly for John C. Breckinridge, the Southern Rights candidate, in the presidential election of 1860, a key indicator of support for secession rather than Union, although the results are very complex and may be interpreted variously. Van Winkle, Pierpont, and Boreman were all industrialists closely allied with the B&O and frustrated with Virginia's antiquated corporation laws. Moreover, Methodists were present in western Virginia in much greater proportion than their Baptist counterparts; a great and unstudied aspect of West Virginia history involves the ethno-cultural-religious denominational cleavage in Mountain State politics.[5]

Central to the state-makers' work was the adoption of a new state constitution, which they completed in February 1862 and submitted with their application to Congress. This little-studied document, West Virginia's first state charter, is central to understanding the complex interpretation of the creation of West Virginia. The 1863 constitution and the subsequent acts of the state's initial legislatures corrected many of the perceived defects of the 1851 Virginia "reform" constitution. Its features included a two-year gubernatorial term; establishment of a lieutenant governor's office in the executive branch; the elimination of the county courts as instruments of local government in favor of the more Northern approach of townships; an appellate court system; printed ballots for all elections, rather than the oral practice still in use in Virginia; naming Wheeling as the state capital; the creation of Grant, Lincoln, and Summers counties, named for key players in the process; the establishment of public education and the chartering of normal schools to train teachers; and the chartering of West Virginia University in Morgantown, and the state prison at Moundsville, a Wheeling suburb. The original document included the infamous Negro Exclusion Clause, which resulted in a three-month delay for admission while Congress demanded that the new state embrace emancipation. Senator Carlile, the consummate conservative unionist, dropped out of the process rather than accept abolition as a condition of statehood. After some debate, the state-makers adopted the name "West Virginia," designed a flag and seal, and agreed to assume an "equitable proportion" of Virginia's antebellum state debt. Most significant for the future of the state, the crucial issues of absentee-owned land values and taxation were addressed.[6]

When the document was presented for congressional approval, a lengthy series of debates in Washington questioned the legality and constitutionality of the events. There are several relevant and ambiguous portions of the U.S. Constitution that might be used to justify either admission or denial. Article IV: section III asserts that "no state shall be formed . . . without the consent of the legislatures of the States concerned." But Article II: section III gives the president "such measures as he shall judge necessary and expedient" to see that "the laws be faithfully executed." At length the statehood bill passed both houses over considerable opposition, and President Lincoln, ever-mindful of political realities, knew that two additional Republican representatives and senators to join the Restored Virginia delegation would only strengthen his fragile congressional majorities in both houses.

After determining that his badly divided cabinet could not help him, Lincoln signed the bill on December 31, 1862.[7]

Unfortunately for the victorious unionist Republican state-makers from the Ohio Valley, their triumph was short-lived and their downfall imminent. The final shape of the state contained fifty counties of the Old Dominion, far more than the founders' original intention. Southern counties had been added for several controversial reasons, some for defense, others perhaps by conservative unionists in anticipation of the politics in the new state. Because they knew that they were in the minority, the founding fathers enacted strict voting restrictions on former Southern sympathizers. Only those who could swear a loyalty oath were enfranchised and permitted to vote and hold office. In some portions of southern West Virginia, it was difficult to find enough candidates who could pass the stiff loyalty test required of officeholders. In Greenbrier County, for example, at one time only seven voters were bold enough to swear the test oath. In this fashion, the Ohio Valley unionists who had created the state kept a tenuous control of their creation.

A factional dispute in the ruling Republican Party in 1870, however, resulted in the removal of the loyalty requirement and promptly enfranchised former Confederates, ending Reconstruction and the brief dominance of the unionist state-makers. The fall 1870 elections completely swept out the founding fathers, replacing them with Democratic majorities in both houses of the state legislature from the "Confederate Counties," who controlled the state government for the next two and a half decades.[8]

They swiftly enacted their revenge, calling a constitutional convention for Charleston the following year. This assembly, the last such meeting in West Virginia's history, promptly undid the work of the state-makers. After first attempting "Restoration," rejoining the Old Dominion—an effort rebuffed by a Supreme Court still packed with Lincoln appointees—the "Redeemers" modeled their charter on the 1851 Virginia document so vilified by the state-makers. They removed the capital south to Charleston; did away with the appellate courts and the lieutenant governor's office; returned the chief executive's term of office to one, nonrenewable four-year term; tried to rename Grant and Lincoln counties for Jefferson Davis and Robert E. Lee; reinstated the county court/justice of the peace system of local government; chartered new normal schools in southern West Virginia; reclaimed a larger proportion of Virginia's state debt, a sum not redeemed until 1939; and most significantly for the future of the Mountain State, expressly reinstated the property rights of alien nonresidents, most of whom lived in Virginia.[9]

This charter, however much it expressed the anger and vengeance of the Southern sympathizers and Virginia supporters, left West Virginia woefully unprepared for the rapid industrialization and natural resource production that began immediately after the war. Experienced Union officers with knowledge of coal, iron, timber, and natural gas could plainly see the rich bounty of the region, and the 1873 completion of the Chesapeake & Ohio Railroad into the New River Valley only presaged the arrival of the Norfolk & Western. By 1880, the iron curtain of industrialization had fallen on West Virginia, but its state government, modeled on the agricultural Virginia constitution, expressly honored absentee ownership, and had no adequate provisions for managing the exploitation of the extractive industries that characterized the state's postwar industrial economy.

Thus the state-makers lost their creation as soon as they had won it, and were promptly cast upon the dustheap of history. There are no streets in the state capital named for Waitman Willey, Arthur Boreman, John Carlile, or Peter Van Winkle; quite the contrary, West Virginians travel on streets named Virginia, Lee, Washington, and Greenbrier to their state capitol building, where a statue of Stonewall Jackson, a man who never set foot in West Virginia as a state, and tried mightily to prevent its very creation, greets them as a state hero. Confederate Civil War figures such as Jackson and the questionable repute of Belle Boyd are glorified in the history books used in the state's schools.

There is no shame in the story; the past has no such emotion. The Civil War witnessed many such ambiguous constitutional issues. The star is not tarnished, but its historiography is certainly questionable. For the story of West Virginia statehood is told in quite a different way to school children from the tale set out above. Instead, students are fed a steady diet of oppression from the slave-owning east, a litany of crimes and misfortunes that forced the loyal and free people of the mountains to declare independence and create a free state. The entire metaphor is taken from the American Revolution, with eastern Virginia substituting for George III's Tory England and the western counties the aggrieved thirteen colonies forced by a long string of "usurpations and abuses" to declare independence and freedom. There is even the famous "Declaration of the People of Virginia" from

June 1861 modeled on Jefferson's famous document from 1776. Misrepresenting the state motto "Montani Semper Liberi" to portray an abolitionist revolt against human bondage, the story takes on greater moral legitimacy.[10]

West Virginia University history professor Charles Henry Ambler was the architect of this most dominant and apparently unshakeable interpretation of West Virginia statehood. In a series of monographs and biographies of the state-makers, he amplified his interpretation that history instills civic pride. His 1910 masterpiece, *Sectionalism in Virginia from 1776–1861*, placed the statehood movement as the inevitable culmination of a century of sectional discord that resulted in the creation of West Virginia. He attacked "corruption and inefficiency" in the Tidewater aristocrats who oppressed the noble men of the mountains. He directed scores of dissertations and master's theses at Morgantown that supported his interpretation.[11]

His followers such as Festus Summers, who succeeded him as chairman of the History Department at West Virginia University, as well as Virgil Lewis, the first official state historian, amplified and codified his interpretation, which has become enshrined in the textbooks used in the state schools. The 1952 text *West Virginia Yesterday and Today* by Phil Conley and Boyd Stutler states that the textbook "is meant to bring a happy experience to the school children of our state. The authors believe it will do so. They have worked zealously in their effort to make this book one that will be enjoyed by both the teachers and the pupils of West Virginia." Kyle McCormick, in a pamphlet written in 1961 and distributed as official canon by the State Department of Archives and History, asked of the statehood episode: "Was the separation for the benefit of mankind? This writer holds that it was." The current fourth-grade West Virginia Studies textbook states solemnly, "people in western Virginia . . . did not feel they were treated fairly. . . . The leaders in western Virginia didn't want to secede."[12]

In the early 1960s the research of Richard Curry and later John Williams demolished this view of statehood as a popular and democratic act by minutely dissecting the vote totals traditionally used as evidence of the overwhelming outpouring of support for statehood. The defenders of the tradition responded with blasts of impassioned rhetoric appropriate for what they perceived as an assault upon the very integrity of the Mountain State. If the statehood process was illegitimate and unconstitutional, then the entire state's history was cast into disrepute. The clash occurred during the Civil War Centennial, which encompassed and brought attention to the

1863 West Virginia star in Old Glory, especially around the June 20, 1963, centennial anniversary of statehood.[13]

When Curry and Williams challenged the evidence utilized by the Morgantown school of interpretation, the response was swift and damning. In an article titled "The West Virginia Incident—An Appraisal," in a 1965 issue of *West Virginia History,* George E. Moore, a West Virginia University history professor, responded vociferously:

> this long-continued vilification has contributed to the apologetic attitude which many West Virginians hold toward their state. . . . Lack of state pride has helped create a national concept of West Virginians as ignorant, loutish hillbillies who live in unfloored shacks and subsist on corn meal mush and mountain dew. Because of this unfavorable national image West Virginians need to develop state pride. We must hold up our heads, look our fellow Americans in the eye and say to them 'We are West Virginians' proud of our origin, proud of our forebears, free Americans, and the peers of any group in this nation. . . . The state of West Virginia was the product of genuine loyalty to the Union, of devotion to democracy and nationality. West Virginians ought, therefore, to take pride in the men who made their state, and in their devotion of values which brought it into being."[14]

The twisted uses of history by national socialism at one extreme, and fascism and communism at the other, the totalitarian tyrannies of the twentieth century, ought to call such misguided assertions into question. History is not an instrument of patriotic sympathy; it is the effort to study the past to understand the present and learn lessons that may help prepare for a brighter future. Obscuring the context of historical interpretation to instill national or state pride only creates dangerous mythology, not patriotism.

As the Methodist minister intoned in his famous invocation at Linsley Institute on the banks of the Ohio in Wheeling that day, June 20, 1863, "Grant us we pray thee Almighty God, that this state born amidst tears, and blood, and fire, and desolation, may long be preserved, and from its little beginning, may grow to be a might and a power that shall make those who come after us look upon it with joy and gladness and pride of heart."[15]

Notes

Earlier versions of this essay were presented at the Kanawha Valley Civil War Roundtable on February 20, 2001, and the Virginia Tech Civil War "Weekend," March 10, 2001. Many thanks to the comments I received at both of these presentations. Special appreciation should be expressed to James I. Robertson Jr., who solicited this paper and encouraged its completion, and my students in West Virginia History classes at West Virginia State College, who patiently endured my exploration of the origins of the Mountain State.

1. Quoted in Richard Orr Curry, *A House Divided: Statehood Politics and the Copperhead Movement in West Virginia* (Pittsburgh: University of Pittsburgh Press, 1964), 55.

2. This account does not differ from the standard interpretation. See Otis K. Rice and Stephen W. Brown, *West Virginia: A History* (Lexington, Ky.: University Press of Kentucky, 1993), 111–64. Recent histories of West Virginia statehood may be found in Kenneth L. Carville, "How West Virginia Got Its Boundaries," *Wonderful West Virginia* 45 (April 2001): 14–21; George Harrison Gilliam, "Reconfiguring Virginia," *The Smithfield Review* 4 (2000): 5–36; Edward Steers Jr., "Montani Semper Liberi: The Making of West Virginia," *North and South* 3 (January 2000), 18–33.

3. Rice and Brown, *West Virginia,* 124–39. Useful also for the military campaigns is Boyd B. Stutler, *West Virginia in the Civil War* (Charleston, W.V.: Education Foundation, 1963), as well as Stan Cohen, *The Civil War in West Virginia: A Pictorial History* (Missoula, Mont.: Gateway Print & Lithography, 1976).

4. Kenneth W. Noe, *Southwest Virginia's Railroad: Modernization and the Sectional Crisis* (Urbana and Chicago: University of Illinois Press, 1994), 105–6.

5. David R. Goldfield, *Urban Growth in the Age of Sectionalism: Virginia, 1847–1861* (Baton Rouge: Louisiana State University Press, 1977), 246–67.

6. Charles H. Ambler, Frances Haney Atwood, and William B. Mathews, eds., *Debates and Proceedings of the First Constitutional Convention of West Virginia, 1861–1863* (Huntington, W.V.: Gentry Brothers Printers, n.d.). See also Robert M. Bastress, *The West Virginia State Constitution: A Reference Guide* (Westport, Conn.: Greenwood Press, 1995), 10–15.

7. For a fresh look at Lincoln's dilemma, see Michael P. Riccards, "Lincoln and the Political Question: The Creation of the State of West Virginia," *Presidential Studies Quarterly* 27 (Summer 1997): 549–64.

8. Rice and Brown, *West Virginia,* 154–64; Curry, *House Divided,* 131–35.

9. Bastress, *West Virginia State Constitution,* 15–21; Rice and Brown, *West Virginia,* 161–63. See also John Alexander Williams, *West Virginia: A Bicentennial History* (New York: Norton, 1976), 76–90.

10. Most of the relevant significant documents may be found in Elizabeth Cometti and Festus P. Summers, eds., *The Thirty-fifth State: A Documentary History of West Virginia* (Morgantown, W.V.: West Virginia University Library, 1966).

11. See John E. Stealey III's superb survey, "In the Shadow of Ambler and Beyond: A Historiography of West Virginia Politics," in Ronald L. Lewis and John C. Hennen Jr., eds., *West Virginia History: Critical Essays on the Literature* (Dubuque, Iowa: Kendal/Hunt Publishing Company, 1993), 1–42. The classic account is Charles Henry Ambler, *Sectionalism in Virginia from 1776 to 1861* (Chicago: University of Chicago Press, 1910; New York: Russell & Russell, 1964).

12. Phil Conley and Boyd B. Stutler, *West Virginia Yesterday and Today* (Charleston, W.V.: Education Foundation of West Virginia, 1952), vii. Tony L. Williams, *West Virginia: Our State* (Charleston, W.V.: West Virginia Historical Education Foundation, 1990), 64–67. Kyle McCormick, *A Story of the Formation of West Virginia* (Charleston, W.V.: Mathews Co., 1961), 16.

13. Curry, *House Divided,* passim, as well as John Alexander Williams, "The New Dominion and the Old: Ante-Bellum and Statehood Politics as the Background of West Virginia's 'Bourbon Democracy,'" *West Virginia History* 31 (July 1972): 317–407. See also Curry's "A Reappraisal of Statehood Politics in West Virginia," *Journal of Southern History* 28 (November 1962): 403–21.

14. George E. Moore, "The West Virginia Incident: An Appraisal," *West Virginia History* 26 (January 1965): 80–85 and reprinted in *West Virginia History* 47 (1988): 23–28.

15. Charles Henry Ambler, *West Virginia: Stories and Biographies* (New York: Rand McNally & Company, 1942), 243.

Diary of a Southern Refugee during the War, 1861

Judith Brockenbrough McGuire
Edited by James I. Robertson Jr.

Some of the most revealing chronicles of life during the Civil War came from the busiest people. Moreover, those who preserved records and observations, and wrote about them, tended to be well educated and farsighted. Judith Brockenbrough McGuire was in those relatively small classes.

Her *Diary of a Southern Refugee during the War* is among the first such works published after the Civil War. The book initially appeared in 1867 published in New York by E.J. Hale and Son, and has been reprinted four times subsequently. It is one of the most widely quoted memoirs by a Confederate lady.[1] Yet until now it has never been edited, nor has a real introduction to Mrs. McGuire and her diary ever appeared.

Modest and private, Judith McGuire identified herself on the title page of the original edition only as "A Lady in Virginia." The chronicle is a riches-to-rags story characteristic of the Southern Confederacy. In 1861 Mrs. McGuire was the middle-aged wife of an Episcopal minister/teacher, a lady of impeccable Old Dominion aristocracy, and comfortably situated in the flourishing Virginia port of Alexandria. Civil war exploded and Federal troops came across the Potomac River. The McGuires were driven from their established and secure way of life into an existence of uncertainty, impoverishment, and despair.

Over the next four years, the Reverend and Mrs. McGuire moved thirty-four times in search of safety and stability. Lacking roots, short of funds, part of a mob drifting here and there as war struck like lightning through Virginia, Mrs. McGuire endured trials and woes that might have broken most people in that plight. Yet she held fast to her faith in God and her fellow man. Thinking first of others rather than brooding about her own misfortunes became her most amazing trait.

Like so many other diarists of that age, Mrs. McGuire tactfully substituted initials or a blank space for the names of individuals she mentioned. Her wide range of family, in-laws, and friends create an editorial nightmare and is a major explanation why no previous historian ever undertook the task of annotating the journal. This reissuance in serial form of Mrs. McGuire's diary marks the first time that most of the people cited obliquely have been identified. Accompanying this edition is also the first in-depth biographical essay of a prominent lady who never sought notoriety. Whereas *Diary of a Southern Refugee* has always been a familiar source, now for the first time it becomes usable as a premier reference work to Confederate social history.

The author of this remarkable journal came from solid Virginia stock. Brockenbroughs were principal settlers of Essex County in the Northern Neck section of the state. Her father was William Brockenbrough (1778–1838), a native of Tappahannock and graduate of the College of William and Mary. In 1802 he was elected to the Virginia General Assembly. That began a long career as a Richmond attorney and judge. Eventually Brockenbrough became a member of the Virginia Court of Appeals. An acquaintance described the judge as "a gentleman distinguished for the soundness of his legal knowledge and honored for the purity of his life, during a period when the old Commonwealth could point with becoming pride to the unsullied ermine of her judiciary."[2]

Brockenrough married Judith White, descended from a long line of Episcopal ministers noted for generosity, affection, and hot tempers. The family home "Westwood" was northeast of Richmond in Hanover County. There, on March 19, 1813, the youngest daughter of the Brockenbrough's six children was born. She was named for her mother. Young Judith Brockenbrough grew up among Richmond's elite. A cousin, Dr. John Brockenbrough, had built a palatial downtown residence that became "the center of social life" in the state capital.[3] It later would be the White House of the Confederate States of America. Private tutors supplied Judith with an excellent education. Her knowledge of poetry and the great authors of literature is evident throughout her diary. In addition, such figures as John Marshall and Benjamin Watkins Leigh were regular dinner guests at the Brockenbrough home.

After the 1838 death of her father, Judith lived at Westwood with her mother and a younger, unmarried brother, Dr. William S.R. Brockenbrough. The family was ardently Episcopalian, as was usually the case among Virginia aristocracy. That association led to a friendship between Judith and the Reverend John Peyton McGuire.

He was from a well-known Winchester family. His father had been an artillerist in the American Revolution. John McGuire, born in 1800, was one of three brothers who became Episcopal ministers. In 1825 young McGuire assumed the rectorate of Saint Anne's and South Farnham parishes in Essex County. Neither had known a regular Episcopal priest for a quarter-century.

Methodists and Baptists had long dominated life in the county. McGuire borrowed their evangelic methods, organized missionary societies, and carried the faith to rich and poor alike. By hard and devoted work, one observer noted, "a dynamic pastor singlehandedly revived the Episcopal Church in Essex and much of the Rappahannock Valley."[4]

In 1827 Rev. McGuire married Mary Mercer Garnett. Her father was a former congressman and the largest landowner in the county. From that union came eight children. Five survived infancy: James, John P. Jr., Mary Mercer, Grace Fenton, and Emily. The unexpected death of the mother left the minister and his five young children in a large void.

Friendship with spinster Judith Brockenbrough led to marriage in November 1846. McGuire was forty-six; Judith was thirty-three; the siblings were thirteen, ten, eight, seven, and six. For six years the new Mrs. McGuire rekindled the family structure while steadily gaining the maternal affection of her stepchildren. Judith McGuire herself never bore any children.

In the late 1840s, Rev. McGuire opened a small school at Loretto in Essex County. "McGuire's English and Classical School" emphasized a traditional curriculum heavy in Latin and Greek languages. The headmaster introduced a new system of monitoring student performance by use of periodic report cards—a system American education came to adopt. Further, all students had to live at the pastor's home, where they were "members of the family circle, and under a firm, vigilant, parental government."[5]

This educational venture was short-lived. Rev. McGuire accepted the call to be rector of influential Christ Church in Alexandria. This too proved a short appointment, for in 1853 he agreed to become the third headmaster of the all-male Episcopal High School in Alexandria. It was then attached as a diocesan academy to the Virginia Theological Seminary, the second-oldest Episcopal seminary in the United States.

McGuire began his new duties with seventy boys. The following year, eighty-two students were enrolled. Steady growth marked the high school's progress over the next eight years. To the boys, Rev. McGuire was "Old Mac." One wrote this description of the headmaster: "He was about five feet ten inches high, dressed in strictly clerical clothes. . . . His head was close set on a stout, robust body, and his every action was with vigor. . . . His face was kept scrupulously free of every sign of beard, his broad, high forehead was crowned with a thick suit of almost snow-white hair, and his penetrating eyes were always protected and aided by gold-rimmed spectacles."[6]

No word-picture or portrait exists of Mrs. McGuire; however, all of the students loved her. One stated that "her marvelous wisdom and goodness, gentleness and tact is the important part she performed as the wife of the principal. . . . Hers was the influence which softened the boarding school life to boys who had never before left home."[7]

The school historian was more laudatory. "Mrs. McGuire was one of those women who came as near to divinity as mortal can do in this world. The High School boys adored her; she was gentle, lovable and tender. . . . She reminded one of Matthew Arnold's description of Mary, the mother of Christ: 'If thou wouldst fetch a thousand pearls from the Arab Sea, one would gleam brightest, the best, the queenliest gem.'"[8]

By 1861 the McGuires enjoyed a solid and respected position in Alexandria society. Rev. McGuire was sixty-one and showing signs of old age. His forty-eight-year-old wife remained active and enthusiastic. Judith McGuire responded to Virginia's secession and the coming of war in typical fashion. She spent tense days sewing and cooking for Virginia troops camped at Alexandria; she faithfully went to services in the now half-empty campus chapel; she tended her flowers as if they would bloom as usual and she would be there to see it. Yet preparing for any eventuality, she buried the family silver in the backyard and packed personal belongings to be taken if she had to leave home. Alexandria's location directly across the Potomac River from Washington, plus her husband's known secessionist views, placed the family in uncertainty if not danger.

On May 3, Rev. McGuire closed the high school. Only thirty students were left to pack their luggage and start home. Sons James and John McGuire were then drilling at a nearby camp; the three daughters were sent for safety to a paternal aunt in Clarke County near the Blue Ridge Mountains. When the McGuire couple learned on May 25 that Union forces were marching toward Alexandria, they abandoned their home and sought refuge elsewhere. They would be among the first of the Civil War refugees, but hardly the last.

To keep her mind occupied, and to record the unusual events she was certain lay ahead, Mrs. McGuire began keeping a diary. The journal would become a rich blend of observations and opinions.

Diary of a Southern Refugee

At Home, May 4, 1861.—I am too nervous, too wretched to-day to write in my diary, but that the employment will while away a few moments of this trying time. Our friends and neighbors have left us. Every thing is broken up. The Theological Seminary is closed; the High School dismissed. Scarcely any one is left of the many families which surrounded us. The homes all look desolate; and yet this beautiful country is looking more peaceful, more lovely than ever, as if to rebuke the tumult of passion and the fanaticism of man. We are left lonely indeed; our children are all gone—the girls to Clarke, where they may be safer, and farther from the exciting scenes which may too soon surround us; and the boys, the dear, dear boys, to the camp, to be drilled and prepared to meet any emergency.[9] Can it be that our country is to be carried on and on to the horrors of civil war? I pray, oh how fervently do I pray, that our Heavenly Father may yet avert it. I shut my eyes and hold my breath when the thought of what may come upon us obtrudes itself; and yet I cannot believe it. It will, I know the breach will be healed without the effusion of blood. The taking of Sumter[10] without bloodshed has somewhat soothed my fears, though I am told by those who are wiser than I, that men must fall on both sides by the score, by the hundred, and even by the thousand. But it is not my habit to look on the dark side, so I try hard to employ myself, and hope for the best. To-day our house seems so deserted, that I feel more sad than usual, for on this morning we took leave of our whole household. Mr. [McGuire] and myself are now the sole occupants of the house, which usually teems with life. I go from room to room, looking at first one thing and then another, so full of sad associations. The closed piano, the locked bookcase, the nicely-arranged tables, the formally-placed chairs, ottomans and sofas in the parlor! Oh for some one to put them out of order! And then the dinner-table, which has always been so well surrounded, so social, so cheerful, looked so cheerless to-day, as we seated ourselves one at the head, the other at the foot, with one friend,—but one,—at the side. I could scarcely restrain my tears, and but for the presence of that one friend, I believe I should have cried outright. After dinner, I did not mean to do it, but I could not help going into the girls' room, and then into C.'s.[11] I heard my own footsteps so plainly, that I was startled by the absence of all other sounds. There the furniture looked so quiet, the beds so fixed and smooth, the wardrobes and bureaux so tightly locked, and the whole so lifeless! But the writing-desks, work-boxes, and the numberless things so familiar to my eyes! Where were they? I paused, to ask myself what it all meant. Why did we think it necessary to send off all that was so dear to us from our own home? I threw open the shutters, and the answer came at once, so mournfully! I heard distinctly the drums beating in Washington. The evening was so still that I seemed to hear nothing else. As I looked at the Capitol in the distance, I could scarcely believe my senses. That Capitol of which I had always been so proud! Can it be possible that it is no longer our Capitol? And are our countrymen, under its very eaves, making mighty preparation to drain our hearts' blood? And must this Union, which I was taught to revere, be rent asunder? Once I thought such a suggestion sacrilege; but now that it is dismembered, I trust I may never, never be reunited. We must be a separate people—our nationality must be different, to insure lasting peace and good-will. Why cannot we part in peace?

May 10.—Since writing last, I have been busy, very busy, arranging and rearranging. We are now hoping that Alexandria will not be a landing-place for the enemy, but that the forts will be attacked.[12] In that case, they would certainly be repulsed, and we could stay quietly at home. To view the progress of events from any point will be sad enough, but it would be more bearable at our own home, and surrounded by our family and friends. With the supposition that we may remain, and that the ladies of the family at least may return to us, I am having the grounds put in order, and they are now so beautiful! Lilacs, crocuses, the lily of the valley, and other spring flowers, are in luxuriant bloom, and the roses in full bud. The greenhouse plants have been removed and grouped on the lawn, verbenas in bright bloom have been transplanted from the pit to the borders, and the grass seems unusually green after the late rains; the trees are in full leaf, every thing is so fresh and lovely. "All, save the spirit of man, is divine."

War seems inevitable, and while I am trying to employ the passing hour, a cloud still hangs over us and all that surrounds us. For a long time before our society was so completely broken up, the ladies of Alexandria and all the surrounding country were busily employed sewing for our soldiers. Shirts, pants, jackets, and beds, of the heaviest material, have been made by the most delicate fingers. All ages, all conditions, meet now on one common platform. We must all work for our country. Our soldiers must be equipped. Our parlor was the rendezvous for our neighborhood, and our sewing-machine was in requisition for weeks. Scissors and needles were plied by all. The daily scene was most animated. The fires of our enthusiasm and patriotism were burning all the while to a degree which might have been consuming, but that our tongues served as safety-valves. Oh, how we worked and talked, and excited each other! One common sentiment animated us all; no doubts, no fears were felt. We all have such entire reliance in the justice of our cause and the valor of our men, and, above all, on the blessing of Heaven! These meetings have necessarily ceased with us, as so few of any age or degree remain at home; but in Alexandria they are still kept up with great interest. We who are left here are trying to give the soldiers who are quartered in town comfort, by carrying them milk, butter, pies, cakes, etc. I went in yesterday to the barracks, with the carriage well filled with such things, and found many young friends quartered there. All are taking up arms; the first young men in the country are the most zealous. Alexandria is doing her duty nobly; so is Fairfax; and so, I hope is the whole South. We are very weak in resources, but strong in stout hearts, zeal for the cause, and enthusiastic devotion to our beloved South; and while men are making a free-will offering of their life's blood on the alter of their country, women must not be idle. We must do what we can for the comfort of our brave men. We must sew for them, knit for them, nurse the sick, keep up the faint-hearted, give them a word of encouragement in season and out of season. There is much for us to do, and we must do it. The embattled hosts of the North will have the whole world from which to draw their supplies; but if, as it seems but too probable, our ports are blockaded, we shall indeed be dependent on our own exertions, and great must those exertions be.

The Confederate flag waves from several points in Alexandria: from the Marshall House, the Market-house, and several barracks. The peaceful, quiet old town looks quite warlike. I feel sometimes, when walking on King's street, meeting men in uniform, passing companies of cavalry, hearing martial music, etc., that I must be in a dream. Oh that it were a dream, and that the last ten years of our country's history were blotted out! Some of our old men are a little nervous, look doubtful, and talk of the impotency of the South. Oh, I feel utter scorn for such remarks. We must not admit weakness. Our soldiers do not think of weakness: they know that their hearts are strong, and their hands well skilled in the use of the rifle. Our country boys have been brought up on horseback, and hunting has ever been their holiday sport. Then why shall they feel weak? Their hearts felt strong when they think of the justice of their cause. In that is our hope.

Walked down this evening to see ——. The road looked lonely and deserted. Busy life has departed from out midst. We found Mrs. —— packing up valuables.[13] I have been doing the same; but after they are packed, where are they to be sent? Silver may be buried, but what is to be done with books, pictures, etc.? We have determined, if we are obliged to go from home, to leave every thing in the care of the servants. They have promised to be faithful, and I believe they will be; but my hope becomes stronger and stronger that we may remain here, or may soon return if we go away. Every thing is so sad around us! We went to the Chapel on Sunday as usual, but it was grievous to see the change—the organ mute, the organist gone; the seats of the students of both institutions empty but one or two members of each family to represent the absentees; the prayer for the President omitted. When Dr. ——[14] came to it, there was a slight pause, and then he went on to the next prayer—all seemed so strange! Tucker Conrad;[15] one of the few students who is still here, raised the tunes; his voice seemed unusually sweet, because so sad. He was feebly supported by all who were not in tears. There was night service, but it rained, and I was not sorry that I could not go.

May 15.—Busy every moment of the time packing up, that our furniture may be safely put away in case of a sudden removal. The parlor furniture has been rolled into the Laboratory, and covered, to keep it from injury; the books are packed up; the pictures put away with care; house linen locked up, and all other things made as secure as possible. We do not hope to remove many things, but to prevent their ruin. We are constantly told that a large army would do great injury if quartered near us; therefore we want to put things out of the reach of the soldiers, for I have no idea that officers would allow them to break locks, or that they would allow our furniture to be interfered with. We have a most unsettled feeling—with carpets up, curtains down, and the rooms without furniture; but a constant excitement, and expectation of we know not what, supplants all other feelings. Nothing but nature is pleasant, and that is so beautiful! The first roses of the season are appearing, and the peonies are splendid; but the horrors of war, with which we are so seriously threatened, prevent the enjoyment of any thing. I feel so much for the Southerners of Maryland; I am afraid they are doomed to persecution, but it does seem so absurd in Maryland and Kentucky to talk of armed neutrality in the present state of the country! Let States, like individuals, be independent—be something or nothing. I believe that the very best people of both States are with us, but are held back by stern necessity. Oh that they could burst the bonds that bind them, and speak and act like freemen! The Lord reigneth; to Him only can we turn, and humbly pray that He may see fit to say to the troubled ways, "Peace, be still!" We sit at our windows, and see the bosom of our own Potomac covered with the sails of vessels employed by the enemies of our peace. I often wish myself far away, that I, at least, might not see these things. The newspapers are filled with the boastings of the North, and yet I cannot feel alarmed. My woman's heart does not quail, even though they come, as they so loudly threaten, as an avalanche to overwhelm us. Such is my abiding faith in the justice of our cause, that I have no shadow of doubt of our success.

May 16.—To-day I am alone. Mr. [McGuire] has gone to Richmond to the Convention, and so have the Bishop and Dr. S.[16] I have promised to spend my nights with Mrs. J[ohns]. All is quiet around us. Federal troops quartered in Baltimore. Poor Maryland! The North has its heel upon her, and how it grinds her! I pray that we may have a peaceful secession.

17th.—Still quiet. Mrs. J., Mrs. B.,[17] and myself, sat at the Malvern windows yesterday, spying the enemy as they sailed up and down the river. Those going up were heavily laden, carrying provisions, etc., to their troops. I think if all Virginia could see their preparations as we do, her vote would be unanimous for secession.

21st.—Mr. [McGuire] has returned. Yesterday evening we rode to the parade-ground in Alexandria; it was a beautiful but sad sight. How many of those young, brave boys may be cut off, or maimed for life! I shudder to think of what a single battle may bring forth. The Federal vessel Pawnee now lies before the old town, with its guns pointing towards it.[18] It is aggravating enough to see it; but the inhabitants move on as calmly as though it were a messenger of peace. It is said that an undefended, indefensible town like Alexandria will hardly be attacked. It seems to me strange that they do not go immediately to the Rappahannock, the York, or the James, and land at once in the heart of the State. I tremble lest they should make a direct attack upon Richmond. Should they go at once to City Point, and march thence to the city, I am afraid it could hardly be defended. Our people are busy in their preparations for defence; but time is necessary—every day is precious to us. Our President and military chiefs are doing all that men can do to forward preparations. My ear is constantly pained with the sound of cannon from the Navy-Yard at Washington, and to-day the drum has been beating furiously in our once loved metropolis. Dr. S[parrow] says there was a grand dress parade—brothers gleefully preparing to draw their brothers' blood!

Day after to-morrow the vote in Virginia on secession will be taken, and I, who so dearly loved this Union, who from my cradle was taught to revere it, now most earnestly hope that the voice of Virginia may give no uncertain sound; that she may leave it with a shout.[19] I am thankful that she did not take so important a step hastily, but that she set an example of patience and long-suffering, and made an earnest effort to maintain peace; but as all her efforts have been rejected with scorn, and she has been required to give her quota of men to fight and destroy her brethren of the South, I trust that she may now speak decidedly.

Fairfax C. H., May 25.—The day of suspense is at an end. Alexandria and its environs, including, I greatly fear, our home, are in the hands of the enemy. Yesterday morning, at an early hour, as I was in my pantry, putting up refreshments for the barracks preparatory to a ride to Alexandria, the door was suddenly thrown open by a servant, looking wild with excitement, exclaiming, "Oh, madam, do you know?" "Know what, Henry?" "Alexandria is filled with Yankees." "Are you sure, Henry?" said I, trembling in every limb. "Sure, madam! I saw them myself. Before I got up I heard sol-

diers rushing by the door; went out, and saw our men going to the cars."
"Did they get off?" I asked, afraid to hear the answer. "Oh, yes, the cars went
off full of them, and some marched out; and then I went to King Street, and
saw such crowds of Yankees coming in! They came down the turnpike, and
some came down the river; and presently I heard such noise and confusion,
and they said they were fighting, so I came home as fast as I could." I lost no
time in seeking Mr. [McGuire], who hurried out to hear the truth of the
story. He soon met Dr. ———,[20] who was bearing off one of the editors in his
buggy. He more than confirmed Henry's report, and gave an account of the
tragedy at the Marshall House. Poor [James William] Jackson (the propri-
etor) had always said that the Confederate flag which floated from the top
of his house should never be taken down but over his dead body. It was
known that he was a devoted patriot, but his friends had amused themselves at this rash speech. He was suddenly aroused by the noise of men
rushing by his room-door, ran to the window, and seeing at once what was
going on, he seized his gun, his wife trying in vain to stop him; as he reached
the passage he saw Colonel [Elmer] Ellsworth coming from the third story,
waving the flag. As he passed Jackson he said, "I have a trophy." Jackson
immediately raised his gun, and in an instant Ellsworth fell dead. One of
the party immediately killed poor Jackson. The Federals then proceeded
down the street, taking possession of public houses, etc. I am mortified to
write that a party of our cavalry, thirty-five in number, was captured.[21] It
can scarcely be accounted for. It is said that the Federals notified the authorities in Alexandria that they would enter the city at eight, and the captain was so credulous as to believe them. Poor fellow, he is now a prisoner,
but it will be a lesson to him and to our troops generally. Jackson leaves a
wife and children. I know the country will take care of them. He is the first
martyr.[22] I shudder to think how many more there may be.

The question with us was, what was next to be done? Mr. [McGuire]
had voted for secession, and there were Union people enough around us to
communicate every thing of the sort to the Federals; the few neighbours
who were left were preparing to be off, and we thought it most prudent to
come off too. Pickets were already thrown out beyond Shuter's Hill, and
they were threatening to arrest all secessionists.[23] With a heavy heart I packed
trunks and boxes, as many as our little carriage would hold; had packing-
boxes fixed in my room for the purpose of bringing off valuables of various
sorts, when I go down on Monday; locked up every thing; gave the keys to

the cook, enjoining upon the servants to take care of the cows, "Old Rock," the garden, the flowers, and last, but not least, J——'s[24] splendid Newfoundland. Poor dog, as we got into the carriage how I did long to take him! When we took leave of the servants they looked sorrowful, and we felt so. I promised them to return to-day, but Mr. [McGuire] was so sick this morning that I could not leave him, and have deferred it until day after to-morrow. Mr. [McGuire] said, as he looked out upon the green lawn just before we set off, that he thought he had never seen the place so attractive; and as we drove off the bright flowers we had planted in full glory; every flower-bed seemed to glow with the "Giant of Battles" and other brilliant roses. In bitterness of heart I exclaimed, "Why must we leave thee, Paradise!" and for the first time my tears streamed. As we drove by "The Seminary," the few students who remained came out to say "Good-by." One of them had just returned from Alexandria, where he had seen the bodies of Ellsworth and Jackson, and another, of which we had heard through one of our servants who went to town in the morning. When the Federal troops arrived, a man being ordered to take down the secession flag from above the market-house, and ran up the "stars and stripes," got nearly to the flag, missed his foothold, fell, and broke his neck. This remarkable circumstance was told me by two persons who saw the body. Is it ominous? I trust and pray that it may be.

When we got to Bailey's Cross Roads, Mr. [McGuire] said to me that we were obliged to leave our home, and as far as we have the right to any other, it makes not the slightest difference which road we take—we might as well drive to the right hand as to the left—nothing remains to us but the barren, beaten track.[25] It was a sorrowful thought; but we have kind relations and friends whose doors are open to us, and we hope to get home again before very long. The South did not bring on the war, and I believe that God will provide for the homeless.

About sunset we drove up to the door of this, the house of our relative, the Rev. Mr. B.,[26] and were received with the warmest welcome. As we drove through the village we saw the carriage of Commodore F.[27] standing at the hotel door, and were soon followed by the C.'s[28] of our neighbourhood and many others. They told us that the Union men of the town were pointing out the houses of the Secessionists, and that some of them had already been taken by Federal officers. When I think of all this my heart quails within me. Our future is so dark and shadowy, so much may, nay must, happen before we again become quiet, and get back, that I feel sad and dreary. I have no fear for the country—that must and will succeed, but our dear ones!—the representatives of every State, almost every family, from the Potomac to the Gulf of Mexico—how must they suffer, and how must we at home suffer in their behalf!

This little village has two or three companies quartered in it. It seems thoroughly aroused from the quiescent state which it was wont to indulge. Drums are beating, colours flying, and ever and anon we are startled by the sound of a gun. At Fairfax Station there are a good many troops, a South Carolina regiment at Centreville, and quite an army is collecting at Manassas Station. We shall be greatly outnumbered, I know, but numbers cannot make up for the zeal and patriotism of our Southern men fighting for home and liberty.

May 29.—I cannot get over my disappointment—I am not to return home!—The wagon was engaged. E.W.[29] had promised to accompany me; all things seemed ready; but yesterday a gentleman came up from the Seminary, reporting that the public roads are picketed far beyond our house, and that he had to cross fields, etc., to avoid an arrest, as he had no pass. I know that there are private roads which we could take, of which the enemy knows nothing; and even if they saw me, they surely would not forbid ingress and egress to a quiet elderly lady like myself. But Mr. [McGuire] thinks that I ought not risk it. The fiat has gone forth, and I am obliged to submit. I hear that the house has been searched for arms, and that J[ames]'s old rifle has been filched from its corner. It was a wonderfully harmless rifle, having been innocent even of the blood of squirrels and hares for some time past. I wonder if they do suppose that we would leave good fire-arms in their reach when they are so much wanted in the Confederacy, or if it is a mere pretext for satisfying a little innocent curiosity for seeing the interior of Southern homes? Ah, how many Northerners—perhaps the very men who have come to despoil these homes, to kill our husbands, sons and brothers, to destroy our peace—have been partakers of the warmhearted hospitality so freely offered by our people! The parlours and dining-rooms now so ignominiously searched, how often have they been opened, and the best cheer which the houses could afford set forth for them! I do most earnestly hope that no Northern gentleman, above all, no Christian gentleman, will engage in this wicked war of invasion. It makes my blood boil when I remember that our private rooms, our chambers, our very sanctums, are thrown open to a ruthless soldiery. But let me not do them injustice. I believe that they took nothing but the rifle, and injured nothing but the sewing-machine. Perhaps they knew of the patriotic work of that same machine—how it had stitched up many a shirt and many a jacket for our brave boys, and therefore did it wrong. But this silent agent for our country's weal shall not lie in ruins. When I get it again, it shall be repaired, and shall

> "Stitch, stitch, stitch,
> Band, and gusset, and seam,"[30]

for the comfort of our men, and it shall work all the more vigorously for the wrongs it has suffered.

I am indulging myself in writing on and on, because I have so little occupation now, and I feel so anxious and restless about those so near and dear to us, who have gone forth to defend us. The loss of property will be as nothing if our boys our spared. I am willing to be poor, but let, oh, let our family circles be unbroken! But I may feel too much anxiety, even on this subject. Our children have gone forth in a just and righteous cause; into God's hands let us consign them; they are doing their duty; to His will let us submit!

29th, Night.—Several of our friends from Alexandria have passed to-day. Many families who attempted to stay at home are escaping as best they may, finding that the liberty of the hoary-headed fathers of patriotic sons is at stake, and others are in peril for opinion's sake.[31] It is too provoking to think of such men as Dr. —— and Dr. —— being obliged to hide themselves in their houses, until their wives, by address and strategy, obtain passes to get them out of town![32] Now they go with large and helpless families, they know not whither. Many have passed whom I did not know. What is to become of us all?

CHANTILLY, June 1.—We came here (the house of our friend Mrs. S.)[33] this morning, after some hours of feverish excitement. About three o'clock in the night we were aroused by a volley of musketry not far from our windows.[34] Every human being in the house sprang up at once. We soon saw by the moonlight a body of cavalry moving up the street, and as they passed below our window (we were in the upper end of the village) we distinctly heard the commander's order, "Halt." They again proceeded a few paces, turned and approached slowly, and as softly as though every horse were shod with velvet. In a few moments there was another volley, the firing rapid, and to my unpractised ear there seemed a discharge of a thousand muskets. Then came the same body of cavalry rushing by in wild disorder. Oaths loud and deep were heard from the commander. They again formed, and rode quite rapidly into the village. Another volley, and another, then such a rushing as I never witnessed. The cavalry strained by, the commander calling out "Halt, halt," with curses and imprecations. On, on they went, nor did they stop. While the balls were flying, I stood riveted to the window, unconscious of danger. When I was forced away, I took refuge in the front yard. Mrs. B[rown] was there before me, and we witnessed the disorderly retreat of eighty-five of the Second United States Cavalry (regulars) before a much smaller body of our raw recruits. They had been sent from Arlington, we suppose, to reconnoiter. They advanced on the village at full speed, into the cross-street by the hotel and court-house, then wheeled to the right, down by the Episcopal church. We could only oppose them with the Warrenton Rifles, as for some reason their cavalry could not be rendered effective. Colonel Ewell, who happened to be there, arranged the Rifles, and I think a few dismounted cavalry, on either side of the street, behind the fence, so as to make it a kind of breastwork, whence they returned the enemy's fire most effectively. Then came the terrible suspense; all was confusion on the street, and it was not yet quite light. One of our gentlemen soon came in with the sad report that Captain Marr of the Warrenton Rifles, a young officer of great promise, was found dead. The gallant Rifles were exulted in their success, until it was whispered that their captain was missing. Had he been captured? Too soon the uncertainty was ended, and their exultant shouts hushed. His body was found in the high grass—dead, quite dead. Two of our men received slight flesh-wounds. The enemy carried off their dead and wounded. We captured four men and three horses. Seven of their horses were left dead on the roadside. They also dropped a number of arms, which were picked up by our men. After having talked the matter over, we were getting quite composed, and thought we had nothing more to fear, when we observed them placing sentinels in Mr. B[rown]'s porch, saying that it was a high point, and another raid was expected. The gentlemen immediately ordered the carriages, and in half an hour Mr. B[rown]'s family and ourselves were on our way to this place. As we approached the house, after a ride of six miles, the whole family came out to receive us. L[aura] and B[ella] ran across the lawn to meet us, with exclamations of pleasure at seeing us. We were soon seated in the parlour, surrounded by every thing that was delightful—Mrs. S[tuart] all kindness, and her daughters making the house pleasant and attractive. It was indeed a haven of rest to us after the noise and tumult of the court-house. They were, of course, in great excitement, having heard wild stories of the fight. We all rejoiced, and returned thanks to God that He had enabled our men to drive off the invaders.

This evening we have been enjoying a walk about these lovely grounds. Nature and art have combined to make it one of the most beautiful spots I ever saw—"So clean, so green, so flowery, so bowery," as Hannah More wrote of Hampstead;[35] and we look on it sadly, fearing that the "trail of the serpent may pass over it all." Can it be that other beautiful homes are to be deserted? The ladies of the family are here alone, the sons are where they should be, in the camp; and should the Northern army sweep over it, they cannot remain here. It is pitiful to think of it. They all look so happy together, and then if they go they must be scattered. Colonel Gregg and others of a South Carolina regiment dined here yesterday.[36] They are in fine spirits, and very sanguine.

June 6.—Still at Chantilly. Every thing quiet, nothing particularly exciting; yet we are so restless. Mrs. C[asenova] and myself rode to the camp at Fairfax Court-House a day or two ago to see many friends; but my particular object was to see my nephew, W.B.N.,[37] first lieutenant in the Hanover troop. He looks well and cheerful, full of enthusiasm and zeal; but he feels that we have a great work before us, and that we have entered upon a more important revolution than our ancestors did in 1775. How my heart yearned over him, when I thought of his dear wife and children, and his sweet home, and how cheerfully he had left all for the sake of his country. His bright political prospects, his successful career at the bar, which for one so young was so remarkable, his future in every respect so full of hope and promise— all, all laid aside. But it is all right, and when he returns to enjoy his unfettered country, his hardships will be all forgotten, in joy for his country's triumphs. The number in camp there has greatly increased since we came away. We came home, and made havelocks and haversacks for the men. The camp at Harper's Ferry is said to be strong and strengthening.

Mrs. General Lee has been with us for several days.[38] She is on her way to the lower country, and feels that she has left Arlington for an indefinite period. They removed their valuables, silver, etc., but the furniture is left behind. I never saw her more cheerful, and she seems to have no doubt of our success. We are looking to her husband as our leader with implicit confidence;[39] for besides his great military abilities, he is a God-fearing man and looks for help where alone it is to be found. Letters from Richmond are very cheering. It is one great barracks. Troops are assembling there from every part of the Confederacy, all determined to do their duty. Ladies assemble daily, by hundreds, at the various churches, for the purpose of sewing for the soldiers. They are fitting out company after company. The large stuccoed house at the corner of Clay and Twelfth streets, so long occupied by Dr. John Brockenbrough, has been purchased as a residence for the President. I am glad that it has been thus appropriated. We expect to leave this place in a day or two for Clarke County for the summer, and we part with this dear family with a sad feeling that they may too soon have to leave it too. Mrs. [Frances Ingraham Sparrow] has already sent off her plate and paintings to a place of safety. Mrs. C[asenova] is here with her mother. She left home when the army approached our neighborhood; she could not stay alone with her little son. Like ourselves, she brought off in her carriage what valuables she could, but necessarily has left much, which she fears may be ruined. Oh, that I had many things that are locked up at home! so many relics—hair of the dead, little golden memorials, etc.—all valueless to others, but very dear to our hearts. Alas, alas! I could not go back for them, and thieves may break through and steal. I trust that the officers will not allow it to be done, and try to rest contented.

The Briars, June 12.—We are now in the beautiful Valley of Virginia, having left Chantilly on the 8th. The ride through the Piedmont country was delightful; it looked so peaceful and calm that we almost forgot the din of war we had left behind us. The road through Loudon and Fauquier was picturesque and beautiful. We passed through the villages of Aldie, Middleburg, and Upperville. At Middleburg we stopped for an hour, and regaled ourselves on strawberries and cream at the house of our excellent brother, the Rev. Mr. K.[40] At Upperville we spent the night. Early next morning we went on through the village of Paris, and then began to ascend the Blue Ridge, wound around on the fine turnpike, paused a moment at the top to "view the landscape o'er," and then descended into the "Valley." The wheat, which is almost ready for the reaper, is rich and luxuriant, foreshadowing an abundant commissariat for our army. After driving some miles over the delightful turnpike, we found ourselves at this door, receiving the warm-hearted welcome of the kindest of relatives and the most pleasant of hosts. Our daughters were here before us, all well, and full of questions about "home." This is all very delightful when we fancy ourselves making a voluntary visit to this family, as in days gone by, to return home when the visit is over, hoping soon to see our friends by our own fireside; but when the reality is before us that we were forced from home, and can only return when it pleases our enemy to open the way for us, or when our men have forced them away at the point of the bayonet, then does our future seem shadowy, doubtful, and dreary, and then we feel that our situation is indeed sorrowful. But these feelings must not be indulged; many are already in our situation, and how many more are there who may have to follow our example! Having no houses to provide for, we must be up and doing for our country; idleness does not become us now—there is too much to be done; we must work on, work ever, and let our country's weal be our being's end and aim.

Yesterday we went to Winchester to see my dear S.[41] and found her house full of refugees: my sister Mrs. C.,[42] and her daughter Mrs. L., from Berkeley County.[43] Mrs. C[olston]'s sons are in the army; her eldest, having been educated at the Virginia Military Institute, drilled a company of his own county men during the John Brown raid; he has now taken it to the field, and is its commander,[44] and Mr. L. is in the army, with the rank of major. Of course the ladies of the family were active in fitting out the soldiers, and when an encampment was near them, they did every thing in their power to contribute to the comfort of the soldiers; for which sins the Union people around them have thought proper to persecute them, until they were obliged to leave home—Mrs. L[eigh] with two sick children. Her house has been searched, furniture broken, and many depredations committed since she left home; books thrown out of the windows during a rain: nothing escaped their fury.

Winchester is filled with hospitals, and the ladies are devoting their energies to nursing the soldiers. The sick from the camp at Harper's Ferry are brought there. Our climate seems not to suit the men from the far South. I hope they will soon become acclimated. It rejoices my heart to see how much everybody is willing to do for the poor fellows. The ladies there think no effort, however self-sacrificing, is too great to be made for the soldiers. Nice food for the sick is constantly being prepared by old and young. Those who are very sick are taken to the private houses, and the best chambers in town are occupied by them. The poorest private and the officer of high degree meet with the same treatment. The truth is, the élite of the land is in the ranks. I heard a young soldier say, a few nights ago, that his captain was perhaps the plainest man, socially, in the company, but that he was an admirable officer. We heard a good story about a wealthy young private whose captain was his intimate friend, but not being rich, he could not afford to take a servant to camp; it therefore fell to the lot of the privates to clean the captain's shoes. When the turn of the wealthy friend came, he walked up, cap in hand, with an air of due humility, gave the military salute, and said, with great gravity, "Captain, your shoes, if you please, sir." The ludicrousness of the scene was more than either could stand, and they laughed heartily. But the wealthy private cleaned the captain's shoes.

June 15.—Yesterday was set apart by the President as a day of prayer and fasting, and I trust that throughout the Confederacy the blessing of God was invoked upon the army and country. We went to church at Millwood, and heard Bishop Meade.[45] His sermon was full of wisdom and love; he urged us to individual piety in all things, particularly to love and charity to our enemies. He is full of enthusiasm and zeal for our cause. His whole heart is in it, and from the abundance of the heart the mouth speaketh, for he talks most delightfully and encouragingly on the subject. He says that if our ancestors had good reason for taking up arms in 1775, surely we had much better, for the oppression they suffered from the mother-country was not a tithe of the provocation we have received from the Government at Washington.

16th.—Rumours are abundant to-day of a Federal force approaching Strasburg.[46] We are not at all credulous of the flying reports with which our ears are daily pained, and yet they make us restless and uneasy. We thank God and take courage from the little successes we have already had at Pigs Point, Acquia Creek, Fairfax Court-House, and Philippi.[47] These are mere trifles, they say; well, so they are, but they are encouraging to our men, and show that we can hold our own.

A most decided revolution is going on in our social system throughout our old State: economy rules the day. In this neighbourhood, which has been not a little remarkable for indulging in the elegancies of life, they are giving up desserts, rich cake, etc. The wants of the soldiers are supplied with a lavish hand, but personal indulgences are considered unpatriotic. How I do admire their self-denying spirit! I do not believe there is a woman among us who would not give up every thing but the bare necessaries of life for the good of our cause.

16th, Night.—I can scarcely control myself to sit quietly down and write of the good news brought by the mail of to-day; I mean the victory—on our side almost bloodless victory—at Bethel.[48] It took place on the 10th. Strange that such brilliant news was so long delayed! The enemy lost 200 men, and we but one. He, poor fellow, belonged to a North Carolina regiment, and his bereaved mother received his body. She lives in Richmond. It seems to me that Colonel Magruder must have displayed consummate skill in the arrangement of his little squad of men. His "blind battery" succeeded admirably. The enemy had approached in two parties from Fortress Monroe, and by mistake, fired into each other, causing great slaughter. They then united and rushed into the jaws of death, or, in other words, into the range of the guns of the blind battery. I feel sorry, very sorry, for the individual sufferers among the Yankees, particularly for those who did not come voluntarily; but they have no business here, and the more unsuccessful they are the sooner their government will recall them. I do believe that the hand of God was in this fight, we were so strangely successful.[49] How we all gathered around M. M.[50] as she read the account given in the paper; and how we exulted and talked, and how Mr. P[age] walked backwards and forwards, rubbing his hands with delight!

The camp at Harper's Ferry is broken up.[51] General Johnston knows why; I am sure that I do not. He is sending out parties of troops to drive off the Yankees, who are marauding about the neighbouring counties, but who are very careful to keep clear of the "Ferry." The Second Regiment, containing some of our dear boys, has been lately very actively in pursuit of these marauders, and we are kept constantly anxious about them.[52]

18th.—We go to-day to dine with Bishop Meade. He wishes us to spend much of our time with him. He says he must have the "refugees," as he calls us, at his house. Dear me, I am not yet prepared to think ourselves refugees, for I do hope to get home before long. How often do I think of it, as I left it! Not only blooming in its beauty, but the garden filled with vegetables, the strawberries turning on the vines, the young peach-orchard in full bloom; every thing teeming with comfort and abundance.

But the family is waiting for me; the carriage is at the door, and my sad thoughts must end.

Night.—The day was passed delightfully; the Bishop, his son, and daughter-in-law, all so kind, hospitable and agreeable.[53] It amused me to see with what avidity the old gentleman watches the progress of events, particularly when I remembered how much opposed he was to secession only a few months ago. He clung to the Union with a whole-souled love for all that he had been educated to revere, as long as he could do it; but when every proposal for peace made by us was spurned, and when the President's proclamation came out, calling for 75,000 troops, and claiming Virginia's quota to assist in fighting her Southern brethren, he could stand it no longer, and I only hope that the revolution may be as thorough throughout the land as it is in his great mind.

"Mountain View" is beautiful by nature, and the Bishop has been collecting exotic trees and shrubs for many years, and now his collection is perfectly magnificent. This country is so far very peaceful, but we are constantly subjected to the most startling rumours, and the frequent though distant, booming of cannon is very trying to our nervous and excitable temperaments. Many, so many, of our dear ones are constantly exposed to danger; and though we would not have it otherwise—we could not bear that one of them should hesitate to give his life's-blood to his country—yet it is heart-breaking to think of what may happen.

June 19.—Yesterday evening we heard rumours of the Federal troops having crossed the Potomac, and marching to Martinsburg and Shepherdstown in large force. General Johnston immediately drew up his army at a place called "Carter's," on the Charlestown road, about four miles beyond Winchester.[54] Messrs. B. and R. M. called this morning, and report that the location of the Federals is very uncertain; it is supposed that they have retreated from Martinsburg.[55] Oh, that our Almighty Father, who rules all things, would interpose and give us peace, even now when all seem ready for war! He alone can do it.

June 24.—We have been in Winchester for the last two days, at Dr. S's.[56] General Johnston's army encamped at "The Lick."[57] Some Southern regiments encamped near Winchester. The army at Manassas said to be strongly reinforced. Measles prevailing there, and near Winchester, among the troops. There has been a slight skirmish in Hampshire, on New Creek, and another at Vienna, in Fairfax County. We repulsed the enemy at both places. Captain Kemper,[58] of Alexandria, led our men in the latter fight, and is much extolled for his dexterity and bravery.

July 1.—A rumour of a skirmish, in which the Messrs. Ashby were engaged, and that Richard Ashby was severely wounded.[59] I trust it may not be true.

July 3.—A real fight has occurred near Williamsport, but on the Virginia side of the Potomac.[60] General Cadwallader crossed the river with, it is said, 14,000 men, to attack our force of 4,000 stationed there under Colonel Jackson. Colonel J. thought it folly to meet such an army with so small a force, and therefore ordered a retreat; but quite a body of artillery remained to keep the enemy at bay. They retained with them but one gun, a six-pounder. The Rev. Dr. Pendleton,[61] now captain of artillery, commanded this gun, and whenever he ordered its discharge, he was heard to say, reverently, "The Lord have mercy upon their souls—fire!" The result was almost miraculous; but four of our men were missing, two of whom were killed; twenty were wounded, and have been brought to the Winchester hospitals; sixty-five prisoners were taken, and are now in Winchester. Many of their men were seen to fall. Our men, who did this deadly firing, retreated in perfect order. I heard this from one who was on the field at the time. It is said that in Dr. Pendleton the soldier and the chaplain are blended most harmoniously. A gentleman who went to the camp to visit his sons, who belong to the "Rockbridge Battery," told me that he arose before daylight, and was walking about the encampment, and when near a dense wood his attention was arrested by the voice of prayer; he found it was the sonorous voice of Dr. P., who was surrounded by his company, invoking for them, and for the country, the blessing of Heaven. What a blessing it is for those young men, away from the influences of home, and exposed to the baneful associations of the camp, to have such a guide! It has almost reconciled me to the clergy going upon the field as soldiers. The Bishop of Louisiana has been to Mountain View, to consult Bishop Meade on the subject of his taking the field.[62] I do not know what advice was given. These reverend gentlemen, who were educated at West Point, are perfectly conscientious, and think it their duty to give their military knowledge to their country, and their presence may do much for the spiritual good of the army.

Brave Richard Ashby is dead; how I grieve for his family and for his country, for we cannot afford to lose such men!

July 4.—This day General Scott[63] promised himself and his Northern friends to dine in Richmond. Poor old renegade, I trust he has eaten his last dinner in Richmond, the place of his marriage, the birthplace of his children, the home of his early friendships, and so near the place of his nativity and early years.

How can he wish to enter Richmond but as a friend? But it is enough for us to know that he is disappointed in his amiable and patriotic wish to-day. So may it be.

I have seen W. H.,[64] who has just returned from Fairfax. Last week he scouted near our house, and gives no very encouraging report for us. Our hills are being fortified, and Alexandria and the neighbourhood have become one vast barracks. The large trees are being felled, and even houses are falling by order of the invader! Our prospect of getting home becomes more and more dim; my heart sinks with me, and hope is almost gone. What shall we do, if the war continues until next winter, without a certain resting-place? Our friends are kind and hospitable, open-hearted and generous to a wonderful degree. In this house we are made to feel not only welcome, but that our society gives them heartfelt pleasure. Other friends, too, are most kind in giving invitations "for the war"—"as long as we find it agreeable to stay," etc.; but while this is very gratifying and delightful, yet we must get some place, however small and humble, to call home. Our friends here amuse themselves at my fears; but should the war continue, I do not think that they have any guarantee that they will not be surrounded by an unfriendly host. They think that they will not leave their homes under any circumstances; perhaps not, because they are surrounded by so much property that they must protect; but the situation will be very trying. Whenever I express a feeling of despondency, Mr. [McGuire] meets it with the calm reply, that the "Lord will provide," so that I am really ashamed to give place to fear. The situation of the people of Hampton is far worse than ours—their homes reduced to ashes; their church in ruins![65] That venerable colonial church, in which for generations they have been baptized, received the Holy Communion, been married, and around which their dead now lie. Their very graves desecrated; their tomb-stones torn down and broken; the slabs, sacred to the memory of their fathers, children, husbands, wives, which have been watched and decorated perhaps for years, now converted into dining-tables for the Yankee soldiery. How can human hearts bear such things and live? We have not yet been subjugated to any thing of the kind, and I humbly trust that so dire a calamity may be averted.

July 5.—Yesterday M[ary] P[age] and myself spent several hours riding about to visit our friends. The news of the day was, that General [Robert] Patterson, with a large force, had crossed the river and taken possession of Martinsburg, and that General Johnston had sent Colonel [J.E.B.] Stuart, with his cavalry, to reconnoitre and cut off his supplies, and to prevent a retreat. All these things make us anxious, particularly as the booming of the cannon is not unfrequent; but my faith in the justice of our cause is strong.

6th.—No army news to be relied on. We spent our time as usual. Knitting for the soldiers is our chief employment. Several suits of clothes for them are in progress in the house.

Sunday. 9th.—About to go to church. I trust that this Sabbath may be instrumental of much spiritual good, and that the hearts of the people may be busy in prayer, both for friends and enemies. Oh, that the Spirit of God may be with the soldiers, to direct them in keeping this holy day! We are on the Lord's hands—He alone can help us.

July 18.—During the last ten days we have been visiting among our friends, near Berryville, and in Winchester. The wheat harvest is giving the most abundant yield, and the fields are thick with corn. Berryville is a little village surrounded by the most beautiful country and delightful society.

Patriotism burns brightly there, and every one is busy for the country in his or her own way. It is cheering to be among such people; the ladies work, and the gentlemen—the old ones—no young man is at home—give them every facility. But Winchester, what shall I say for Winchester that will do it justice? It is now a hospital. The soldiers from the far South have never had measles, and most unfortunately it has broken out among them, and many of them have died of it, notwithstanding the attention of surgeons and nurses.[66] No one can imagine the degree of self-sacrificing attention the ladies pay them; they attend to their comfort in every respect; their nourishment is prepared at private houses; every lady seems to remember that her son, brother, or husband may be placed in the same situation among strangers, and to be determined to do unto others as she would have others to do unto her.

War still rages. Winchester is fortified, and General Johnston has been reinforced. He now awaits General Patterson, who seems slowly approaching.

While in Winchester, I heard of the death of one who has been for many years as a sister to me—Mrs. L. A. P., of S. H., Hanover County.[67] My heart is sorely stricken by it, particularly when I think of her only child, and the many who seemed dependent on her for happiness. She died on Saturday last. With perfect resignation to the will of God, she yielded up her redeemed spirit, without a doubt of its acceptance. In coelo quies. There is none for us here.

We have been dreadfully shocked by the defeat at Rich Mountain and the death of General Garnett![68] It is the first repulse we have had, and we should not complain, as we were overpowered by superior numbers; but we have so much to dread from superior numbers—they are like the sand upon the sea-shore for multitude. Our men say that one Southern man is equal to three Yankees. Poor fellows! I wish that their strength may be equal to their valour. It is hard to give up such a man as General Garnett. He was son of the late Hon. Robert S. Garnett, of Essex County; educated at West Point; accomplished and gallant. His military knowledge and energy will be sadly missed. It was an unfortunate stroke, the whole affair; but we must hope on, and allow nothing to depress us.

I have just returned from a small hospital which has recently been established in a meeting-house near us.[69] The convalescent are sent down to recruit for service, and to recover their strength in the country, and also to relieve the Winchester hospitals. The ladies of the neighbourhood are doing all they can to make them comfortable. They are full of enthusiasm, and seem to be very cheerful, except when they speak of home. They are hundreds of miles from wife, children, and friends. Will they ever see them again? I have been particularly interested in one who is just recovering from typhoid fever. I said to him as I sat fanning him: "Are you married?" His eyes filled with tears as he replied, "Not now; I have been, and my little children, away in Alabama, are always in my mind. At first I thought I could not leave the little motherless things, but then our boys were all coming, and mother said, 'Go, Jack, the country must have men, and you must bear your part, and I will take care of the children;' and then I went and 'listed, and when I went back home for my things, and saw my children, I 'most died like. 'Mother,' says I, 'I am going, and father must take my corn, my hogs, and every thing else he likes, and keep my children; but if I never get back, I know it will be a mighty burden in your old age; but I know you will do your best.' 'Jack,' says she, 'I will do a mother's part by them; but you must not talk that way. Why should you get killed more than another? You will get back, and then we shall be so happy. God will take care of you, I know He will.'" He then took a wallet from under his pillow, and took two locks of hair: "This is Peter's, he is three years old; and this is Mary's, she is a little more than one, and named after her mother, and was just stepping about when I left home." At that recollection, tears poured down his bronzed cheeks, and I could not restrain my own. I looked at the warm-hearted soldier and felt that he was not the less brave for shedding tears at the recollection of his dead wife, his motherless children, and his brave old mother. I find that the best way to nurse them, when they are not too sick to bear it, is to talk to them of home. They then cease to feel to you as a stranger, and finding that you take interest in their "short and simple annals," their natural reserve gives way, and they at once feel themselves among friends.

July 19.—This day is perhaps the most anxious of my life. It is believed that a battle is going on at or near Manassas. Our large household is in a state of feverish anxiety; but we cannot talk of it. Some sit still, and are more quiet than usual; others are trying to employ themselves. N. is reading aloud, trying to interest herself and others; but we are all alike anxious, which is betrayed by the restless eye and sad countenance. Yesterday evening we were startled by the sound of myriad horses, wheels, and men on the

turnpike. We soon found the whole of General Johnston's army was passing by, on its way to join [Gen. P.G.T.] Beauregard, below the mountain. A
note from J. M. G.,[70] written with a pencil at the Longwood gate, was soon
brought in, to say that they would halt at Millwood. The carriages were
soon ready, and as many of the family as could go went to Millwood to
meet them. I gave up my seat to another, for I felt too sad to meet with
those dear boys marching on to such danger. Mr. [McGuire] and the girls
went. They saw my nephews, R. C. W. and B. B., and others who were very
dear to us.[71] They report them all as in fine spirits. The people all along the
road, and in the village of Millwood, went out to meet them with refreshments. While halting at Millwood, General Johnston announced to them
that General Beauregard had been successful in a fight the day before, near
Manassas, and that another fight was hourly pending. The troops became
wild with excitement. It is said that General Patterson has gone to join
McDowell.[72] I trust that General Johnston may get there in time. They were
passing here from about four in the afternoon until a late hour in the night.
After midnight the heavy army wagons were lumbering by, and we ever and
anon heard the tap of the drum. We did not retire until all was still, and
then none of us slept.

July 20.—R[obert] P[age] arrived yesterday, and saw J.[73] very busy with
the wounded. The fight of the 18th quite severe; the enemy were very decidedly repulsed; but another battle is imminent. We were shocked by the
death of Major C. Harrison.[74] J[ames] wrote to his father. He fears to-
morrow may be a bloody Sabbath. Oh, that Providence would now interpose and prevent further bloodshed! Oh, that strength may be given to our
men. Let not the enemy overcome them. Oh, God of Nations! have mercy
on the South!

The fight on Thursday lasted several hours; our loss was fifteen killed,
about forty wounded; in all about eighty to eighty-five missing. It is believed that at least 900 of the enemy were left on the field; 150 of their
slightly wounded have been sent to Richmond as prisoners.[75] Their severely
wounded are in the hands of our surgeons at Manassas.

Sunday, 21.—We were at church this morning and heard Bishop Meade,
on the subject of "Praise." He and his whole congregation greatly excited.
Perhaps there was no one present who had not some near relative at

Manassas, and the impression was universal that they were then fighting. This suspense is fearful; but we must possess our souls in patience.

Monday.—We can hear nothing from Manassas at all reliable. Men are passing through the neighbourhood giving contradictory reports. They are evidently deserters. They only concur in one statement—that there was a battle yesterday.

Tuesday.—The victory is ours! The enemy was routed! The Lord be praised for this great mercy.

Evening.—Mr. [McGuire] and myself have just returned from a neighbouring house where we heard the dread particulars of the battle. We saw a gentleman just from the battlefield, who brought off his wounded son. It is said to have been one of the most remarkable victories on record, when we consider the disparity in numbers, equipments, etc. Our loss, when compared with that of the enemy, was small, very small; but such men as have fallen![76] How can I record the death of our young friends, the Conrads of Martinsburg, the only sons of their father, and such sons! Never can we cease to regret Tucker Conrad, the bright, joyous youth of the "High School," and the devoted divinity student of our Theological Seminary! Noble in mind and spirit, with the most genial temper and kindest manners I have ever known. Mr. [McGuire] saw him on Thursday evening on his way to the battle-field, and remarked afterwards on his enthusiasm and zeal in the cause. Holmes, his brother, was not one of us, as Tucker was, but he was in no respect inferior to him—loved and admired by all. They were near the same age, and there was not fifteen minutes between their deaths.[77] Lovely and pleasant in their lives, in their deaths they were not divided. But my thoughts constantly revert to that desolated home—to the parents and sisters who perhaps are now listening and waiting for letters from the battle-field. Before this night is over, loving friends will bear their dead sons home. An express has gone from Winchester to tell them all. They might with truth exclaim, with one of old, whose son was thus slain, "I would not give my dead son for any living son in Christendom." But that devoted father, and fond mother, have better and higher sources of comfort than any which earthly praise can give! Their sons were Christians, and their ransomed spirits were wafted from the clash of the storm of the battle-field to those peaceful joys, "of which it has not entered into the heart of man to conceive." I have not heard which was there to welcome his brother to his home in the skies; but both were there to receive the spirit of another, who was to them as a brother. I allude to Mr. Peyton Harrison, a gifted young lawyer of the same village. He was lieutenant of their company, and their mother's nephew, and fell a few moments after the last brother. He left a young wife and little children to grieve, to faint, and almost die, for the loss of a husband and father, so devoted, so accomplished, so brave. Like his young cousins, he was a Christian; and is now with them rejoicing in his rest. Martinsburg has lost one other of her brave sons; and yet another is fearfully wounded. I thank God, those of my own household and family, as far as I can hear, have escaped, except that one has a slight wound.

We certainly routed the enemy, and already wonderful stories are told of the pursuit. We shall hear all from time to time. It is enough for us now to know that their great expectations are disappointed, and that we have gloriously gained our point. Oh, that they would now consent to leave our soil, and return to their own homes! If I knew my own heart, I do not desire vengeance upon them, but only that they would leave us in peace, to be forever and forever a separate people. It is true that we have slaughtered them, and whipped them, and driven them from our land, but they are people of such indomitable perseverance, that I am afraid that they will come again, perhaps in greater force.[78] The final result I do not fear; but I do dread the butchery of our young men.

"Mountain View," July 29.—Mr. [McGuire] and myself came over here on Friday, to spend a few days with the Bishop and his family. He delivered a delightful address yesterday in the church, on the thankfulness and praise due to Almighty God, for (considering the circumstances) our unprecedented victory at Manassas. Our President and Congress requested that thanks should be returned in all of our churches. All rejoice for the country, though there are many bleeding hearts in our land. Among our acquaintances, Mr. Charles Powell, of Winchester, Col. Edmund Fontaine, of Hanover, and Mr. W. N. Page of Lexington, each lost a son; and our friend, Mr. Clay Ward, of Alexandria, also fell.[79] The gallant Generals [Barnard] Bee and [Francis] Bartow were not of our State, but of our cause, and we all mourn their loss. Each mail adds to the list of casualties. The enemy admit their terrible disaster, and are busy inquiring into causes.

This house has been a kind of hospital for the last month. Several sick soldiers are here now, men of whom they know nothing except that they are soldiers of the Confederacy. They have had measles, and are now recruiting for service. One who left here two weeks ago, after having been carefully nursed, was killed at Manassas. The family seem to lament him as an old friend, though they never saw him until he came here from the Winchester hospital. Two sons of this house were in the fight; and the Bishop had several other grandchildren engaged, one of whom, R. M., lost his right arm.[80] His grandfather has been to Winchester to see him, and is much gratified by the fortitude with which he bears his suffering. He says, "R. is a brave boy, and has done his duty to his country, and I will try to do my duty to him, and make up the loss of his arm to him, as far as possible." It is delightful to be with Bishop Meade. There is so much genuine hospitality and kindness in his manner of entertaining, which we perhaps appreciate more highly now than we ever did before. His simple, self-denying habits are more conspicuous at home than anywhere else. We sit a great deal in his study, where he loves to entertain his friends. Nothing can be more simple than its furniture and arrangements, but he gives you so cordial a welcome to it, and is so agreeable, that you forget that the chair on which you sit is not cushioned. He delights in walking over the grounds with his friends, and as you stop to admire a beautiful tree or shrub, he will give you the history of it. Many of them he brought with him from Europe; but whether native or foreign, each has its association. This he brought in his trunk when a mere scion, from the tide-water section of Virginia; that from the "Eastern Shore;" another from the Alleghany mountains; another still from the Cattskill Mountains. Here is the oak of old England; there the cedar of Lebanon; there the willow from St. Helena, raised from a slip which had absolutely waved over the grave of Napoleon. Here is another, and prettier willow, native of our own Virginia soil. Then he points out his eight varieties of Arbor Vitae, and the splendid yews, hemlocks, spruces, and firs of every kind, which have attained an immense size. Our own forest trees are by no means forgotten, and we find oaks, poplars, elms, etc., without number. He tells me that he has more than a hundred varieties of trees in his yard. His flowers, too, are objects of great interest to him, particularly the old-fashioned damask rose. But his grape-vines are now his pets. He understands the cultivation of them perfectly, and I never saw them so luxuriant. It has been somewhat the fashion to call him stern, but I wish that those who call him so could see him among his children, grandchildren, and servants. Here he is indeed a patriarch. All are affectionately respectful, but none of them seem at all afraid of him. The grandchildren are never so happy as when in "grand papa's room;" and the little coloured children frequently come to the porch, where he spends a great deal of his time, to inquire after "old master's health," and to receive bread and butter or fruit from his hands.

July 30th.—I have just been conversing with some young soldiers, who joined in the dangers and glories of the battle-field. They corroborate what I had before heard of the presence of Northern females.[81] I would not mention it before in my diary, because I did not wish to record any thing which I did not know to be true. But when I receive the account from eye-witnesses whose veracity cannot be doubted, I can only say, that I feel mortified that such was the case. They came, not as Florence Nightingales to alleviate human suffering, but to witness and exult over it. With the full assurance of the success of their army they meant to pass over the mutilated limbs and mangled corpses of ours, and to go on their way rejoicing to scenes of festivity in the halls of vanquished, and to revel over the blood of the slain, the groans of the dying, the wails of the widow and the fatherless. But "Linden saw another sight,"[82] and these very delicate, gentle womanly ladies, where were they? Flying back to Washington, in confusion and terror, pell-mell, in the wildest excitement. And where were their brave and honourable escorts? Flying, too; not as protectors to their fair friends, but with self-preservation alone in view. All went helter-skelter—coaches, cabriolets, barouches, buggies, flying over the roads, as though all Fairfax were mad.

"Ah, Fear! Ah, frantic Fear!
I see-I see thee near.
I know thy hurried step, thy haggard eye!
Like thee, I start; like thee, disordered fly!"[83]

Each bush to their disordered imaginations contained a savage Confederate. Cannon seemed thundering in the summer breeze, and in each spark of the lightning-bug, glinted and gleamed the sword and Bowie-knife of the blood-thirsty Southerner. Among the captured articles were ladies' dresses, jewels, and other gew-gaws, on their way to Richmond to the grand ball promised to them on their safe arrival. There were also fine wines, West India fruits, and almost everything else rich, or sweet, or intoxicating, brought by the gay party, for a right royal pic-nic on the field of blood. The wines and brandies came in well for our wounded that night, and we thank God for the superfluities of the wicked.

July 30.—News from home. Mr. McD.,[84] of the Theological Seminary, an Irish student, who was allowed to remain there in peace, being a subject of Great Britain, has just arrived at this house as a candidate for ordination. He says that our house has been taken for a hospital, except two or three rooms which are used as headquarters by an officer. Bishop Johns' house is used as headquarters; and the whole neighbourhood is one great barracks. The families who remained, Mrs. B., the Misses H.,[85] and others, have been sent to Alexandria, and their houses taken. Mr. J's[86] and Mr. C[asenova]'s sweet residences have been taken down to the ground to give place to fortifications, which have been thrown up in every direction. Vaucluse,[87] too, the seat of such elegant hospitality, the refined and dearly-loved home of the F[airfax] family, has been leveled to the earth, fortifications thrown up across the lawn, the fine old trees felled, and the whole grounds, once so embowered and shut out from public gaze, now laid bare and open— Vaucluse no more! There seems no probability of our getting home, and if we cannot go, what then? What will become of our furniture, and all our comforts, books, pictures, etc.! But these things are too sad to dwell on.

Mr. McD. gives an amusing account of the return of the Northern troops on the night of the 21st, and during the whole of the 22d. Such a wild, alarmed, dispirited set he had never an idea of. He had seen them pass by thousands and thousands, first on one road and then on the other, well armed, well mounted, in every respect splendidly equipped, only a few days before. As a Southern sympathizer, he had trembled for us, and prayed for us, that we might not be entirely destroyed. He and one or two others of similar sentiments had prayed and talked together of our danger. Then what was their surprise to see the hasty, disordered return!

August 1.—This whole neighbourhood is busy to-day, loading a wagon with comforts for the hospital at Fairfax Court-House. They send it down once a week, under the care of a gentleman, who, being too old for the service, does this for the sick and wounded. The hospitals at Centreville and the Court-House are filled with those who are too severely wounded to be taken to Richmond, Charlottesville, and the larger hospitals. They are supplied, to a very great degree, by the private contributions. It is beautiful to see the self-denying efforts of these patriotic people. Everybody sends contributions on the appointed day to Millwood, where the wagon is filled to overflowing with garments, brandy, wine, nice-bread, biscuit, sponge cake, butter, fresh vegetables, fruit, etc. Being thoroughly packed, it goes off for a journey of fifty miles.

The Briars, August 10.—Nothing new from the army. All seems quiet; no startling rumours within the past week. The family somewhat scattered: M[ary] P[age] has gone to the "Hot Springs," J[ames] to Capon Springs, both in quest of health; E. P. and E. M.[88] are at "Long Branch" (Mr. H. N's)[89] on a visit to a young friend.

J. P.[90] has just called, having resigned his commission in the United States Navy, and received one in the Confederate; he is on his way to Richmond for orders. He tells me that my dear W. B. P.[91] has come in from Kentucky, with the first Kentucky Regiment, which is stationed near Centreville. It is right he should come; and I am glad he has, though it is another source of painful anxiety to me.

12th.—Still nothing from the army. We go on here quietly and happily—as happily as the state of the country will allow. The household peaceful and pleasant. The ladies—all of us collect in one room—work, while one reads some pleasant book. We are mercifully dealt with, and I hope we are grateful for such blessings.

The Northern papers tell us that General Patterson has withdrawn from the Northern army.[92] The reason thereof is not mentioned; but we are shrewdly suspect that the powers at Washington are not entirely satisfied that he was so completely foiled by General Johnston. General Johnston was fighting the battle of Manassas before General P. knew that he had left the Valley. The rumour that he had gone to join McDowell was unfounded. For many days there was no intercourse between the section occupied by the Federal army and that occupied by ours; pickets were placed on every road, to prevent any one from passing towards General P. Gentlemen who had come to Winchester and Berryville on business for a few hours, were not allowed to return home for days. So how could the poor man know what was going on? We only fear that his place may be supplied by one more vigilant. General Scott, too, has been almost superseded by General McClellan,[93] who seems just now to be the idol of the North. The Philadelphia papers give a glowing description of his reception in that city. It was his luck, for it seems to me, with his disciplined and large command, it required no skill to overcome and kill the gallant General Garnett at Rich Mountain. For this he is feted and caressed, lionized and heroized to the greatest degree. I only hope that, like McDowell and Patterson, he may disappoint their expectations.

August 20.—We are rejoicing over a victory at Springfield, Missouri—General Lyon killed and his troops routed.[94] Our loss represented large. I have only seen the Northern account.

No news from home, and nothing good from that quarter anticipated. We are among dear, kind friends, and have the home feeling which only such genuine and generous hospitality can give; but it sometimes overpowers me, when I allow myself to think of our uncertain future.

Norwood, Near Berryville, August 26.—On a visit of a few days to our relative, Dr. M[urphy]. The people of this neighbourhood occupied as they are in the one I left. All hearts and hands seem open to our army. Four heavily laden wagons have left Berryville within a few days, for the hospitals below. We are all anxious about Western Virginia, of which we can hear so little. General Lee and General Floyd are there, and if they can only have men and ammunition enough we have nothing to fear.[95]

The army in Fairfax seems quiet. Colonel Stuart, with his cavalry, has driven the enemy back, and taken possession of "Chestnut Hill" as headquarters.[96] There they are over-looking Washington, Georgetown, and our neighbourhood, all bristling with cannon, to prevent their nearer approach. Some of those young men can almost point from the hills on which they are encamped, to chimneys of their own firesides, the portals of their own homes. The woods are cleared away for miles; even the yard trees are gone, leaving the houses in bold relief, with nothing to shade, nothing to obscure them. I do pity those who were obliged to stay in Southern homes, with Southern hearts, surrounded by bitter and suspicious enemies. My old friend Mrs. D[97] is sometimes in their lines, sometimes in ours. When our men are near her, they are fed from her table, and receive all manner of kindness from her hands. Some of my nephews have been invited to her table, and treated as her relations. When they entered her house she advanced towards them with outstretched hands. "You don't know me, but I knew your mother, father, and all your relations; and besides, I am connected with you, and you must come to my house while near me, as to that of an old friend." Nothing could be more grateful to a soldier far away from home and friends. But these were her bright moments. She has had many trials while in the enemy's lines. Her husband and grown son are in the Confederate service; she has sent her two young daughters to her friends in the lower country, and has remained as the protector of her property, with her two sons of eight and ten, as her companions. On one occasion her servant was driving the cows from her yard to be milked; from very loneliness she called to the servant to remain and milk them where they were; the very-tinkling of the cow-bell was pleasant to her. It was scarcely done when a posse of soldiers came with their bayonets gleaming in the moonlight, and demanded, "Why did you have a bell rung in your yard this evening?" "Do you mean, why did the cow-bell ring? Because the cow shook her head while she was being milked." "But you don't have the cows milked in the yard every evening. It was a signal to the rebels—you know it was—and your house shall be burnt for it." She then had to plead her innocence to save her house, which they pretended not to believe until the servants were called up to prove her statements. They then, with threats and curses, went off. Another night she carried a candle from room to room to seek some missing article. In a short time several soldiers were seen running to her house with lighted torches, yelling "Burn it, burn it to the ground!" She ran to the yard to know the cause; instantly this lonely woman was surrounded by a lawless, shouting soldiery, each with a burning torch, revealing, by its lurid and fitful light, a countenance almost demoniac. They seemed perfectly lawless, and without a leader, for each screamed out, "We are ordered to burn your house." "Why?" said she. "Because you have signal-lights at your windows for the d——d rebels." She immediately suspected that no such order had been given, and summoning firmness of voice and manner to her aid, she ordered them off, saying that she should send for an officer. They did go, uttering imprecations on her defenceless head. But a still more trying scene occurred a short time ago. Our soldiers were surrounding her house, when Colonel Stuart sent off a raiding party. During that night the

Yankees advanced, and our men retired. The Yankees at once heard that the raiders were out; but in what direction was the question. They came up to her house, and knowing the mother too well to attempt to extort any thing from her, ordered the little boys to tell them in what direction Colonel Stuart had gone. The boys told them that they could tell nothing. Threats followed; finally handcuffs and irons for the ankles were brought. Still those little heroes stood, the one as pale as ashes, the other with his teeth clenched over his under lip, until the blood was ready to gush out, but not one word could be extorted, until, with a feeling of hopelessness in their efforts, they went off, calling them cursed little rebels, etc. The mother saw all this, and stood it unflinchingly—poor thing! It is harrowing to think of her sufferings. Yet, if she comes away, her house will be sacked, and perhaps burnt.

We are sometimes alarmed by reports that the enemy is advancing upon Winchester; but are enabled to possess our souls in patience, and hope that all may be well. I see that they are encroaching upon the Northern Neck. I trust they may be repulsed from that fair land.

"The Briars," Sept. 6.—We returned home, as we are wont to call this sweet place, yesterday, and are just now taken up with family matters of deep interest. The army in Virginia seems quiet; but our arms had a severe reverse on Thursday. Fort Hatteras was bombarded and taken by Federal vessels. They also secured many prisoners.[98]

General Floyd, in Western Virginia, had a severe skirmish with the enemy, about a week ago, and drove them off with considerable loss.[99] Our loss was small.

Sept. 12th.—Yesterday was the wedding of our dear ——.[100] The marriage of a child is always melancholy when it involves separation, but particularly so under such circumstances. But surely never were refugees so blessed with friends. Our plan was to have the ceremony in the church, and then to proceed to Winchester, where the bridal party would take the stage for Strasburg, and thence by the cars to Richmond; but we were overruled by Mr. P[age], who invited his and our friends for the evening, and a beautiful entertainment was prepared for them. We all exercised our taste in arranging the table, which, with its ices, jellies, and the usual etceteras of an elegant bridal supper, made us forget that we were in a blockaded country.[101] A pyramid of the most luscious grapes, from Bishop Meade's garden, graced the centre of the table. The bridesmaids were three, and the grooms-man one, and he, poor fellow, had to go off in the storm of last night, be-cause his furlough lasted but forty-eight hours, and his station is Culpepper Court-House. The groom had a furlough of but three days, to come from and return to Richmond. The Bishop and Mrs. J[ohns] arrived in the morn-ing. The party consisted of ladies, and gentlemen too old for the service. Bishop J[ohns] performed the ceremony. Bishop Meade professed to be too old for such occasions, and declined coming. We feel very lonely this morning, and turn to the newspapers more than we have done for some time.

I saw a young soldier the other day, who told me he could see the top of our house distinctly from "Munson's Hill." Oh, that I could know what is going on within those walls, all encompassed by armies as it is. With my mind's eye I look into first one room and then another, with all the associa-tions of the past; the old family Bible, the family pictures, the library, con-taining the collection of forty years, and so many things which seemed a part of ourselves.[102] What will become of them? Who are now using or abus-ing them?

Sept. 16th.—Just returned from Annfield, where we have spent a charm-ing day, with most delightful society.[103] The papers brought us news of suc-cess in the West, General Floyd having overcome Rosecranz on Ganley River.[104] This gave us great satisfaction, as we are peculiarly anxious about that part of Virginia. We passed the time in talking over the feats of our heroes, as well as in enjoying the elegancies by which we were surrounded.

Sept. 18th.—I have been greatly interested in a letter, which has been sent me, written by my nephew, Lt. W. B. N[ewton], to his wife, the day after the battle of Manassas.[105] I copy it here because I want his little rela-tions, for whom I am writing this diary, to have a graphic description of the fight, and to know what their family and friends suffered for the great cause.

"Centreville, July 22, 1861.

"MY DEAR [MARY]:—For the last four days we have never been longer than two hours in any one place, have slept upon the ground in good weather and bad, eaten nothing but crackers and fried ba-con, and rested little at any time; for all of which privations and a thousand others we have been more compensated (thanks to the just God who governs the councils of history and decrees the destiny of nations) in the glorious results of yesterday. On the morning of the 17th, we had received reliable information that the enemy was advancing, over 50,000 strong, and were not surprised, at five o'clock in the morning, to hear the fire of our pickets, who were slowly retiring before the advancing foe. The order was given to pack. In ten minutes baggage was packed, tents struck, and the wagons driven to the rear; and the whole command forward to line of battle. In a few minutes the glittering bayonets of the enemy lined the neighbouring hills. From the heavy signal-guns being fired at intervals along our line—commencing at Germantown and stretching along to Fairfax Court-House—it was evident that the enemy was endeavouring to surround our little band; but our "Little Trump," as the men call Beauregard, was not to be taken by any such game.[106] Every preparation was made to deceive the enemy, by inducing him to believe that we meditated a vigorous resistance. Meantime our column defiled through a densely wooded road, and was far on the way to Centreville when the enemy discovered his mistake. He followed on very cautiously. To our troop, with Kemper's Battery,[107] was assigned the post of honour, and charged with the duty of covering the retreat. We were the last to leave the village, and as we went out at one end of the street, his column appeared at the other. We halted at this place about four o'clock in the afternoon, and again made show of battle—slept until twelve o'clock at the heads of our horses. We silently left the place, the enemy's pickets being within hailing distance of our own. At daybreak we were across Bull Run, having marched very slowly to keep pace with the infantry. We found beds of leaves in the woods, wrapped ourselves in our blankets, and slept for an hour or two, until we were aroused by the roar of the enemy's guns as he opened his batteries upon our lines. For two mortal hours shot and shell flew thick along our whole line. This day's work was evidently intended only to draw the fire of our artillery, and show where our batteries were. In consequence of which our gunners were ordered not to fire a single shot, unless within point-blank range. After thus opening the ball, two dense masses of infantry were sent to defile to the right and left, to make two separate attacks. It was indeed a beautiful sight as they came down in the perfect order, and with the stealthy step of veterans. They came nearer and yet nearer, and yet no shot from our guns. Our men began to mutter, and say that we were preparing for another retreat. But in a few moments the appointed time arrived. A single shot from the Washington Artillery[108] gave the signal of death, and for half an hour there was nothing but a continuous sheet of flame along the right of our lines. The enemy fell back, rallied, and charged again, with a like result. Again they rested, and rushed forward, but old Virginia was true to herself, and the gallant Seventeenth and Eighteenth Regiments charged them with the bayonet, and drove them back in utter confusion. The cavalry were held in reserve, and although within range of the artillery, and constantly experiencing the sensation which men may be supposed to indulge, who know there is a hidden danger hovering in the air, without knowing where it is to light, took no part in the action. Our time came yesterday, however. Our troop was for four hours in the hottest of the fight, and every man in it won the applause and approbation of the whole camp. The action commenced at eight o'clock on the sweet Sabbath morning. The enemy commenced with quite a heavy cannonade upon our right, which proved to be a mere feint, to distract our attention, as his main attack was directed to our left wing. At ten o'clock the enemy had crossed the river on our left, and then the fighting commenced in earnest. From the hill on which we stood, we could see, from the smoke of dust, though at the distance of several miles, how the fight was waging on our left. Some thought the enemy was retreating; others that our men had fallen back. It was an hour of painful interest. At eleven o'clock an aid-de-camp rode up in a gallop, and said our men were retiring—the cavalry was ordered to the left. We were temporarily attached to Radford's regiment[109]—ours was the first company, and mine the first platoon. On we dashed in a gallop, and as we passed within range of a battery of rifled cannon a ball was fired at us which passed between Wickham[110] and myself, knocking up a cloud of dust. Without wavering in their ranks, the men and horses dashed forward at a gallop. As we reached the scene of action the sight was discouraging in the extreme. The enemy had at first the advantage of every attacking party. He had concentrated his forces for an attack upon one point. The First Louisiana Regiment and the Fourth Alabama, attacked in flank and centre by 30,000 men, were literally cut to pieces.[111] They refused to surrender, but retired slowly, disputing every inch of ground. As we rode up we could meet parts of companies which had been utterly overwhelmed—the men wounded, their arms broken, while some of them were carrying off their dead in blankets. Every thing looked like retreat. We were ordered up to within five hundred yards of the enemy's artillery, behind a hill which afforded some protection against their destructive fire. For one hour the fire raged with incessant fury. A ball passed over the hill and through our ranks, grazing one of our men. A shell exploded just under Radford's horse, and every minute shot and shell were continually whistling by us. I can give you no conception of that awful hour. Not a man shrank from his post. Two of our men were taken exceedingly sick, one fainting from the heat and excitement. Such calmness and composure I never witnessed. To make the matter worse, despondency, if not despair, was fast writing itself upon every face. The fire was evidently approaching us. Our friends were retiring, and the whispered rumour passed from lip to lip that our artillery ammunition was running low. In a moment, however, a cloud of dust in our rear showed the approach of our wagons, coming up at a dashing rate, with a fresh supply. Our reinforcements now commenced pouring in. Georgia, South Carolina, Alabama, Mississippi, and Tennessee swept by in their glittering array with calm light of battle in their faces, and their bayonets gleaming in the quiet Sabbath sunshine. No man faltered, no man lagged behind. Neither the groans of the dying nor the shrieks of the wounded, as they passed by in crowded ambulances, seemed to produce any impression except to fix determination upon the countenances of all, to win or to die upon the field. The tide now seemed to ebb, just enough to keep us from despair. The firing did not advance, although the explosion of their shells was terrific in the extreme. A gleam of hope, too gradually broke in upon us, when Kemper's Battery, which had been posted in our centre, galloped up and opened a destructive fire upon our extreme left. The advance was evidently checked, when a loud cheer in the front told us that something unusual had happened. What was it? Was it the triumph of our enemies over our poor stricken friends; or was it some advantage gained by courage in defence of right? The suspense was awful. Men stood straight in their stirrups and stretched their eyes as if they could pierce the rugged bosom of the barren hill which raised its scarred front between them. An aid passed up. His message is written on his face, and before he speaks a word a wild shout breaks from the throats of thousands. When he speaks, another, another and another round of cheers told the story to our hitherto sinking hearts.[112] The Fourth Virginia Regiment had taken Sprague's Rhode Island Battery of six pieces, at the point of the bayonet. Scarcely had the echo of our cheers died away when again the noise of shouting broke upon the air. What was it? Had the enemy rallied and retaken the guns? Fear struggled with hope. But no: the gallant Twenty-seventh, envious of the glorious achievement of the Fourth, at a single dash had charged a regiment of regulars, swept them from the field, and taken every gun in Sherman's Battery. The firing of musketry and the rattling of bayonets was now terrible beyond description. For one hour there was an incessant cracking of rifles, without a single moment's pause. The enemy were evidently retiring, and unless reinforced from the left and centre, the day was ours.

"To prevent this, our field telegraph had already given the signal for movement upon our own right, and a heavy fire of musketry and artillery told us that [Gen. Milledge Luke] Bonham's Brigade, to which we had been attached in the morning, had crossed the run and were pouring it into the enemy's centre. The South Carolina boys dashed up the hill in face of a murderous fire, bayoneted their gunners, and took quiet possession of their central battery. It was three o'clock, and the day was ours. The Washington Artillery galloped up the hill on which we were posted, and opened a perfect Vesuvius of shot and shell upon the receding foe. Colonel Lay[113] then rode up and told us that the time for us to act had arrived. Our whole body of cavalry, 2,700 strong now rushed like the wind to the front. It was indeed a brilliant spectacle, as, with slackened rein and sabers drawn, the whole command dashed past. The whole line resounded with continued cheering. The force was divided into different detachments. Colonel Radford, with six companies, was ordered to cross a short distance below the enemy's extreme right, and intercept his column. Our company was in front, and I was riding in front of my platoon, when, after crossing the swamp, we came suddenly on a detachment of the enemy concealed in the bushes, with their pieces leveled. The Colonel ordered the charge, and our boys rushed on. Poor E[dmund] F[ontaine] was at my side when we rode over two of them, and they grounded their arms to E[dmond] W[inston] who was just in our rear. We galloped on in pursuit of the rest, who retreated across a field, towards the road on which the enemy was retreating. Fontaine was just behind me. [Richard W.] Saunders, a fine young fellow, just twenty-four years of age, and splendidly mounted, dashed by us. The enemy had concealed themselves behind a fence; we rode up, and I demanded their surrender; they made no reply. I ordered Saunders to fire; before he levelled his carbine the whole squad poured in a volley. Saunders fell dead at my feet, and Edmund Fontaine reeled in his saddle, exclaiming, "Save me, boys; I am killed!" He was caught in the arms of his cousin, who was just in my rear. Three of my platoon fired, and the two who had shot Fontaine and Saunders fell dead in their tracks. We were now in full view of the enemy's columns, passing in rapid and disorderly retreat along the road, with two pieces of artillery, a large number of baggage-wagons, and some officers' carriages. Colonel Radford, who is a soldier of experience, knew the strength of the enemy and ordered a halt, commanding the men to form. But such a thing was utterly impossible. The men seemed perfectly delirious with excitement, and with a wild shout of, "The guns, the guns!" our whole company rushed pell-mell upon the battery, which proved to be another detachment of the Rhode Island Artillery. Such a scene of wild excitement I never witnessed. My platoon had been detached from the company, and the company from the regiment. There were two caissons and two guns; the guns behind the caissons. My platoon, which was furthest down the road, rushed upon the men who guarded them. One fellow was standing on the caisson, whipping the horses to make them run; they had become so much alarmed that they stood perfectly still, and trembled. I made a blow at him with my sabre, knocked him off the caisson, and he was shot twice before he reached the ground. Meantime W[ickham] (who behaved admirably), with the main body, crossed the road higher up, and when the main body of the regiment came up, our company, with some of the Alexandria cavalry, had killed and wounded every man at the guns, and driven the infantry supports in rapid retreat. When we left we expected to be supported by infantry and artillery, and you may imagine our astonishment when, with not quite 300 men, we found that we had nearly cut into the enemy's column, and upon looking one hundred yards down the road, we found them preparing to open on us with two guns supported by six regiments of infantry. The Colonel at once ordered a retreat, so we shot the horses to the caissons, so as to block up the road, and retreated, not, however, before they had poured in upon us four rounds of grape and canister at one hundred and fifty yards' distance. How we escaped a perfect massacre I cannot say. Had they not been so close to us the slaughter would have been terrible. Four of our men were killed. Captain Radford,[114] brother of the Colonel, was literally blown to pieces. I escaped without a scratch, (as did all the rest of the officers,) excepting quite a severe bruise caused by my horse having pressed my leg against the wheel to the gun-carriage. We brought off several prisoners, a great many pistols, and several horses. Just ahead of the guns was a very handsome open carriage. As soon as they saw us, such a rush! It is suspected, or rather hoped, that Wilson, of Massachusetts, (who was, it is known, on the field,) was in it. One of our men, Linkey by name, took it into his head that General Scott was in it, pursued and overtook it, but at the distance of thirty steps fired his musketine, with eighteen buck-shot, right into the back window.[115]

"As we returned, a melancholy mistake occurred. [Baldman H.] Bowles, our second lieutenant, who was carrying poor Fontaine to the hospital, with one or two others, met a detachment of four of the Appomattox cavalry, who hailed him. It is said that, instead of giving the signal agreed upon in our camp, by raising the hand to the top of the head, he took them for the enemy, and answered "Federal troops." They fired and he fell dead. Our company received, upon its return, the congratulations of every officer on General

Bonham's staff, to whom Colonel R[adford] had spoken of the conduct or our men. To-day it has been raining incessantly. Our column pushed on this morning to this place. Our company was assigned the advance-guard, and this morning at ten o'clock, I had the honor of occupying the city of Centreville. The citizens tell us that about twelve o'clock last night the cry passed through the camp that the Virginia horsemen were upon them, when they left in wild confusion. Our triumph has been complete. In two days our noble army has driven them back to Alexandria, captured forty-two guns, many colors, and how many prisoners I will not venture to say. After we reached this place, we were ordered to explore the surrounding country in quest of fugitives. We took eighteen prisoners, and got back just at night, very wet. You never saw such a collection of property as was left in their flight. Hundreds of muskets, gun carriages, wagon horses; thousands of knapsacks, oil-cloths and blankets, hogsheads of sugar, barrels of pork, beans, etc.; in short, every thing you can conceive. We found to-day over five hundred splendid army overcoats.

"The men are amusing themselves to-night reading letters, of which there were thousands left on the field. Some of them were directed to Mr. So-and-So, expected at Manassas Junction. Some asked for a piece of the floor of the house in which Ellsworth was killed, with blood on it; while others confidently express the belief that Beauregard's scalp was to be carried to Washington. When I tell you that we supped to-night on Yankee crackers, Yankee coffee, and a nice beef-tongue, actually left on the hearth of one of the officers' quarters, in a kettle, ready to be set on fire—that this is written with a Yankee pencil, given me by one of the men, and on Yankee paper, taken from their wagons, and that I am sitting on a Yankee camp-stool, and writing by a Yankee candle, you can form some idea of the utter rout. I have a pincushion for L[ucy], picked up on the field, a needle-case for K[atherine], and a sword taken from a Vermont volunteer, for W.[116] Our troops occupy Fairfax Court-House to-day. I will try and see you soon. Good-night. God bless and protect you. I feel that he has protected me in the last few days, in answer to the prayers of a pious wife. I hope that I feel grateful for my preservation."

"*MOUNTAIN VIEW,*" *September 22.*—Came down here with Mr. [McGuire], a few days ago. Spent this day not quite so profitably as I desired. The ride to the "old chapel," where we had service, is so long, that we spent a great deal of time upon the road. Bishop Meade delivered a most interesting address. He mentioned with great feeling the death of Mr. John A. Washington, of Mount Vernon, who fell at "Cheat Mountain" a few days ago, while, with some other officers, he was observing the movements of Rosecranz.[117] It is heart-rending to hear of the number of valuable lives which are lost in this cruel war.

25th.—The last two days spent with pleasant friends—one day with Miss M. M.,[118] and the other with my old acquaintance, Mrs. Dr. F.,[119] of the "White Post." These ladies, like all others, are busy for the soldiers. To-day we have been helping the Bishop to pack a barrel of grapes, and another with tomatoes and other fresh vegetables; and yet another Mrs. M[eade] has packed with bread, biscuit, and a variety of things for the sick. To-day I received a copy of "Headly Vicars,"[120] abridged for the camp, by friend J. J.

"*THE BRIARS,*" *October 2d.*—We returned yesterday, everybody anxious and apprehensive. Battles seem to be imminent, both in Western Virginia and on the Potomac. Constant skirmishing reported in both places.

General Price, it is said, has taken Lexington, Missouri, with a large number of prisoners.[121] Our army in Fairfax has fallen back from "Munson's Hill" to the Court-House; thus leaving our dear homes more deeply buried in the shades of Yankeeism than ever. There are many refugees in the neighbourhood, like ourselves, wandering and waiting. Mrs. General Lee has been staying at Annfield, and at Media,[122] sick, and without a home. All Virginia has open doors for the family of General Lee; but in her state of health, how dreadful it is to have no certain abiding place. She is very cheerful, and showed me the other day a picture of "Arlington," in a number of Harpers' Magazine, which had mistaken its way and strayed to Dixie. She thought the representation good, as it certainly is of what Arlington was; but it is said that those fine trees are living trees no more—all felled to make room for the everlasting fortifications. She clings to the hope of getting back to it; but I begin to feel that we may all hang our harps upon the willows; and though we do not sit by the waters of a strange land, but among our whole-souled friends in our own Virginia, yet our "vine and figtree" is wanting. Home and its surroundings must ever be our chief joy, and while shut out from it and its many objects of interest, there will be a feeling of desolation.[123] The number of refugees increases fearfully as our army falls back; for though many persons, still surrounded by all the comforts of home, ask why they do not stay, and protect their property, my only answer is, "How can they?" In many instances defenceless women and children are left without the means of subsistence; their crops destroyed; their business suspended; their servants gone; their horses and other stock taken off; their houses liable at any hour of the day or night to be entered and desecrated by a lawless soldiery. How can they remain without even the present means of support, and nothing in prospect? The enemy will dole them out rations, it is said, if they will take the oath! But who so base as to do that? Can a Southern woman sell her birthright for a mess of pottage? Would she not be unworthy of the husband, the son, the brother who is now offering himself a willing sacrifice on the alter of his country? And our old men, the hoary-headed fathers of the heroic sons, can they bear the insults, the taunts of an invading army? Can they see the spot of earth which they have perhaps inherited from their fathers covered with the tents of the enemy; their houses used as head-quarters by officers, while they and their families are forced into the poorest accommodations; ancestral trees laid low, to make room for fortifications, thrown across their grounds, from which cannon will point to the very heart of their loved South? How can the venerable gentlemen of the land stay at home and bear such things? No—let them come out, and in some way help the Confederacy. Our new government will want officers, and the old men had better fill them, and leave the young ones free to swell the army. But I will no longer indulge in this strain; it makes me sad, and it is my duty to give at least the meed of cheerfulness to our kind friends; in truth, we have a right cheerful household. It would be amusing to an observer to see us on mail days. The papers are read aloud, from "Terms" to "finis," by N[annie T. Page], who, being a good reader, and having the powers of endurance to a great degree, goes on untiringly, notwithstanding the runner commentaries kept up throughout from many voices.

October 5.—M[ary] P[age] and myself drove to Millwood yesterday, and heard various rumours of victories in Western Virginia, and in Missouri; but we are afraid to believe them. At home we go on as usual.

October 8.—At church yesterday; the services interesting; the Communion administered. Rev. Dr. A.[124] delivered an address, perhaps a little too political for the occasion.

The news from Western Virginia not confirmed. Another rumour of a fight on Cheat Mountain, in which General Jackson, with some regiments of Georgians, repulsed the Federal General Reynolds.[125]

11th.—Every thing apparently quiet, and we, in the absence of bad news, are surrounded by a most peaceful and pleasant atmosphere. Our communication with the outer world cut off by the freshet in the Shenandoah, so that we had no mail yesterday. Mr. [McGuire] has gone to Richmond on business. He wrote from Culpeper Court-House, at which place he stopped to see J[ames], a most pleasing account of the hospitals, and the care taken of the sick.

12th.—M[ary] P[age] and myself drove to Millwood for the mail, and then made an agreeable visit to Mr. and Mrs. J.[126] We found several letters from family and friends; one from my sister, Mrs. C[olston] who with her whole family (except her sons,) married daughters and single, are about to rent the Presbyterian Parsonage, in Hanover, and keep house. As they are all refugees, and have the means, it is a most pleasant idea. The Rev. Mr. H.,[127] who was the occupant of the house, has gone to the army as captain of a company which he raised for the purpose.

The papers mentioned the capture of a vessel called "The Fanny," on the coast of North Carolina, laden with blankets, greatcoats, arms and ammunition.[128] A most valuable prize.

October 16.—We had a pleasant evening. While N[annie] read the papers we were knitting for the soldiers. An account is given of some small successes. Our men, near Pensacola, have broken up the camp of "Billy Wilson's Zouaves," of which we have heard so much;[129] and Captain Hollins of the navy has broken the blockade at New Orleans, sunk the "Vincennes," and captured a sloop, without the least damage to himself and men.[130] Rosecranz has retreated before our men at Big Sewell Mountain.[131] For these things we desire to be truly grateful, without rejoicing in the misfortunes of our enemies, except as they tend to the welfare of our invaded and abused country.

Sunday Night.—To-day went to church, and heard an admirable sermon from Mr. J[ones]. As we returned, we called at the post-office, and received a newspaper from Dr. Drane, of Tennessee, in which is recorded the death of his son James.[132] He belonged to the army in Western Virginia, and died there of typhoid fever. He was one of the late pupils of the E. H. S., a most amiable, gentlemanly youth; and it seems but as yesterday that I saw him, light-hearted and buoyant, among his young companions. He is constantly before my mind's eye. His parents and young sister—how my heart bleeds for them! Our poor boys! What may not each battle bring forth? Scarcely a battalion of the army, in any part of the Confederacy, where they are not.

Thursday, 24th.—An account reached us to-day of a severe fight last Monday (21st), at Leesburg—a Manassas fight in a small way.[133] The Federals, under General Stone, came in large force to the river; they crossed in the morning 8,000 or 10,000 strong, under command of Colonel Baker, late Senator from Oregon. They came with all the pomp and circumstance of glorious war, and rushed on as if to certain victory over our small force. "But when the sun set, where were they?" They were flying back to Maryland, that her hills might hide and her rocks shelter them. They crowded into their boats, on their rafts; multitudes plunged into the water and swam over; any thing, any way, that would bear them from "old Virginia's shore." Our men were in hot pursuit, firing upon them incessantly, until the blue waters of the Potomac ran red with blood. It was a "famous victory," as old Caspar would say,[134] and I am thankful enough for it; for if they come to kill us, we must kill or drive them back. But it is dreadful to think of the dead and the dying, the widows and the orphans. Mr. William Randolph,[135] who brought us this account, says there were between five and six hundred prisoners, a number of wounded, and 400 killed and drowned—among them Colonel [Edward] Baker killed. They had no business here on such an errand; but who, with a human heart, does not feel a pang at the thought that each one had somebody to grieve for him—somebody who will look long for the return of each one of the four hundred! The account goes on to state with exultation, that we lost but twenty-seven killed. There are but twenty-seven bereaved households in the length and breadth of this Confederacy from this one fight—a great disparity, and very few considering the violence of the fight; but it is difficult to think with composure of the lacerated hearts in those twenty-seven homes!

Tuesday, 29th.—A little reverse to record this morning. It is said that Colonel McDonald's cavalry[136] made an unfortunate retreat from Romney the other day, as the enemy approached. It may have been wise, as the enemy outnumbered us greatly.

Mr. [Page] and myself have just returned from a delightful walk to Pagebrook.[137] We were talking of our future, about which he will not allow me to despond. The Lord will provide, he says, and begins at once to count up our mercies. We constantly hear that our children and near relatives are well—none of them have been wounded, all mercifully spared; so that we would be ungrateful indeed to encourage or allow a feeling of despondency.

Wednesday.—Captain and Mrs. W. N.[138] dined with us to-day. It was gratifying to see him look so well, after the intense suffering through which he has passed. He was borne from the field of Manassas, with what seemed to be a mortal wound; a ball had passed through his body. But, thanks to a merciful Providence, good nursing and surgery have saved his valuable life. We are now planning to go to the lower country, but when and where we do not know.

November 3d.—To-day we were at church, and heard a good sermon from the Rev. Mr. [Cornelius] Walker, of Alexandria—a refugee in pursuit of an abiding-place.

An immense Federal fleet left Hampton Roads a few days ago, for what point destined we do not know.[139] Oh, that it may find its resting-place in the bottom of the ocean! The terrific storm yesterday gave us comfort. The mighty rushing of the winds was music to our ears. We thought of the Spanish Armada, thanked God and took courage. Was this wicked? I think not. They must lose their lives, or we must lose ours; and if it will please the Almighty Ruler of the wind and waves to use them in our defence, we shall be most grateful.

6th.—Mr. [McGuire] gone to the prayer-meeting at Millwood, accompanied by Mr. [Page]; both will cast their votes for Mr. Davis to be President of these Confederate States for the next six years. We yesterday dined at "Mountain View," with the Rev. Mr. Walker and family. He has been called to South Carolina to be professor in the Episcopal Theological Seminary of that State. He will go, as there is no hope of his getting back to Alexandria during the war.

Nothing from the "Fleet."

November 9.—Our hearts cheered by news from the fleet. A part of it stranded—one vessel on the coast of North Carolina, from which seventy prisoners have been taken; others on the coast of South Carolina. Unfortunately, a part is safe, and is attacking Tybee Island.[140] The fortifications there are said to be strong and well manned.

10th.—Returning from church to-day, we were overtaken by W. B. C.,[141] on horseback. We were surprised and delighted. He soon explained his "position." Jackson's Brigade[142] has been ordered to take charge of the Valley, and is coming to-day to Strasburg, and thence to Winchester. He rode across on R's horse. He dined with us, and told us a great deal about the army, particularly about our own boys. We are greatly relieved to have that noble brigade in our midst; we have felt, for a long time, the want of protection.

Monday Night.—To-day M. P.[143] and myself went to Winchester, and thence to the camp. We took Mr. P. N.'s[144] children to see their father. There we saw W. B., J. M. G.,[145] and many other young friends, and were much pleased at their cheerfulness. They look sunburnt and soldierly. I returned to Winchester to see my dear S[allie] S[mith]. R. C.[146] was sitting with her, looking well and happy. Camp-life agrees with him. These poor boys expect to be ordered to Romney; but wherever they go, they hope, by God's help, to repel the invaders.

15th.—This was fast-day—a national fast proclaimed by our President. I trust that every church in the Confederacy was well filled with heart-worshippers. The Rev. Mr. Jones preached for us at Millwood. This whole household was there—indeed, the whole neighbourhood turned out.

We have been anxiously awaiting the result of an anticipated fight between Price and Fremont; but Fremont was superseded while almost in the act of making the attack.[147] We await further developments.

WINCHESTER, December 9.—Mr. [McGuire] and myself have been here for three weeks, with Dr. S[mith] and our dear niece. Jackson's Brigade still near, which gives these warm-hearted people a good opportunity of working for them, and supplying their wants. We see a great deal of our nephews, and never sit at the table without a large addition to the family circle. This is always prepared for, morning, noon, and night, as it is a matter of course that soldiers will be brought in just at the right time, and so cordially received that they feel that they have a perfect right to come again when it is convenient to them.

A regiment or two have been sent to protect the Chesapeake and Ohio Canal near Honeywood. Affairs in the army are very quiet. I hope that the calm does not portend a storm; I pray that it may be averted.

"THE BRIARS," December 18.—Sadly negligent of my diary lately. Nothing new has occurred. We pleasantly pursue the even tenor of our way, but are now preparing to go to my brother's, in Hanover, next week. We have been to "Mountain View" for a couple of days, on a farewell visit to the family. The Bishop has sent his study-carpet to the camp, along with every thing he could possibly spare, for the soldiers' comfort. He looks cheerfully upon our prospects, and is now listening to "Motley's Dutch Republic"[148] with "infinite zest." It is read to him by his daughter-in-law, on these long winter nights. His manner of life is certainly most amiable, as well as pleasant to himself and instructive to others.

Newspapers have just come, giving an account of a fight at Cheat Mountain, on the 13th of December, in which we were successful.[149] Rumours also of a fight on the Chesapeake and Ohio Canal;[150] and another rumour that England has demanded the restoration of "Mason and Slidell," and in case of non-compliance with the demand, that Lord Lyons should demand his passports.[151] How ardently I do wish that England would break up the blockade!

Notes

1. For example, see Charles T. Quintard, *Doctor Quintard, Chaplain, C.S.A., and Second Bishop of Tennessee: The Memoir and Civil War Diary of Charles Todd Quintard,* Sam Davis Elliott, ed. (Baton Rouge: Louisiana State University Press, 2003), 41; Matthew Page Andrews, comp., *Women of the South in War Times* (Baltimore: Norman, Remington Company, 1920), 71–103, 155–89, 372–412; Mary Elizabeth Massey, *Bonnet Brigades* (New York: Knopf, 1966), 190–91.

2. Charles D. Walker, *Memorial, Virginia Military Institute: Biographical Sketches of the Graduates . . . Who Fell during the War between the States* (Philadelphia: J.B. Lippincott & Company, 1875), 120.

3. *Confederate Veteran* 33 (1925): 253.

4. James B. Slaughter, *Settlers, Southerners, Americans: The History of Essex County, Virginia, 1608–1984* (Tappahannock, Va.: Essex County Board of Supervisors, 1985), 109.

5. Slaughter, *Settlers,* 102.

6. Arthur Barksdale Kinsolving, *The Story of a Southern School: The Episcopal High School of Virginia* (Baltimore: Norman, Remington Company, 1922), 45.

7. Willie T. Weathers, "Judith W. McGuire: A Lady of Virginia," *Virginia Magazine of History and Biography* 81 (1974): 107.

8. Kinsolving, *Southern School,* 39–40.

9. The two McGuire boys were probably drilling with a volunteer home guard unit. No James McGuire served in a Virginia unit this early in the war. The other son, John P. Jr., became a captain in the Third Virginia Regiment, Local Defense. The McGuire daughters were Mary, Grace, and Emily.

10. Civil War came with the April 12–13, 1861, Confederate bombardment of Fort Sumter, S.C. Some four thousand shells were fired in the thirty-four-hour contest. Astoundingly, no casualties occurred, but one man was killed and one mortally wounded in the surrender process.

11. In 1868 Mrs. McGuire took the printed copy of her diary owned by her good friend, Mrs. Margaret Dickins, and identified in the margins many of the individuals she had originally cited by initials only. "C's" was "Clark's—my son's wife." Hereafter, these additions will be cited as Dickins Copy.

12. No earthen fortifications of note defended Alexandria. However, following John Brown's 1859 raid on Harpers Ferry and Abraham Lincoln's 1860 election, three infantry companies had been formed in Alexandria. Several home guard units were also active.

13. Mrs. McGuire was referring to Angelina Southgate Johns, wife of the assistant bishop for the Episcopal Diocese of Virginia. John Sumner Wood, *The Virginia Bishop: A Yankee Hero of the Confederacy* (Richmond: Garrett & Massie, 1961), 38.

14. Rev. Joseph Packard was dean and a professor at Virginia Theological Seminary. His memoirs, *Recollections of a Long Life* (Washington, D.C.: B.S. Adams, 1902), are revealing for the Episcopal Church at that time.

15. Henry Tucker Conrad, a native of Martinsburg, Virginia, was twenty-two years old at the time and a divinity student at the seminary. He would be killed little more than two months later.

16. The Right Reverend John Johns was a native of Delaware and had been president of the College of William and Mary during the 1849–1854 period. Officially, he was assistant bishop of the Virginia diocese; but with Bishop William Meade ailing, Johns was basically in charge of Virginia Episcopal matters. He, seminary president Sparrow, and Rev. McGuire had gone to Richmond for the annual meeting of the diocese. See *The Life and Correspondence of Rev. William Sparrow, D.D.* (Philadelphia: J. Hammond, 1876), 241–46.

17. Although Mrs. McGuire later identified the lady as "Mrs. Brooks," no such family appears on any of the usual research avenues. In all likelihood, this was Mrs. Miriam M. Brown. She and her Episcopal minister-husband had eight children. Dickins Copy; 1860 Virginia Census—Fairfax County.

18. The warship *Pawnee* was returning from an ill-fated attempt to reinforce the besieged Union garrison at Fort Sumter. Three days after Mrs. McGuire's mention of the vessel, it provided protection for Federal soldiers marching into Alexandria.

19. For the first time, many American women were actively expressing opinions on political subjects. One Virginia matron wrote of the spring 1861 situation: "Governed by feeling, we thrust judgment in the background, and were for immediate action. We taunted our grand old mother State with her prudence, her slowness—indeed we were so unfilial as to say that she was in her dotage." Francis W. Dawson, ed., *Our Women in the War* (Charleston, S.C.: The News and Courier Book Presses, 1885), 169.

20. Francis T. Murphy appears on the 1860 Fairfax County census as a fifty-three-year-old unmarried physician.

21. Union Gen. Samuel P. Heintzelman reported ordering troops to occupy Alexandria. "This was done without opposition, capturing in the town a few rebel cavalry." United States War Department, *War of the Rebellion: A Compilation of Official Records of the Union and Confederate Armies* (Washington, D.C.: Government Printing Office, 1880–1901), series I, vol. 2, 41. Cited hereafter as *OR;* unless otherwise stated, all references will be to series I.

22. Actually, Ellsworth and Jackson both were the first martyrs for their respective sides.

23. Shuter's Hill was an elevation a half-mile west of downtown. It would become the site of Union-constructed Fort Ellsworth.

24. James Mercer Garnett McGuire was the eldest son of Rev. McGuire.

25. The displaced generally fell into three categories: those who had a specific destination in mind, those with no real plans but who hoped to stay with relatives and friends for the time being, and those with no idea where they were going or where they would stop. Many refugees would fit all categories in the course of the war.

26. Richard Templeman Brown was rector of Zion and Falls Church parishes in Fairfax County.

27. "Claremont" was the home of French Forrest, who became the third ranking officer in the Confederate States Navy. Forrest shortly took charge of the South's largest navy yard at Norfolk, Virginia.

28. A former member of the Virginia General Assembly, William G. Casenova was an influential Alexandria businessman and a vestryman in the Episcopal Church. His wife was the former Mary Elizabeth Stanard. Ruth Lincoln Kaye, to editor, March 29, 2004.

29. Mrs. McGuire later identified this person as "E. Wilmer," but no one by that name appears in the 1860 censuses for northern Virginia. Dickins Copy.

30. These lines are from Thomas Hood's poem, *The Song of the Shirt*.

31. The McGuires were certainly not alone as they made their way westward. Spinster Anne Frobel wrote from her Fairfax County home: "The turnpike road, and all the roads as far as we could see were filled with vehicles of all sorts and description, filled with women and children, and goods of all kinds, men on horseback and on foot, and continual stream. Old Fairfax [County] surely never saw such commotion before." *The Civil War Diary of Anne S. Frobel* (McLean, Va.: EPM Publications, 1992), 18.

32. Based on Mrs. McGuire's marginal notations in the Dickins Copy, these two physicians were Orlando A. Fairfax and William J. Williams.

33. Cornelia Lee Turberville Stuart was the widow of Charles C. Stuart, who had built the mansion "Chantilly" in the 1820s. It was considered one of the most beautiful estates in all of Fairfax County. The Stuarts had nine children, all but two of whom lived elsewhere at the time of the Civil War. Edward T. Wenzel, Vienna, Va., to editor, July 8, 2004.

34. Here Mrs. McGuire described a June 1 skirmish at Fairfax Court House. Fifty troopers of the Second U.S. Cavalry dashed into the village on a reconnaissance. They encountered John Quincy Marr's "Warrenton Rifles," an infantry company from Fauquier County. Lt. Col. Richard S. Ewell directed Confederate efforts in the brief action. Marr was killed in one of the early exchanges of gunfire. *OR*, II, 60–64.

35. Hannah More (1745–1833) was a prolific English writer whose works did much to advance the cultural, ethical, and spiritual standards of the people of her day.

36. Col. Maxcy Gregg commanded the First South Carolina Infantry Regiment.

37. Twenty-nine-year-old William Brockenbrough Newton of Richmond had enlisted in the "Hanover Troop" of the Fourth Virginia Cavalry. He would be promoted to captain in late September 1861.

38. Since being driven from her Arlington estate, Mary Custis Lee had been living in Fairfax County at her mother's ancestral home, "Ravensworth." The fifty-three-year-old Mrs. Lee was rapidly becoming an invalid from arthritis.

39. At Virginia's secession, Robert E. Lee abandoned a distinguished thirty-year career in the United States Army. He was now in command of all the military forces of his native state.

40. Ovid Americus Kinsolving was rector of Meade Parish in Loudoun County. His home was in Middleburg.

41. Sally Bland Newton, the daughter of Willoughby Newton of Westmoreland, was the wife of Dr. J. Philip Smith in Winchester. Ben Ritter to editor, March 29, 2004.

42. Edward and Jane Brockenbrough Colston resided at "Honeywood" in Berkeley County.

43. Susan Colston Leigh was the wife of Benjamin Watkins Leigh, then a captain in the First Virginia Battalion. He rose to major and staff assignments before his death at Gettysburg.

44. Raleigh Thomas Colston joined the Second Virginia as a company captain and by 1863 was lieutenant colonel of the regiment. He died of complications from a wound received at Mine Run. His brother, William Brockenbrough Colston, also became a captain in the Second Virginia.

45. The son of a member of George Washington's military staff, the Right Reverend William Meade was at the time the senior bishop in all of the Confederate dioceses. His health was failing steadily when the McGuires visited his home.

46. One of the basic foundations of any war are unfounded rumors. Mrs. McGuire was citing one here.

47. The skirmishes at Aquia Creek (May 31), Fairfax Court House (June 1), and Pig Point (June 5) involved repulsing weak Federal probes. In a brief action at Philippi (June 3), Confederates were routed.

48. On June 10, some 2,500 Federals from Fort Monroe attacked 1,200 Confederates under Col. John B. Magruder at Big Bethel (also called Bethel Church). The Union efforts were hesitant, confused, and repulsed within an hour. Union losses were 76 men. Southern casualties were 1 killed and 7 wounded. The lone fatality was Pvt. Henry Lawson Wyatt of the First North Carolina.

49. Confederate victories and deliverances from immediate peril struck many Southern women as acts of a favorable Providence. In North Carolina, a diarist asserted that "He it is that giveth us victory & in His own good time He will grant us peace!" Catherine Ann Devereux Edmondston, *Journal of a Secesh Lady* (Raleigh, N.C.: Division of Archives and History, 1979), 564.

50. Mary Mercer McGuire was the eldest daughter of Rev. McGuire. Family members at the time were houseguests at "The Briars," home of Dr. Robert Powell Page and his second wife, the former Susan Grymes of Clarke County. Richard Channing Moore Page, *Genealogy of the Page Family in Virginia* (Bridgewater, Va.: Carrier Press, 1965), 147. For more on the home, see John W. Wayland, *Stonewall Jackson's Way* (Staunton, Va.: McClure Printing Company, 1956), 196–97.

51. Gen. Joseph E. Johnston commanded defenses at the northern end of the Shenandoah Valley. On June 14, having concluded that Harpers Ferry was untenable, he abandoned the post and shifted his forces southward toward Winchester.

52. Ten companies from Berkeley, Clarke, Frederick, and Jefferson counties comprised the Second Virginia. It was part of a brigade commanded by Col. Thomas J. Jackson. During the last two weeks of June, wrote a private, the ever-active Jackson "marched us back and forth every day, and at least half of every night." The regiment changed camps seven times in seventeen days. Dennis E. Frye, *2nd Virginia Infantry* (Lynchburg, Va.: H.E. Howard, 1984), 9.

53. Bishop Meade was in virtual retirement at his home near Millwood. He was insistent that the righteousness of this second revolution in 1861 exceeded that of the Revolution of 1776. Wood, *Virginia Bishop*, 39.

54. The Carter farm was on the west side of the Valley Turnpike, four miles north of Winchester and between McCann's Lane and Old Charlestown Pike. Ben Ritter to editor, April 6, 2004.

55. Mrs. McGuire identified the latter figure as R.C. Mason. He was then in his late fifties. Dickins Copy; 1860 Virginia Census—Clarke County.

56. John Philip Smith, a Winchester native, had been professor of medicine at Winchester Medical College since 1848. In July 1861, he accepted appointment as surgeon of the Second Virginia; yet for most of the war, he was on hospital duty at four different locations. Ben Ritter to editor, March 29, 2004.

57. This site was three miles north of Winchester on the Martinsburg Turnpike. Garland R. Quarles, *Occupied Winchester, 1981–1865* (Winchester, Va.: Farmers & Merchants National Bank, 1991), 57.

58. Summaries of the June 19 skirmish at New Creek and the June 17 action at Vienna are in *OR*, II, 124–26, 130–32. At the latter engagement, Col. Maxcy Gregg reported that Capt. Delaware Kemper's "skill in the management of guns left nothing to be desired." *OR*, II, 130.

59. Turner Ashby of Fauquier County became the beau ideal of a Confederate cavalry leader to the residents of the lower Shenandoah Valley. On June 26,

in a running fight with Union horsemen near Kelly's Island in the Potomac, Ashby's younger brother was killed. A good account of the action is in Millard K. Bushong, *General Turner Ashby and Stonewall's Valley Campaign* (Verona, Va.: McClure Printing Company, 1980), 38–40.

60. Mrs. McGuire was referring to the July 2 action at Falling Waters, near Martinsburg. Confederate success there led to the promotion of Thomas J. Jackson to brigadier general. James I. Robertson Jr., *Stonewall Jackson: The Man, the Soldier, the Legend* (New York: Macmillan, 1997), 247–51.

61. William Nelson Pendleton was a West Point graduate and Episcopal priest. He commanded the four-gun Rockbridge Artillery at Falling Waters. See Robertson, *Stonewall Jackson,* 248–49, 831. Pendleton ultimately rose to general's rank, but he proved to be a better minister than military leader.

62. Although trained at West Point, Bishop Leonidas Polk had little military experience when civil war came. He owed his general's stars to his powerful standing in Louisiana and to friendship with President Jefferson Davis.

63. The Virginia-born Winfield Scott had been general-in-chief of the U.S. Army since 1841. Three weeks after Mrs. McGuire's entry, the wife of a Texas congressman wrote: "Poor old Scott! If he had only died after the Mexican War, how much better it would have been for his military fame." Mrs. D. Giraud Wright, *A Southern Girl in '61* (New York: Doubleday, Page, 1905), 73–74.

64. William Taylor Hammond had been a student at Episcopal High School. On May 25, he had joined a Fairfax County company that became part of the Sixth Virginia Cavalry. Hammond fell mortally wounded in June 1864, at Reams's Station. Michael P. Musick, *6th Virginia Cavalry* (Lynchburg, Va.: H.E. Howard, 1990), 120.

65. On May 17, Confederates abandoned Hampton from fear of being flanked by superior Union numbers massed at Fort Monroe. The "venerable colonial church" to which Mrs. McGuire referred was St. John's Church, built in 1728 and the oldest Episcopal parish in continuous service in the United States. John V. Quarstein, *Hampton and Newport News in the Civil War: War Comes to the Peninsula* (Lynchburg, Va.: H.E. Howard, 1998), 14, 27–28.

66. The most contagious disease that struck Civil War soldiers was rubeola, or red measles. One of every seven Confederates in Virginia in 1861 contracted the malady. Untreatable at the time, measles was often fatal.

67. Lucy Ann Nelson and Charles Page married in 1831 and lived at the Page estate, "Summer Hill," in Hanover County. Adjacent to the Page property was "Westwood," home of the Brockenbroughs.

68. On July 11, some two thousand Federals overwhelmed a Confederate force that Gen. Robert Selden Garnett Jr. had posted atop Rich Mountain in western Virginia. Garnett retired with the remnant of his small command to

Corrick's Ford. There, on July 13, Union forces again routed the Southerners. Garnett was killed in the fighting.

69. The Quaker Meeting House stood on a Winchester square bounded by Steuart, Monmouth, Washington, and Germain streets. The building was so extensively damaged by Union occupation during the war that it ceased to operate after 1865. Ben Ritter to editor, March 29, 2004.

70. James Mercer Garnett was then a lieutenant and, in November 1861, would join the staff of Gen. "Stonewall" Jackson. He was from the Aldie community of northern Virginia.

71. "R.C.W." was probably Robert C. White, a Richmond native who served in the Twenty-first Virginia before transferring to the Richmond Howitzers. John Bowyer Brockenbrough, known widely as "Beau," was a lieutenant in the Rockbridge Artillery. He eventually rose to the rank of major of artillery.

72. This statement was untrue. Johnston used secrecy and a series of ruses to disappear from Patterson's front. The aged Union commander was befuddled by it all and allowed Johnston's army to unite at Manassas with Beauregard's untested forces. Union Gen. Irvin McDowell's equally green command fought a sharp July 18 action at Blackburn's Ford and were now moving toward a major engagement at Manassas.

73. James M. G. McGuire, the diarist's eldest stepson, was a physician practicing in Berryville at the outset of the war.

74. "An accomplished, promising officer," Carter Henry Harrison of the Eleventh Virginia was mortally wounded on July 18 while leading two companies in an attack. *OR*, II, 445.

75. Union casualties at Blackburn's Ford were nineteen killed, thirty-eight wounded, and twenty-six missing. Confederate losses were fifteen killed and fifty-three wounded. E.B. Long, *The Civil War Day by Day* (Garden City, N.Y.: Doubleday, 1971), 96.

76. At First Bull Run or Manassas, Federals suffered 482 killed, 1,126 wounded, and 1,740 missing (most of them captured). Confederates lost 363 killed, 1,465 wounded, and 9 missing. John Hennessy, *The First Battle of Manassas* (Lynchburg, Va.: H.E. Howard, 1989), 130–35.

77. David Holmes Conrad and Henry Tucker Conrad were the sons of Martinsburg's influential David Holmes Conrad. The brothers, along with their cousin, Peyton R. Harrison, served in the "Berkeley Border Guards" of the Second Virginia. Legend has it that the three soldiers were killed by the same shell. Cornelia McDonald, *A Diary with Reminiscences of the War and Refugee Life in the Shenandoah Valley, 1860–1865* (Nashville: Cullom & Ghertner Company, 1934), 29.

78. Mrs. McGuire would not join with others in the celebrations of First

Manassas because she was thinking of the soldiers who would yet pay for victories and defeats. The anxiety that Union armies would come back to resume the fighting was infectious and became the thinking of growing numbers of Southern women.

79. The four soldiers to whom Mrs. McGuire alluded were Pvt. Lowell F. Powell of the Second Virginia, Sgt. Maj. Edmund Fontaine and Pvt. William Nelson Page of the Fourth Virginia, plus Lt. Henry Clay Ward of the Forty-ninth Virginia.

80. Pvt. Richard Kidder Meade of the "Winchester Riflemen," Second Virginia, lost his right arm at First Manassas. He later served on Gen. "Stonewall" Jackson's staff.

81. As the Battle of First Manassas began that Sunday in July, hundreds of Washington civilians came in carriages and wagons to enjoy a picnic and watch the show. The Union retirement from the field caused frantic civilians to exit as well, and all too soon the retreat became a rout.

82. Mrs. McGuire was making a loose reference to Thomas Campbell's *Hohenlinden*.

83. These are the opening lines of William Collins's poem *Ode to Fear*.

84. Englishman George Victor Macdona attended the seminary and was about to graduate in 1861 when the school closed. He then returned to England, was ordained an Anglican priest, and had a long, varied clerical career. Julia Randle to editor, March 29, 2004.

85. The Dickins Copy identified these individuals as "Mrs. Brooks and the Misses Herbert." At that time, Alexandria shoemaker Edward W. Herbert had four daughters ranging in age from twenty-four to eight. 1860 Virginia Census—Alexandria.

86. This is probably Robert Jamieson, a respected president of one of the local banks.

87. "Vaucluse" was an ancestral home in Alexandria for part of the great Fairfax family. Through marriage, Fairfaxes and Carys inhabited the mansion at the time of the Civil War. See Mrs. Burton Harrison, *Recollections Grave and Gay* (New York: Charles Scribner's Sons, 1911), 22–23, 36, 44–45.

88. Elizabeth Page was the oldest child from Robert P. Page's second marriage. Emily McGuire was Mrs. McGuire's stepdaughter.

89. This is probably Hugh M. Nelson, from one of Clarke County's most prominent families.

90. Jefferson Phelps, of Essex County, had attended the U.S. Naval Academy and served in the Navy prior to civil war.

91. William B. Phelps was sergeant major of the First Kentucky.

92. Robert Patterson had fought in two wars and was a highly successful

businessman. Yet commanding a three-month militia in northern Virginia was beyond the ability of the sixty-nine-year-old officer. The failure to hold Johnston's men at Winchester ended Patterson's Civil War career.

93. Following the Union defeat at First Manassas, Lincoln replaced McDowell with Gen. George B. McClellan. The handsome, well-organized, and confident McClellan brought an instant rise in Northern morale.

94. On August 10, at Wilson's Creek, Missouri, new Union Gen. Nathaniel Lyon led a green, undersized force into battle. The results included Lyon's death, a resounding Union defeat, and opportunities for Confederates to threaten southern and western Missouri.

95. President Davis sent Lee to western Virginia in an attempt to bring cohesion among quarreling Confederate generals John B. Floyd, William W. Loring, and Henry A. Wise. Jealousies and ambitions among the trio, plus rough terrain and atrocious weather, blocked all of Lee's efforts. This failed campaign opened the way for the eventual creation of the state of West Virginia.

96. Subsequent to First Manassas, James Ewell Brown "Jeb" Stuart established a series of cavalry outposts on Mason's, Munson's, and Upton's Hills in the area of modern-day Arlington. Stuart's headquarters for several weeks was at Munson's Hill. H.B. McClellan, *The Life and Campaigns of Major-General J. E. B. Stuart* (Boston and New York: Houghton, Mifflin, and Company, 1885), 41.

97. Margaret Randolph Dickins was married to a successful Washington attorney. The couple lived at "Ossian Hall," a Fairfax County estate. Mrs. Dickins was one of Mrs. McGuire's closest friends. See Estella Bryans-Munson and Robert M. Moxham, *Annandale, Virginia: A Brief History* (Fairfax, Va., 1992), 55.

98. During August 27–28, Federal naval vessels with infantry attacked Forts Clark and Hatteras. Almost seven hundred Confederates surrendered. This offensive closed Albemarle and Pamlico sounds as havens for blockade-runners.

99. Mrs. McGuire actually was referring to skirmishes by Gen. Henry A. Wise's troops at Hawks Nest on August 20 and Piggot's Mill five days later.

100. The McGuires' eldest daughter Mary wed Lt. John Johns Jr., son of the Episcopal bishop. The bridegroom performed staff duties in Richmond for the duration of the war.

101. At another wedding feast in Virginia during this time, the offerings were a roast fowl, dried apple pies, cracked walnuts, and coffee made of okra seed and sweet potatoes. Dawson, *Our Women in the War,* 126.

102. Women found it painfully difficult to leave their homes and household furnishings. Mrs. McGuire was no exception. When Mrs. Elvira Scott prepared to abandon her home, she remembered ten years of effort to "improve

ornament and beautify" her residence. "Every tree and bush in the yard," she lamented, "was dear to me." Edward D.C. Campbell Jr. and Kym S. Rice, eds., *A Woman's War: Southern Women, Civil War, and the Confederate Legacy* (Richmond, Va.: Museum of the Confederacy/Charlottesville, University Press of Virginia, 1996), 35.

103. "Annfield" was the Clarke County home of the Thomas Carter family.

104. On September 10, Union forces under Gen. William S. Rosecrans attacked Floyd's position at Carnifex Ferry but failed to break the Confederate line. Under cover of darkness, Floyd's outnumbered command abandoned the field.

105. Mary Page Newton was the wife of the cavalryman. She had three small children at the time. 1860 Virginia Census—Hanover County.

106. Gen. P.G.T. Beauregard was in command of the Confederate army at First Manassas. A Louisiana Creole and professional soldier, he stood five feet, seven inches tall and weighed 150 pounds. Many who saw Beauregard likened him to Napoleon Bonaparte. T. Harry Williams, *P.G.T. Beauregard: Napoleon in Gray* (Baton Rouge: Louisiana State University Press, 1954), 51.

107. Capt. Delaware Kemper's battery was known as the "Alexandria Artillery."

108. The "Washington Artillery" of New Orleans became the most famous battery from Louisiana in the Civil War.

109. Colonel of the Second Virginia Cavalry, Richard Carlton Walker Radford commanded a mounted brigade at First Manassas.

110. Williams Carter Wickham was captain of the "Hanover Light Dragoons" in the Fourth Virginia Cavalry. When Wickham received promotion to lieutenant colonel in September 1861, Newton succeeded him as company commander.

111. Captain Newton fell victim to exaggeration at this point. At no time were 30,000 Federals engaged in battle at Manassas. The First Louisiana suffered only 48 casualties, but the Fourth Alabama lost 197 men. *OR,* II, 570.

112. Newton was describing the unbending stand of Gen. Thomas J. Jackson's brigade and its capture of two Union batteries seeking to deliver an oblique fire. See Robertson, *Stonewall Jackson,* 259–67. The artillery battery attached to Union Col. William T. Sherman's infantry brigade never crossed Bull Run or entered the action. *OR,* II, 369, 373.

113. Col. George William Lay was an aide to General Bonham in the battle.

114. Capt. Edmund Winston Radford's official service record states that he was killed by a shot in the abdomen. Robert J. Driver Jr. and H.E. Howard, *2nd Virginia Cavalry* (Lynchburg, Va.: H.E. Howard, 1995), 263.

115. An active and outspoken abolitionist, Henry Wilson was a United

States senator from Massachusetts. Gen. Winfield Scott was too infirm to be at First Manassas. The soldier in the "Hanover Light Dragoons" was William G. Lindsey. Kenneth L. Stiles, *4th Virginia Cavalry* (Lynchburg, Va.: H.E. Howard, 1985), 122.

116. William was one of Lieutenant Newton's sons.

117. John Augustine Washington was the great-nephew of George Washington and the last member of the family to farm the Mount Vernon estate. He was serving on Robert E. Lee's staff when he was killed in a September 13 skirmish at Elkwater, near Cheat Mountain in western Virginia.

118. The sister of Bishop Meade, Mary Meade lived in the White Post area of Clarke County.

119. Few men were more widely beloved in Clarke County than Dr. John Fauntleroy. See Thomas D. Gold, *History of Clarke County, Virginia* (Berryville, Va.: C.R. Hughes, 1962), 50, 57.

120. Capt. Hadley Vicars served with the Ninety-seventh Regiment, His Majesty's Royal Regiment. His exploits in the Crimean War added to his reputation as "The Christian Soldier."

121. After the victory at Wilson's Creek, Confederate Gen. Sterling Price advanced westward along the Missouri River and gathered recruits as he moved. His 18,000 men laid siege to 3,500 Federals inside Lexington, Missouri. On September 20, the garrison surrendered.

122. Fitzhugh relatives of Mrs. Mary Lee had built "Annfield" in Clarke County. Another relative, Thomas Carter, was living there at the time. "Media" was the residence of Mary Meade.

123. "The household was the center of emotional gravity, the hearth in every sense, the place where most women gave birth to their children, welcomed visits from kinfolk and friends, and attended the deathbeds of their relatives. Here much of their labor bore fruit, in the meals on the table, the clothes their children wore, and the quilts that covered the family at night." Most women "were profoundly attached to the household as a physical place and as a symbol of all they held dear." Campbell and Rice, *Woman's War*, 33.

124. Charles W. Andrews was a Northern-born clergyman who married a relative of Bishop Meade and made his home in Virginia. "Brought up on politico-moral sermons," Andrews became "heart and soul for the Confederacy." Andrews, *Women of the South*, 103.

125. Opposing troops under generals Joseph J. Reynolds and Henry R. Jackson fought a number of minor actions between Cheat Mountain and Greenbrier during the September-early October period. See *OR*, V, 184–86, 224–29.

126. Rev. Joseph R. Jones was rector of Frederick Parish in Clark County. His wife was Courtney B. Jones. 1860 Virginia Census—Clarke County.

127. A native of Albemarle County and graduate of Princeton Seminary, Dabney Carr Harrison was then thirty years old. He was captain of the "Harrison Guards," a company in the Fifty-sixth Virginia.

128. On October 1, three Confederate vessels captured the Union supply steamer *Fanny* in Pamlico Sound, North Carolina. That the boat was loaded with men and supplies made the seizure more of a success than it appeared.

129. Before dawn on October 9, a large Confederate force landed on Santa Rosa Island, Florida. It surprised and burned the camp of Col. William Wilson's Sixth New York. The Zouaves fell back on the main Federal encampment, and the Confederates were soon forced to retire. The Union commander of the sector reported that the New Yorkers "did not behave well on the occasion." *OR,* VI, 442.

130. Cdr. George N. Hollins led the Confederate ram *Manassas* and two armed steamers down the Mississippi River and, on October 12, challenged a Union naval squadron near Head of Passes at the mouth of the river. USS *Richmond* and *Vincennes* ran aground in the brief action.

131. Federals under William S. Rosecrans and Confederates under Robert E. Lee skirmished for three days in the Big Sewell Mountain area of western Virginia. Rosecrans was hesitant to launch an attack against strong enemy entrenchments. He thereupon retired to the Gauley Bridge-Kanawha River line.

132. James McClure Drane, an Episcopal High School student in 1859–1861, enlisted in the Fourteenth Tennessee. On September 20, Drane died of typhoid fever in camp in Pocahontas County, Virginia. Richard P. Williams Jr., *The High School: A History of the Episcopal High School in Virginia at Alexandria* (Boston: Vincent-Curtis, 1964), 208.

133. On October 21, Federals shuttled across the Potomac River on inadequate boats and assailed the Confederates at Ball's Bluff near Leesburg. The resultant action cost the North 920 casualties. Southern losses were 153 men. Many of the Union fatalities drowned in the Potomac while seeking safety.

134. Actually, the phrase is from Robert Southey, *The Battle of Blenheim.*

135. William Welford Randolph of Clarke County attended the University of Virginia prior to joining the Second Virginia. He was killed in the 1864 Battle of the Wilderness.

136. On October 26, Union forces overwhelmed a small Confederate garrison around the important post of Romney, west of Winchester. For the action of Col. Angus William McDonald's regiment in the engagement, see Richard L. Armstrong, *7th Virginia Cavalry* (Lynchburg, Va.: H.E. Howard, 1992), 11–13.

137. "Pagebrook" was the Clarke County home of William Byrd Page and

Eliza Atkinson Page. It was near "The Briars," the estate of Dr. Robert Powell Page. Page, *Page Family,* 146.

138. William Norborne Nelson was captain of Company C ("Nelson Rifles") of the Second Virginia. At First Manassas, Nelson was wounded so severely in the left breast that he was unable to return to duty thereafter. His wife was Mary A. Nelson. Frye, *2nd Virginia,* 121; 1860 Virginia Census—Clarke County.

139. On October 29, a huge land and sea expedition departed Hampton Roads for action along the Carolina coasts. The undertaking consisted of seventy-seven vessels and twelve thousand troops.

140. The Union armada fought off violent storms at Cape Hatteras and gained a November 7 victory by seizing Port Royal, South Carolina, thirty miles north of Savannah, Georgia. Tybee Island controlled the entrance to the Savannah River. On November 24, Union forces occupied the island, which became a foothold for a subsequent attack on Fort Pulaski, Georgia.

141. Sgt. William Brockenbrough Colston of the Second Virginia received wounds at both Kernstown and Fredericksburg. These injuries removed him from field service for the remainder of the war. Frye, *2nd Virginia,* 90.

142. The Stonewall Brigade, nicknamed with Gen. Thomas J. Jackson at First Manassas, consisted almost entirely of soldiers from the Shenandoah Valley and its southern extension. The five regiments in the brigade were the Second, Fourth, Fifth, Twenty-seventh, and Thirty-third Virginia.

143. Mary Frances Page, a daughter of Dr. Robert P. Page, was then in her early twenties. In 1867 she married well-known writer John Esten Cooke.

144. The Nelson and Page families intermarried often. Philip Nelson, cited here, and his wife, the former Emily Page, then had two young children. Page, *Page Family,* 184.

145. William Strother Barton of the Second Virginia had been wounded in the leg at First Manassas and was home at the time on sick furlough. Lt. James M. Garnett was then about to join the staff of Gen. "Stonewall" Jackson.

146. This reference is to Capt. Raleigh T. Colston of the Second Virginia.

147. In the last weeks of 1861, Union Gen. Samuel R. Curtis maneuvered Confederates under Gen. Sterling Price completely out of Missouri. Gen. John C. Frémont had been in charge of the Union's western department, but was transferred after issuing an unauthorized emancipation proclamation in his department.

148. John Lathrop Motley, *The Rise of the Dutch Republic* (New York: Harper & Brothers, 1856), was a popular historical chronicle of the day.

149. After a brief action on December 13 at Camp Alleghany (or Buffalo Mountain), in which the opposing sides suffered 283 casualties, Federals retired to Cheat Mountain and Confederates withdrew to Staunton.

150. Mrs. McGuire was referring to a December 14 skirmish near Dam No. 4 on the Chesapeake & Ohio Canal.

151. In November, Confederate emissaries James M. Mason and John Slidell were en route to Europe on the English steamer *Trent* when the warship USS *San Jacinto,* under Capt. Charles Wilkes, stopped the boat and removed the passengers. This highly illegal seizure almost brought a new war between England and the United States. Lord Lyons was British ambassador to the United States.

Selected Bibliography

Ambler, Charles Henry. *Sectionalism in Virginia from 1776 to 1861.* Chicago: University of Chicago Press, 1910; New York: Russell & Russell, 1964.

Andrews, Matthew Page, comp. *Women of the South in War Times.* Baltimore: Norman, Remington Company, 1920.

Basler, Roy P., ed. *The Collected Works of Abraham Lincoln.* New Brunswick, N.J.: Rutgers University Press, 1953–1955.

Bastress, Robert M. *The West Virginia State Constitution: A Reference Guide.* Westport, Conn.: Greenwood Press, 1995.

Bergman, Peter M. *The Chronological History of the Negro in America.* New York: Harper & Row, 1969.

Blackerby, H.C. *Blacks in Blue and Gray: Afro-American Service in the Civil War.* Tuscaloosa, Al.: Portals Press, 1979.

Blassingame, John W., ed. *Slave Testimony: Two Centuries of Letters, Speeches, Interviews, and Autobiographies.* Baton Rouge: Louisiana State University Press, 1977.

Brewer, James H. *The Confederate Negro: Virginia's Craftsmen and Military Laborers, 1861–1865.* Durham, N.C.: Duke University Press, 1969.

Brooke, George M., Jr., ed. *Ironclads and Big Guns of the Confederacy: The Journal and Letters of John M. Brooke.* Columbia, S.C.: University of South Carolina Press, 2002.

Campbell, Edward D.C., Jr., and Kym S. Rice, eds. *A Woman's War: Southern Women, Civil War, and the Confederate Legacy.* Richmond: Museum of the Confederacy/Charlottesville: University Press of Virginia, 1996.

Casdorph, Paul D. *Prince John Magruder: His Life and Campaigns.* New York: John Wiley & Sons, 1996.

Chesnut, Mary Boykin Miller, ed. C. Vann Woodward. *Mary Chesnut's Civil War.* New Haven and London: Yale University Press, 1981.

Cohen, Stan. *The Civil War in West Virginia: A Pictorial History.* Missoula, Mont: Gateway Print & Lithography, 1976.

Cometti, Elizabeth, and Festus P. Summers, eds. *The Thirty-fifth State: A Docu-*

mentary History of West Virginia. Morgantown, W.V.: West Virginia University Library, 1966.

Coski, John M. *Capital Navy: The Men, Ships, and Operations of the James River Squadron.* Campbell, Ca.: Savas Woodbury Publishers, 1996.

Coulter, E. Merton. *The Confederate States of America 1861–1865.* Baton Rouge: Louisiana State University Press, 1950.

Crofts, Daniel W. *Reluctant Confederates: Upper South Confederates in the Secession Crisis.* Chapel Hill: University of North Carolina Press, 1989.

Curry, Richard Orr. *A House Divided: Statehood Politics and the Copperhead Movement in West Virginia.* Pittsburgh: University of Pittsburgh Press, 1964.

Davis, William C. *"A Government of Our Own": The Making of the Confederacy.* New York: Free Press, 1994.

———. *Battle at Bull Run: A History of the First Major Campaign of the Civil War.* Garden City, N.Y.: Doubleday, 1977.

———. *Duel between the First Ironclads.* Garden City, N.Y.: Doubleday, 1975.

———. *Rhett: The Turbulent Life and Times of a Fire-Eater.* Columbia, S.C.: University of South Carolina Press, 2001.

Dew, Charles W. *Apostles of Disunion: Southern Secession Commissioners and the Causes of the Civil War.* Charlottesville: University Press of Virginia, 2001.

———. *Ironmaker to the Confederacy: Joseph R. Anderson and Tredegar Iron Works.* New Haven, Conn.: Yale University Press, 1966.

Durden, Robert F. *The Gray and the Black: The Confederate Debate on Emancipation.* Baton Rouge: Louisiana State University Press, 1972.

Farwell, Byron. *Ball's Bluff: A Small Battle and Its Long Shadow.* McLean, Va.: EPM Publications, 1990.

Fischer, David Hackett, and James C. Kelly. *Bound Away: Virginia and the Westward Movement.* Charlottesville and London: University Press of Virginia, 2000.

Foote, Shelby. *The Civil War: A Narrative,* I. New York: Random House, 1958.

Franklin, John Hope. *The Militant South, 1800–1861.* Boston: Belknap Press of Harvard University Press, 1956.

Freeman, Douglas Southall. *R.E. Lee: A Biography.* New York: Scribner, 1934.

Goff, Richard. *Confederate Supply.* Durham, N.C.: Duke University Press, 1969.

Goldfield, David R. *Urban Growth in the Age of Sectionalism: Virginia, 1847–1861.* Baton Rouge: Louisiana State University Press, 1977.

Hall, Granville Davisson. *The Rending of Virginia: A History.* Chicago: Mayer and Miller, 1902; Knoxville: University of Tennessee Press, 2000.

Jordan, Ervin L., Jr. *Black Confederates and Afro-Yankees in Civil War Virginia.* Charlottesville and London: University Press of Virginia, 1995.

Keckley, Elizabeth. *Behind the Scenes, or, Thirty Years a Slave and Four Years in the White House.* New York: G.W. Carleton & Co., 1868; New York: Penguin Books, 2005.

Lewis, Ronald L., and John C. Hennen Jr., eds. *West Virginia History: Critical Essays on the Literature.* Dubuque, Iowa: Kendall/Hunt Pub. Co., 1993.

Luraghi, Raimondo. *A History of the Confederate Navy.* Annapolis, Md.: Naval Institute Press, 1996.

Manarin, Louis H., ed. *Richmond at War: The Minutes of the City Council, 1861–1865.* Chapel Hill, N.C.: University of North Carolina Press, 1966.

Massey, Mary Elizabeth. *Bonnet Brigades.* New York: Knopf, 1966.

McGregor, James C. *The Disruption of Virginia.* New York: Macmillan, 1922.

McMurray, Richard M. *Two Great Rebel Armies: An Essay in Confederate Military History.* Chapel Hill: University of North Carolina Press, 1989.

Morris, George, and Susan Foutz. *Lynchburg in the Civil War.* Lynchburg, Va.: H.E. Howard,1984.

Newell, Clayton R. *Lee vs. McClellan: The First Campaign.* Washington, D.C.: Regnery Pub., 1996.

Noe, Kenneth W. *Southwest Virginia's Railroad: Modernization and the Sectional Crisis.* Urbana and Chicago: University of Illinois Press, 1994.

Perdue, Charles L., Jr., Thomas E. Barden, and Robert K. Phillips, eds. *Weevils in the Wheat: Interviews with Virginia Ex-Slaves.* Charlottesville: University Press of Virginia, 1976.

Quarstein, John V. *C.S.S. Virginia: Mistress of Hampton Roads.* Appomattox, Va.: H.E. Howard, 2000.

———. *Hampton and Newport News in the Civil War: War Comes to the Peninsula.* Lynchburg, Va.: H.E. Howard, 1998.

Quintard, Charles T., ed. Sam Davis Elliott. *Doctor Quintard, Chaplain, C.S.A., and Second Bishop of Tennessee: The Memoir and Civil War Diary of Charles Todd Quintard.* Baton Rouge: Louisiana State University Press, 2003.

Rice, Otis K., and Stephen W. Brown. *West Virginia: A History.* Second Edition. Lexington: University Press of Kentucky, 1993.

Riggs, David F. *Embattled Shrine: Jamestown in the Civil War.* Shippensburg, Pa.: White Mane Pub. Co., 1997.

Robertson, James I., Jr. *18th Virginia Infantry.* Lynchburg, Va.: H.E. Howard, 1984.

———. *Stonewall Jackson: The Man, the Soldier, the Legend.* New York: Macmillan, 1997.

Ruffin, Edmund, ed. William Kauffman Scarborough. *The Diary of Edmund Ruffin.* Baton Rouge: Louisiana State University Press, 1972–1989.

Scharf, J. Thomas. *History of the Confederate States Navy: From Its Organization to the Surrender of Its Last Vessel.* New York: Rogers & Sherwood, 1887.

Schwarz, Philip J. *Slave Laws in Virginia.* Athens, Ga.: University of Georgia Press, 1996.

Shanks, Henry T. *The Secession Movement in Virginia, 1847–1861.* Richmond: Garrett and Massie, 1934.

Slaughter, James B. *Settlers, Southerners, Americans: The History of Essex County, Virginia, 1608–1984.* Tappahannock, Va.: Essex County Board of Supervisors, 1985.

Starobin, Robert S., ed. *Blacks in Bondage: Letters of American Slaves.* New York: New Viewpoints, 1974; New York: M. Wiener, 1988.

Sterling, Dorothy, ed. *We Are Your Sisters: Black Women in the Nineteenth Century.* New York: W.W. Norton, 1984.

Still, William. *The Underground Rail Road: A Record of Facts, Authentic Narratives, Letters, &c.* Philadelphia: Porter & Coates, 1872; Chicago: Johnson Pub. Co., 1970.

Still, William N., Jr. *Iron Afloat: The Story of the Confederate Armorclads.* Nashville: Vanderbilt University Press, 1971.

Stutler, Boyd B. *West Virginia in the Civil War.* Charleston, W.V.: Education Foundation, 1963.

Sutherland, Daniel E. *Seasons of War: The Ordeal of a Confederate Community, 1861–1865.* New York: Free Press, 1995.

Thomas, Emory M. *The Confederate State of Richmond: A Biography of the Capital.* Austin: University of Texas Press, 1971.

Trout, Robert J. *With Pen and Saber: The Letters and Diaries of J.E.B. Stuart's Staff Officers.* Mechanicsburg, Pa.: Stackpole Books, 1995.

U.S. War Department. *War of the Rebellion: A Compilation of Official Records of the Union and Confederate Armies.* Washington, D.C.: Government Printing Office, 1880–1901.

Williams, John Alexander. *West Virginia: A Bicentennial History.* New York: Norton, 1976.

Williams, T. Harry. *Lincoln and His Generals.* New York: Knopf, 1952.

Wills, Mary Alice. *The Confederate Blockade of Washington, D.C., 1861–1862.* Parsons, W.V.: McClain Print. Co., 1975; Shippensburg, Pa.: Burd Street Press, 1998.

Woodson, Carter G. *The Mind of the Negro as Reflected in Letters Written dur-*

ing the Crisis 1800–1860. Washington, D.C.: Association for the Study of Negro Life and History, 1926.

Wooster, Ralph A. *The Secession Conventions of the South.* Princeton, N.J.: Princeton University Press, 1962.

Index